Being Gregory

Bill Forsyth, *Gregory's Girl*, the lot

First published in 2023
by Crackle + Hiss

Cover design by Jamie Keenan

A CIP catalogue record for this book is available from the British Library.

ISBN 978-1-3999-5045-9

Being Gregory

Bill Forsyth, *Gregory's Girl,*
the lot

TIM BLANCHARD

CRACKLE
+HISS

Foreword

By Jonathan Coe

I have a vivid memory of seeing *Gregory's Girl* for the first time. At least, I don't remember exactly *where* I saw it, but I do remember the company that I was in.

The screening did not take place, as far as I remember, in a commercial cinema, but at a college film society. It was autumn 1981, I was just starting my second year at Cambridge, and the audience was therefore just as you'd expect: young, posh, entitled, privileged. (Words which all applied to me as well, even if I hadn't been to public school like most of them.) In other words, the world being shown to us in *Gregory's Girl* that afternoon, the world of new towns, housing estates, Cumbernauld, state schools, could hardly have been more remote from the life experience of the people watching.

And yet I've rarely been witness to a film screening which brought such joy. It was a double bill, in fact: Bill Forsyth's debut feature *That Sinking Feeling* was shown first, and went down a storm. But it was *Gregory's Girl* that really hit the spot: half of the dialogue was lost beneath the laughter, and yet this crowd of toffs and Sloanes were not laughing scornfully at Gregory and his friends, there was no condescension or mockery in their response. With this charming, featherweight, finely-judged comedy Bill Forsyth had simply bridged the class divide and tapped into a vein of humour which appealed to everyone, which was beautifully grounded in our shared humanity.

As it happened, Forsyth had already been on my radar for a few weeks. On 30 August that year, BBC 2 had screened *That Sinking Feeling* in its Sunday evening 'Film of the Week' slot. I'd watched the broadcast and thought it brilliant. For me, this new director's films immediately became a must-see. Next up was *Local Hero*, which I watched at a cinema just off Piccadilly Circus in 1983 and which came, I must say, as something of a surprise: a masterpiece, for sure, but different to *Gregory's Girl*, much slower in pace, rooted in environmental and political themes and working on a far broader canvas. After which, it was the turn of that finely-judged comedy of depression, abandonment and the search for a purpose in life — *Comfort and Joy*, which according to my diary I saw in a central London cinema on 3rd September, 1984.

The perennially-grumpy Leslie Halliwell, whose *Halliwell's Film Guide* was still my go-to reference book, considered it "a distinct descent from *Local Hero*, which was a comedown after *Gregory's Girl*". My own response, I think, was a bit more accurate: my diary simply described the film as 'slightly baffling'. What was beginning to become clear, at any rate, was that Forsyth was a more interesting and complicated director than the (wholly delightful) comedy of *Gregory's Girl* had led us to believe. When I saw *Housekeeping* in its week of release at the Chelsea Cinema in 1987, this became even clearer. Being familiar with Forsyth's work, but not with that of Marilynne Robinson (author of the source novel), I was anticipating laughs, but there didn't seem to be any. The film is tender, melancholy, disturbing, strange, and totally faithful to Robinson's book. I was haunted by it for weeks afterwards. But it seemed further away than ever from the world of *That Sinking Feeling* or Abronhill High School.

And that, for me, was more or less it. Forsyth would shoot his next two films in America, and I missed them both. The idea of a Burt Reynolds caper movie (*Breaking In*) didn't appeal at the time, and a few years later the desperately ill-fated *Being Human* seemed impossible to find, even in its recut form. It would be years before I caught up with either of them. I did see *Gregory's Two Girls* (1999) in London at the time of release, and I liked it much more than the reviewers did, although as a sequel to the original film it could hardly have been more wayward and perverse. It was certainly nice to find a film written and directed by Forsyth again, and I would have been shocked and dismayed if anyone had told me it was the last he would make.

His is a brief filmography, then: just eight features, plus the virtually-unknown *Andrina*, his measured adaptation of a George Mackay Brown short story, shot for the BBC in 1981. And what had been the peak of that career? When I had the pleasure of meeting Bill Forsyth twelve years ago and interviewing him on stage, he told the audience that *Housekeeping* was his favourite among his own films, and did not speak especially fondly of *Gregory's Girl*. It was clear that, like Woody Allen, he felt a certain frustration with fans of his movies who preferred 'the early, funny ones'. And it's certainly true that *Housekeeping*, *Local Hero* and *Being Human* are all visually richer than *Gregory's Girl*, while *Comfort and Joy*, for instance, is much more complex and nuanced in tone.

All the same, there's something special about *Gregory's Girl* that never has been — and probably never could be — replicated. It's partly just the ceaseless flow of comic invention: I find it hard to think of any other film comedy where the script just trips from one great line to another and there isn't a single scene where the quality dips. (This is why, whenever it comes on television, I tell myself I'm just going to watch the first few minutes and always end up seeing the whole thing.) But it's more than the script, and more than the performances. There's a magic to Michael Coulter's cinematography, and Colin Tully's music, which turns the final act of the film — and especially Gregory's date with Susan in the park — into something quite luminous, the distillation of every perfect date we've ever been on and every lost teenage summer that we've ever lived through.

Anyway, you will read about all this and more, expressed far more eloquently than I can manage, in the excellent book which you now hold in your hands. It will reawaken precious memories of *Gregory's Girl* and inspire you, I hope, to dive deeper into Forsyth's work. You're in for a treat. *"Bella Bella"*, as I believe they say in Italy.

February 2023

Acknowledgments

Thank you to the brilliant folk of *Gregory's Girl* and the Glasgow Youth Theatre. In particular to Adrienne Atkinson, John Baraldi, Rab Buchanan, Gerry Clark, Clare Grogan, Caroline Guthrie, Dee Hepburn, Alan Love and Douglas Sannachan for their input and support. And to the town of Cumbernauld and its residents. Still a special kind of place.

Contents

1.

Windows

"If I don't see you through the week, I'll see you through a windae eh?"

Streetlights are coming on across Luton on a grey Saturday afternoon. Pink at first, the violet-pink of chocolate wrappers from the Christmas tin. Rows of them glowing in empty streets, over one hill and down another, around the Vauxhall works and into town.

A boy in winter, my finger follows a procession of chimney smoke across the glass of the window and leaves a wet trail in condensation made from breathing so close. Dusk is falling on the wastes of a Luton afternoon. Nothing happening except *Grandstand*: Warrington and Widnes and the mud of the North. No classified football results until it's black outside, then Findus Crispy Pancakes, potatoes and peas; *The Generation Game* after tea.

I go and sit in the corner with my comics and wonder where the magic is hiding. In stories, enchantment was everywhere. The dullest and meanest of houses was permeable, it would have portals to the fantastic in its old doors and wardrobes, a cupboard, a mirror, a fireplace. But my experience of so many long days in Luton hadn't yet produced any evidence to support the claims of storybooks. I'd investigated the darkest corners of the house on my hands and knees and found wood-chip wallpaper, carpet and dust. The mind of an eight-year old — simple as a mushroom — doesn't rule anything out, and I had casually accepted that any day, especially on an empty day like this, the magic would arrive; coalesce with an uncanny gleam, in a slow whorl of new colours. After all, the signs of possibility were everywhere: we stood and sang songs about God and heard the history of his miracles every morning in the school hall; our coal fire had all the reds, blacks and crackle of Hell.

One book in particular was troubling me. Among the thickish, age-softened pages of a collection of children's stories was a picture of a girl. Not the kind of girl I knew from school (eggy-white skin, socks pulled up to her chapped knees), she was almond-eyed and dressed in purple and jade. I don't remember the story, but I would sit in the corner and look into the picture where the girl was trapped by some spell or curse or law, serene and alone, looking back at me out of the picture. This was the window I wanted to climb through, the place where I longed to be. If I could only concentrate hard enough, I would be in the picture. Luton would be on the other side, the hopeless fantasy.

Neuroscience offers some explanation of why I believed this was going to happen. Brains don't come preloaded with rationality, it says. They don't start out with a 'default mode network', the structure of knowledge our brain falls back on when we're not actively thinking about much at all; a reliable, empirical history of what we've experienced: of what's hard and solid, what's cold, what's painful. It works as an energy-saver that reduces unnecessary brain activity (and tells us not to bother looking for secret doorways in wardrobes). Young children's brains don't have much of this structure, meaning there's plenty of space for believing in the fancies of imagination. They're a loose affair, more like a treehouse that's open to the elements — a place where the moonlight can shine in. An adult's default mode tends to be triple-glazed and double-locked with an Audi in the drive, which means we know, instinctively, that the things of the imagination are baseless, detached from the reality we have (partly) learned first-hand, and (mostly) been told about. Imagination is a toy. For entertainment, distraction, and making things up.

But there are flaws and leaks in the system. As modern people, much of our experience comes mediated through TV and radio, books and films. So imagination slips inside anyhow. It messes about with the default mode and suggests all kinds of contradictions. Which is why, even now in a century where science has dissected every part of our hard-surfaced real world, where digital media has turned life into a fishbowl, we can still feel haunted. Haunted by a sense of loss and longing; by something in the look of far-off clouds and treetops, wet pavements and brickwork, or in the receding light of a day; something that's a mystery beyond the limits of any rational knowledge or calculation. We're muddled and torn. Maybe because we're in a state of revolt against a default mode that doesn't allow for imaginative conclusions or half-truths, leaving us with a nagging impression, more sensation than thought, that we're missing something. A painful alternation between belief and disbelief that makes us romantic about unlikely things.

I can only assume that's why I'm 52 years old and want to go to Cumbernauld. I want to be Gregory, walking through the concrete and asphalt of a grey housing estate on a summer's evening. At least once, I want to be in every one of those places from the film: the corrugated underpass on the way to school, the red ash sports pitches, under the clock in the Plaza. Just the particular look of the economy landscaping, the trees and shrubs razzled by a breeze, even the images of passing lorries in a watery sunlight, are richly bittersweet and confusing. Somehow overwhelming. I want to go to Cumbernauld even though I know it's only a wet and windy 'new' town with the reputation of having a town centre like an aborted Stalinist experiment. Horrible Sixties' overspill with no more magic than Luton, or any other town where there are careers to pursue, a closed rhythm of performance appraisals and retail therapy, leisure time spent with Netflix and celebrity gossip on Instagram.

And anyway, aren't there better old films to climb into? *Il Postino* (1995) would be a lot warmer, a blissful cerulean escape; *8½* (1963) more pleasingly sexy. But I don't want any of them. I only want to know the pallid twilight of Cumbernauld's country park.

*

Gregory's Girl was first screened in British cinemas on Thursday 23rd April 1981. The lines of punters snaking over dirty foyer carpets that Easter school holiday wouldn't have been expecting much. They'd come inside from the snowy streets and were now more interested in buying a box of Maltesers from the kiosk than *Gregory's Girl*, still bickering over whether they wouldn't be better off seeing *Superman II* at the Odeon instead. Because this was a 'British film', another low-budget offering from an industry that had become increasingly desperate over the preceding decade. Toilet humour and big women in nightgowns and curlers were just accepted as a given. Few of the customers taking their ticket stubs would have heard, or cared, that *Gregory's Girl* had been given a warmish welcome at the London Film Festival. Any excitement around Britain's film industry belonged to *Chariots of Fire*, a new brand of 'bigger budget' movie that had been launched into cinemas only a few weeks before. Somehow producer David Puttnam had been able to milk American affection for the Old World to fund a piece of soft culture with scenes of gorgeous élitism and a stirring electro soundtrack.

Gregory's Girl wasn't part of that universe. Not really a British film at all but something unheard of — a Scottish feature movie — and if audiences had known more about the film and how it was made, they would have been even less enthusiastic. *Gregory's Girl* was the first effort at a screenplay by a 34 year-old Glaswegian who'd been scratching a living making commercial promo films about the fishing industry and home improvement grants. The production had been scraped together with small resources and a glue of goodwill, using mostly inexperienced actors and some child extras bribed with bags of sweets. Filming had to be shoe-horned into the space of just seven weeks to keep the costs down, and had been constantly thwarted by Cumbernauld's grisly summer weather. The whole atmosphere was casual and the teenage cast liked to disappear off to local pubs.

Too late now. Our unwary audience has shuffled into the big auditorium. The usherette with the bubble perm and tray of Lyons Maid tubs and choc ices has made a cursory wave of her torch and they've crept along the aisles, muttered some 'scuse me's and avoided eye contact with the owners of legs and bags and tried to find the seats without fag burns and rubbish. The curtains have been tugged back and Pearl & Dean is booming out its crackly adverts, the same old stuff for Stork margarine and Hamlet cigars. There's a photo of Barry and his reliable motors at Hi-life Cars, followed by the madly-grinning staff at the Passage to India, only two minutes up the High Street. Local heroes in bilious technicolour. They make their appearance on reels of celluloid so blotted and hairy it's like the projectionist's cat has been at them. Sweets are doled out and the chatting gets noisier. When the lights finally dim, the ABC's seedy velvet softens into something more like a shadowy sophistication, and there's a revelation of immense vaulted space, a silver cave, an entry into a realm of brilliant dust: "This is to certi-fy that *Gregory's Girl* has been passed 'A'" (because the British Board of Film Censors gets to stamp its mark of sense and officialdom on even the wildest and most subversive of dreams). Snoggers have no reason to wait any longer. More pop and crackle until the opening scene starts and everyone cheers up. It's settling and reassuring. How else was a British film going to begin? There's a night-time window where a young woman is undressing, oblivious to the Peeping Tom teenagers. Everyone gets a cheeky peek and we're off and running.

*

It so happened that the formula of "young love and football" worked out. *Gregory's Girl* played in London for a run of 75 weeks and, after it was given a US release by Sam Goldwyn, went on to make more than £25 million in ticket sales. The little Scottish newcomer grossed about £10 million more than Martin Scorsese's classic from the same year, *Raging Bull* — and in terms of profit margin, made an extra £20 million. Great numbers to put in front of industry executives and financiers (although their smiles would have been merely polite, they would have been thinking about Stephen Spielberg's *Raiders of the Lost Ark*, which took $389.9 million in the same year; *Superman II*: $190.4 million; and an average addition to the James Bond franchise, *For Your Eyes Only*, $195.3 million).

Critics were disoriented by what they saw. Movies were meant to be a circus of big name stars and their thrills and spills; adventures that used the primary colours of emotion; or, at the other end of the scale, at least be a serious exercise in art. *Gregory's Girl* was unexpected. Quietly otherworldly and disarming. Film writers found a "peculiar fascination" in the film's meandering approach, the "tangential scenes, limning each character's odd obsession, be it food, girls, soccer, or just watching the traffic drive by."[1] "No character, emotion, gesture or response is too commonplace not to be re-examined and, in the process, miraculously seen anew," decided Vincent Canby in the *New York Times* (the man who had recently destroyed *Heaven's Gate* (1980) and the ambition of Michael Cimino). "In this fashion, what might have been an ordinary comedy about the perils and pressures of growing up is transformed into something as exotic as a visit to another planet, a place that looks and sounds familiar but whose gravitational pull is about one-tenth of Earth's."[2] Regional press got to applaud a local success story (and re-write the film's plot): "a charming, spunky little tale of a couple of teenagers, with the football field as its background. He loses his place in the school team to her (cheers for Women's Lib) and he isn't at all pleased. Then he falls in love with her all the same, and there's an idyllic ending with the two youngsters walking away together in the moonlight…proof, once again, of the age-old truth that there is nothing to beat the genuine, indigenous movie, even just a modest one."[3]

The modesty was the problem. There was no peril in the film, no perceivable edge of 'issues' at all — and that couldn't be right. *Variety* called it a "friendly, unmalicious approach" to cinema. But others were more worried, their teeth set on edge. "Very, very modest whimsy from Scotland…The only ambition of writer-director Bill Forsyth is to beguile — he has no insights worth mentioning — and I guess he succeeds, though it's hard to warm to a film as intentionally slight and safe as this."[4] "Is there not something amiss with comedies that offend absolutely no-one?" asked Neil Sinyard in *Films Illustrated* (who, ironically, seemed quite offended). "Forsyth's naturalistic mode in his films might ultimately demand from him a toughness, honesty and comic fearlessness that as yet he seems unwilling to display."[5]

The British Academy for Film and Television Award for 'Best Screenplay' in 1982 went to Bill Forsyth. There were BAFTA nominations for Best Film and Best Director as well, but these prizes went to *Chariots of Fire*, and to one of the original members of the French New Wave, Louis Malle, for his dewy-eyed scam movie *Atlantic City*. There were no Oscar nominations for *Gregory's Girl*, not that anyone expected any. Deliberations over the significance of such a minor piece revolved more around what might be coming next. Had Forsyth started something? Before now, Scottish filmmakers had been stuck in TV or making documentaries and shorts. *Gregory's Girl* was home-grown with Scottish TV money and Scottish talent, and was an exemplar of how a national cinema could tell its own stories and shake off the burden of clichés. Tartan clans and their whisky jigs, drug gangs and stabbings. The film's international success led, one way or another, to the setting up of the Scottish Film Production Fund and the Glasgow Film Fund. Its reputation among movie fans as a film "still worth watching" has lived on. Just about. In the British Film Institute's poll of the 'Top 100 British films' in 1999, *Gregory's Girl* came 30th, some way behind *Chariots of Fire*, *Whisky Galore!* and *Trainspotting*. In 2021, *Entertainment Weekly* placed the film 29th out of 50 in a list of the 'Best High School Movies' topped by John Hughes' *The Breakfast Club* (1985), but had slipped to 95th in *Empire* magazine's ranking of the '100 Best British Films'. Bill Forsyth's story has at least become a fixture on the

GCSE English lit curriculum (as a consequence of being an opportunity to write about gender representation). More feebly, it's rumoured to have been an influence on Wes Anderson and Shane Meadows; and, maybe, it's one of Scorsese's favourite films — if we believe what a restaurant owner 'friend' of Scorsese once said to Clare Grogan's mum.

An affection hasn't survived within Bill Forsyth himself. His films have become something distant from him, and his relationship with them can be awkward. "I used to say that if I saw them across the street, I wouldn't cross to say hello to them. I still feel that way...It's like having kids. They kind of wander away and do their own thing."[6] He's less than sentimental about *Gregory's Girl* in particular, always determined to avoid any romanticising of his intentions. He'd wanted his first screenplay to be a "calling card", a way to raise funds for more interesting projects. That's why a documentary-maker with no interest in Old Firm derbies had chosen to write about love and football. "Sorry if it bursts your bubble," said Bill to an interviewer in 2008[7] (and you know he'd enjoyed playing the wily old cynic when he said it). "I'm not fond of any of my films in an intimate way, but *Gregory's Girl* would be number four on my list."[8] He's been humble, as well as honest, about his contribution to the Scottish movie business: "Back then [in the late 70s and early 80s] there must have only been around 20 people in the whole industry," he explained. "God, there must be double that now."[9] There has been very little culturally-distinctive film-making coming out of Scotland since (or any other part of the UK for that matter), no 'Scollywood'. The globalising impulses of the film business, along with the expediencies of raising finance, have been too strong, too all-consuming, for there to be many mainstream films as pure as *Gregory's Girl*. While film-makers in other parts of Europe, as well as countries like Taiwan and South Korea, keep on adding to an idiosyncratic and independently-minded catalogue, British films, generally, are vehicles trying to win international distribution deals. The movies quoted as owing their existence to bodies like the Glasgow Film Fund have been a mishmash. *Shallow Grave* (1994) might have had a screenplay written by a Scot and been mostly filmed in Glasgow, but it also had an English director and funding from Channel 4; Lynne Ramsay's *Ratcatcher* (1999) was made possible by money from the BBC and French company Pathé.

Lined up alongside the muscular blockbusters of film history, their legends and star-power, *Gregory's Girl* is a shy and skinny-looking thing, apologetic about being remembered at all. Yes, there's an affectingly simple naturalism and humour; there's the universal themes of school days and first love. As a piece of uncomplicated nostalgia, what's not to like? *Empire* summed up what's been generally accepted as the denouement to the film's story in its review of a DVD re-release in 2000: "in the end, *Gregory's Girl* didn't prove to be a particularly influential movie: there was a brief trend in quirky Scotcom such as *Restless Natives* [1985] and *The Girl In The Picture* [1985]…perhaps *Gregory's Girl* was just too darned idiosyncratic to replicate. Daft and deft, innocent yet knowing, it remains the growing up spread you never grow out of."[10]

There's no reason why the basic ingredients of *Gregory's Girl* couldn't be re-assembled. But there have never been any successful imitations of Forsyth's films. It's only disheartening when a new release suggests it re-captures the spirit of Forsyth (low-key performances? Scottish scenery? running visual gags?) — because it has never worked and it never will. The mystery is too tightly furled and encoded. Other attempts to tap into the bittersweet resonance of school days have demonstrated the problem. David Puttnam's first project after *Chariots of Fire* was *P'tang Yang Kipperbang* (1982): another simple plot involving a socially-awkward hero and first love; the same innocence, this time with box office-friendly 1940s window-dressing. There was a £395,000 budget and a hot ticket director in Michael Apted, who'd recently made the big money-maker *Coal Miner's Daughter* (1980), attracting seven Oscar nominations. The result is plastic and unconvincing. Jokey. Un-affecting.

*

The mystery starts (but doesn't end) with Bill Forsyth. From one article, review and blurb after another, we've been left with the impression of an affable director of 'whimsy'. Other labels used to describe his films include 'light', 'gentle', 'wry', 'quirky' and 'quaint'. He's been classified as part of the tea-and-toast Ealing comedy tradition[11]. Also known as someone who didn't make it in Hollywood, and by the industry, more pointedly, as a man who lost them lots of money. In an interview in 2019 he was typically phlegmatic:

> "I don't really think a lot now about the films
> I've made; for me, when the movies are over,
> they're over. I don't want the world to love

my films, although it's nice if they do. I don't ever remember having a hit, although maybe I didn't know what a hit was. One time, I drove past the Odeon on Sauchiehall Street in Glasgow and saw people queueing up to see *Gregory's Girl* – that was a bit of a thrill. But the films don't linger a lot with me, and I think that's OK."[12]

Bill Forsyth is a man whose trade has been celluloid but whose personal culture has always been rooted in an older and richer world of literature, art and music. A maker of art installations that just happen to involve moving pictures.

"The only ambitions I have for the films I make," he once said, "is that they're appreciated as poetical works. Either film is too crude a medium to handle that or else I can't make it do these things."[13] He's felt thoroughly misunderstood over the years. "Three movies were greeted as comedies and labelled as charming, lyrical…when I was trying to be much more serious in the things I was trying to say. In those early films I was trying to please too much…too cute in the way I was saying those things." Out of tune with film critics, often mystified by their response. "No matter that film-makers are attempting some kind of personal film-making, the critics don't seem capable of making that journey…I would respect any opinion of my work if I could see the logic of it."[14]

Forsyth was, instead, always more naturally constituted as an underground film-maker. "I feel subversive in

13

everything I do. At every stage of the process I'm thinking how can I subvert this. How can I make this less like a 'real' movie."[15] A practical man without a trace of careerism in him — who, at the same time, has known very well he's been pigheaded about making poetry for an industry that didn't want it: "There's always something you want to say. I would not want to make a film that did not say anything, I'm not interested in getting into something that's just a piece of entertainment, a James Bond or an adventure film. I don't enjoy filming that much, in fact I don't enjoy filming at all, and to go through all that for the sake of money would just not interest me."[16]

It's grandly Quixotic. A shy thirty-something with no money behind him runs away from his familiar stomping ground of commercial films to make mainstream feature movies; doing what he's always admitted was painful for him: having to turn up every day and be the boss of a shoot, manage the actors and all of their expectations, deal with questions from the crew. Why expose yourself, your little creations and their sometimes contrary sensibility, to the most harshly fluorescent of examinations? For the writer/director, the movie industry has never really been a dream factory but more the destroyer of illusions. In some ways it's our modern world in microcosm. On the surface there's glamour and delight, a democracy of opportunity that means anyone can rise to an unimaginable level of fame, claim a rapt audience of billions who understand and share the same passions. Underneath, exacting structures of money and power.

Roughly-speaking, there have been more than 100,000 film releases since 1981. Each of them has been a new business venture in itself, with far more money to spend on an enticing package of celebrity, action and cinematography than a provincial, clubhouse kind of enterprise like *Gregory's Girl*. There's also been an acceleration in the scale of the competition and its clamour, a doubling in the average number of releases into UK cinemas between 2000 and 2016 (peaking at 16 new films per week), made possible by digital technologies and lower production costs, alongside shorter cycles of attention and impatient business models[17]. Films bloom one week and fade the next.

Since then, film entertainment has become more like a utility service, streamed on-demand into our homes with a single click, removing many of the traditional obstacles between film-makers and their audiences: the physical distance, the bundle of costs, the rainy nights, having to find a parking space and put up with the terminally inconsiderate presence of 'other people'. The proliferation of streaming platforms and their mass subscription model of funding means the flow of investment into film-making is different in character. More writers and directors have the chance to create, and at the same time, reach guaranteed audiences. Mostly that means products made to be confections of emotional treats and pleasures, that fit a comfortable genre and press buttons of popularity; but it could, in theory, also mean being able to realise visions and ambitions, to bring the most worthwhile of literary artefacts to life, or say something new about the changing times and our changing human condition. Digital technology means cinema can do anything. Each and every pixel can be manipulated to deliver an imaginative hyper-reality or metaverse — but at the same time it's become less interested in the mess of reality in itself (and, arguably, less able to convey it). With so much possibility, the film industry should be a machinery of inspiration, our culture's conversation, its genius. And yet; and yet. How many of the 100,000 films produced have we wanted to watch again; how many have been anything more than a moment of distraction?

Through it all, *Gregory's Girl* has stayed with us. Among romantics of many different varieties. The people who would never normally bother with a rom-com; among men who were geeks as boys (and maybe still are); as well as those who know that, somehow, there's more to the film than just nostalgia; and those who recognise that nothing like it could ever be made again. For one generation at least, it's an unforgettable love song.

This is a book about the impossibility of *Gregory's Girl*. How it shouldn't really exist. I think the reason it does says a great deal about the period it was made, as well as the singular talent of its maker, Bill Forsyth. Why it still occupies such a luminous place in our minds says something about us, and also about the film as a cultural phenomenon, now walking around on its own two feet.

There are secrets in all of this, and I've tried to follow them to their end — still on my hands and knees in a dusty corner — because the surfaces of our dispassionate and unpromising world are strewn with windows.

[1] *Gregory's Girl* review, *Variety*, December 31, 1981.

[2] Vincent Canby, *Gregory's Girl* review, *New York Times*, 26 May 1982.

[3] Molly Plowright, 'Scottish story scores success for Forsyth', *Glasgow Herald*, 1 May 1981.

[4] Dave Kehr, *Chicago Reader*, December 5 1984.

[5] Neil Sinyard, 'The Forsyth Saga', *Films Illustrated*, August 1981.

[6] Abbey Bender, 'From Sponsored Movies to Coming-of-Age Classics: Bill Forsyth Talks About Pioneering Scottish Cinema', MUBI, 3 October 2019.

[7] Tim Teeman, 'Bill Forsyth: the reluctant father of *Gregory's Girl*', *The Times*, 6 February 2008.

[8] Gerald Peary, 'Bill Forsyth', www.geraldpeary.com, September 1985.

[9] From the 'Bill Forsyth Lifetime Achievement Award Film', Scottish BAFTA Awards, 8 November 2009.

[10] Ian Freer, *Gregory's Girl* review, *Empire*, 1 January 2000.

[11] Alwyn W. Turner, *Rejoice! Rejoice! Britain in the 1980s*, Aurum Press, 2010, p19.

[12] Bill Forsyth interview, 'On Making *Breaking In* with Burt Reynolds', *Talkhouse*, 4 October 2019.

[13] Allan Hunter, 'Being Human', *Sight and Sound*, August 1994.

[14] James Park, *Learning to Dream: The New British Cinema*, Faber & Faber, 1984, p22.

[15] Bill Forsyth interview, *Fresh Air with Terry Gross*, 6 October 1989.

[16] Allan Hunter and Mark Astaire, *Local Hero: the making of the film*, Polygon Books, 1983.

[17] Nick Clark, 'Too many films are released each year, says British Film Institute', *The Independent*, 24 July 2016.

2. Bill

"Come on! you're worse than my dad, and he's old. At least he's got an excuse for bein a prick."

In Edinburgh's old industrial harbour, the salty horseshoe bay of Granton, a portrait of Bill Forsyth is kept in storage. It's only one curiosity among millions of drawings and paintings hung on rows of wire racking like a scrapbook made up of bumpy pages of shells, feathers and bottle caps. A climate-controlled morgue for the arts. The oil painting — a fair size, about two metres tall — was commissioned from Steven Campbell in 1995 as part of the Scottish National Gallery's series of portraits of the country's "worthies".

History works its way, quietly, into physical forms. As a result of processes of recognition and popularity and their filters, certain people are remembered in more formal representations for the public to see. The visitors to the Queen Street portrait gallery, tiny figures in the caverns of Edinburgh's own Venetian palace, instinctively feel a reverence for what has been validated as a work of art: like the stately portraits of Sir Walter Scott and Robert Burns. Those faces that look out from a time so distant from our own they seem to belong less to a foreign country than an alien planet. We understand other likenesses in the gallery much better. Billy Connolly. Alex Ferguson. Chris Hoy. Ian Rankin. Robbie Coltrane. Unlike those celebrities though, Bill Forsyth's portrait hasn't often been on public display, left in storage since 2007. His name wasn't on the original list of commissions and it had taken lobbying by the artist for Forsyth to be included at all.

Because of the Internet, even a little-known painting like this has been in plain sight — we can still come upon the shock of Steven Campbell's portrait and the questions it asks. If Bill Forsyth had been dressed up in a penguin suit it would have made perfect sense. If he was coming out of a red phone box with an ice-cream fritter, we would warm to it instantly. What we have instead is a glassy-eyed figure in a suit and tie. A night-time scene with a coating of cold sweat. The challenge of the portrait makes it easy to ignore: it's confusing to the point of being dis-engaging, and when something looks so wilfully obscure it becomes another picture that can be sent to Granton. We need to keep looking though, because this isn't just a portrait of a minor celebrity who we may or may not be interested in anymore, but a landscape depicting the chemistry of man and place. Forsyth is in the hills above Glasgow in the moonlight. There's a lush meadow, bright-flowered with both wild and cultivated plants, and we're looking down onto the city's homes and the Kingston Bridge ring road. Time must have stopped or the world ended for Glasgow's roads to be so car-less and deserted. The motorway lights are like burning lollipops — or maybe little heads on fire — and Forsyth is entwined around the trunk of a tree, one arm oddly elongated, stretching a claw-like hand to cover the moon. He's there with his children, Sam and Doone, who are similarly glassy-eyed.

They're playing with a hoop on their zombie family outing, holding onto different headshot portraits of their father: the 'public' faces that might seem more human but are also more self-conscious and troubled than the 'real' Dad who's with them. There's someone else in the painting, looking out from around Forsyth's legs, someone with an unhealthy-looking combination of white face, yellow hair and yellow goatee beard. It's the artist himself in impish form, (probably) holding a red paintbrush in his hand and responsible for the faint blood streaks on the portrait's foreheads.

What makes the painting really matter is that Bill and Steven were close friends. Not industry friends or occasional drinking pals but friends who talked. They met in New York in the mid-1980s as a pair of expats with young families in Manhattan. They'd both gone from struggling to make a living in Glasgow to sudden and heady episodes of worldly fame. More importantly for their friendship, they were both ambivalent about what that fame meant and what they should do with it. They hated the parties, the schmooze, the fudge of superficiality that seemed to be an unavoidable part of their respective industries. Steven (well known as a prickly kind of character) and Bill (quieter and more tactful but equally single-minded) would spend whole days together fishing; fellow riverbank philosophers and curmudgeons. One of Steven's works of collage — a dreaming, drowning 'Fake Ophelia' — was on Bill's wall at home for many years (before he donated it to the Glasgow School of Art, the institution where Steven had been a student[1]). "I feel closer to him than I do to most film-makers," said Bill. "I don't want to sound pretentious, but we relate as artists. If I'm talking to other film-makers, I'll end up talking about practical things, fees, budgets; but with Steven we can cut straight through to the fundamentals, the perennials, the universals."[2]

When it came to the portrait, Steven wasn't much bothered about getting Bill to sit for him, he'd already seen enough and knew enough. "The kids and I tramped along to his studio to see what he was up to. The disconcerting thing was, he had nine or 10 painted sketches of my head strewn all over the floor. He asked me which one I liked best — I don't know if he was allowing me to choose or offering me the illusion that I was allowed to choose. But anyway, I picked the nicest, sweetest, most enigmatic one." Bill has been non-committal about the unexpectedly chilly result. "I didn't feel desperately personal about it, I wasn't assessing it in an egotistical way. I don't feel it's me so much as that Steven has put me in one of his stories." A diplomatic response, a straight bat that deflects any further delving. It doesn't seem likely his friend was simply having a joke, it's not his style, and the painting is perfectly in keeping with the rest of Steven's output, with his interest in psychological extremes, in danger and death and absurdity. And it's meaningful because over the years, Steven said, he'd learnt that Bill was a "dark and mysterious creature"[3]. He had wanted to paint Bill for a reason, to share some of his understanding of a man with far more to him than the reductions of publicity machines might suggest or allow. As Forsyth's former partner Adrienne Atkinson has said of the different heads stuck onto the portrait's canvas: "I think the multiple images are quite telling."[4]

*

Resurrected and breathing warm life again, Bill is down from the hill and back into the marketplace of movies and its round of promotional press interviews. He turns up at the downtown hotel suite on time, wearing a flat cap and an old jacket. The journalists are waiting for him, grinning like sharks. He takes off his cap and jacket, revealing a tank-top and an obviously un-ironed shirt, and places them at the other end of the sofa where he'll be sitting for the duration. His trousers ride up to give a glimpse of pink socks.

Straightaway there's the colour for the piece, thinks the first magazine writer, making mental notes of how un-Hollywood Forsyth is, so rumpled and nervy. His hands are clasped in front of him like paws; other times he's fiddling at the cuff of his shirt. He's often avoiding eye contact (which is a shame, because those attractive dolphin-blue eyes are his best feature, along with the dimple on his chin), and he makes those quirky little films right? So that's going to be him all over, lots of self-deprecating jokes, the British kind of nerviness that makes him an over-talker, talking more than he wants to because he knows he's meant to be an entertainer. Have to listen carefully because he's not only softly-spoken but there's that Scottish accent misting it all over. Genial though. Even if I throw a curveball I know he's not gonna get sharp or say something to the PR. Those jokes keep coming, followed by a shy, soundless chuckle like he's just hoping he's being funny. I'll laugh a little for him, but not so much he won't try harder with the gags. Because Forsyth doesn't keep up the sparkle like the big studio regulars, he's not giving either himself or the film the huckster push; there are no keeper anecdotes about swapping pyjamas with

Robert de Niro — which is okay for a budget film-maker, he's not on the circuit and probably won't turn up again for a long time. Maybe never again if this one's a dud. Hey, they come and go Mr Forsyth. "So, you expecting a call from Hollywood now?"

What's most surprising about the press interviews over the years is that Bill doesn't just get it over with, play the game and talk about the wonderful experience he's been so proud to be a part of. He gives up bits of himself, in a self-immolating kind of way, through a series of unnecessary admissions of fallibility. Admissions or distractions? Either way, interviews come with the suggestion of a fatalistic out-look. He's not really a film director, he says, not really a writer either. He could be very shy as a younger man ("not fit to be around people")[5], and has mostly hated the film-making process. The character he has identified with most of all has been Dickie Bird in *Comfort & Joy*, he told Rita Kempley of the *Washington Post* in 1989: the DJ dumped by his girlfriend and left stranded and confused, driving his car aimlessly around Glasgow's ring road.

> "Because he is the most pathetic and the most like me in a sense. Because he's just not in control of anything...I don't think anyone ever is, you know. I mean, I think everything is predestined in the sense that the end is assured and pretty much the journey towards the end is pretty well assured. I think the idea of free will is just a joke. Yeah, it's just here you are and you just float down and hit a

rock and you can bounce off it and float
down a bit more and that's all you can do."[6]

He's not been worried about contradicting the persona the
media have wanted for him ("I'm a very serious person, trying to say serious things"[7]); or whether what he's said sounds
like a dig at both the critics and customers: "the films I've
made have always had a much darker side to them than I
think people have perceived, and it makes me wonder if
there is really all that much understanding of what irony is."[8]

The Campbell portrait isn't such a weird fancy after
all, but fascinatingly suggestive of a rebel who never wanted
to be the manufacturer of cinema product. Only by understanding the making of Bill can we find the dreamer who'd
want to make *Gregory's Girl*.

*

Born in 1946, he grew up with the river Clyde. A boy watching the oil tankers, cargo ships and ferries churn through the
grey waters and the criss-crossing of their wake, one sliding
pattern after another and how they move and meet; where
the waves go racing to the bank, each of them topped by a
cavalry charge of little white horses. Every day a new map of
formations and attacks. Fast ones, slow ones. Then an angry
one, the best of all, with its suck and slap and spray onto the
bank. Whatever fuss they make for a moment or two, he
knows those waves will eventually lose themselves in the
same wide reaches of the Clyde and be emptied far away in
the sea. Seagulls swing and circle above him, higher and

higher until they disappear into the endless space, leaving their wild sea cries behind them like they're made from nothing and nowhere.

There's more to the Clyde than water, it's a highway belonging to the local race of giants. The shipyard's cranes: the stiff-armed monsters of the smirr; their hulking great sheds have bellies of fire. Legions of people work for the river and its giants, the great black crowds of them in big heavy boots and overcoats with their fags and cursing. But Bill also knows the river stink — rank and rotten and oily — as being the smell of an adventure into technology, Festival of Britain stuff, and the surrounding storms of industry have both a familiar rhythm and a character of romance to them.

Looking back, Bill remembered: "the constant sound of steam hammers, metal on metal. You always woke up to it, you lived with it, but it was a gorgeous sound. I remember it in primary school. Five years old sitting at our little desks with a lid, like a sound box, you could put your ear to it and hear all the sounds from the shipyard vibrating in your little school desk. A kind of magical thing."[9]

The place he lives in is connected to every faraway port on the planet. A transporting kind of place. "In our house on the kitchen door handle there was a little cotton sock full of cane sugar — an awful lot of sugar was imported to Glasgow. Probably why the Scottish have such bad health, because we liked sweets too much. You could put your hand in there and get a handful of sugar."[10] On gala days he takes himself down to the Clyde to see a tugboat pulling one of the giant ocean liners setting sail, like a luxury skyscraper wallowing in his local street; a vessel soon to be basking off foreign shores, drifting under evening lights strung out over one of the great American bridges; a floating white miracle among a flotilla of junks on China seas.

Home was around the corner from the river in a soot-blackened Victorian tenement building in Whiteinch. It was close to the Barclay's shipyard on one side, and the enormous 13-storey Meadowside granary on the other: a constructivist monolith that marked the triumphs involved in feeding Glasgow's masses. Facing Whiteinch across the river there was the Stephens yard, building mostly cargo ships and ferries; then Lithgows and its big Royal Navy warships and cruisers. Father had himself once been one of the heroically dour men of the shipyard, working as a plumber, but now he kept a grocer's store. These outside places were as much like home as the inside, and Bill would be exploring them all, kicking stones through the pathways of Victoria Park; with his pals running down the Mekon (the big green dobber); wandering free over the waste grounds between the warehouses and factories, picking up old pieces of rope and furniture to make dens. As good as woods and fields in their secret corners and unexpected discoveries. And when summer came, they would fill and froth over just the same with high grasses and thistles, dandelions and bitter cress.

The river was the gateway to the Forsyth family's annual holiday to the island town of Millport around the Firth of Clyde. Mrs Martha Forsyth would travel on the steamer with her three children, the two older girls and Bill, excited over who would have the first sight of the Crocodile Rock, looking forward to the penny slot machines, the sandy beaches and misty evening views over to the Isle of Arran.

Mr William Forsyth would finally join them at the end of the week, the Friday evening when he would take the family out for a holiday fish supper.

This was Glasgow in the 1950s. A city of smoking mouths. Chimneys big and small that covered everything in soot: the washing hung out in the yard, the net curtains, the window sills and their potted ferns, the children out playing in the streets. The wettest of cities in a country already steeped in the lore and language of rain, that knew the slow, unmoving occupation of the smirr; the bluster and splash of yillen; the misery of a rain that's stoatin', sparking white off the pavements. The work of the Luftwaffe was still visible in the local landscape around Whiteinch when Bill was a boy. From early in the war, the Clydeside shipyards had been singled out by German bomber fleets. Factories like Harland & Wolff were given a heavy red outline on intelligence maps, marked up as small but significant targets among the massed rooftops of tenement homes, lying below the bombers in the wilds of an unknown country and its night-time darkness. The ruins and rubble created by the raids of 1940 and 1941 were only a small part of the story of Glasgow's landscape; a city of hills and water, riven by canyons of mouldering Victorian architecture, like a necropolis that had been turned over to the workers and shop-keepers once the families of imperial adventurers had gone. After the war there were still the same trails of smoke moving over the same low clouds, a horizon of cranes and pylons and factory chimneys; the grey river moving slow. But in these years it was an industrial city built on a premise that, after two hundred years, had become unsustainable. The heavy industries

were turgid and costly, too reliant on demand from international markets; its massed population had become too much
for the tenements to contain.

Glasgow was made from geography and geology: a
land stuffed with coal and ironstone, served by a river as
good as any arterial road. The city's potential energy was
released by a neighbouring power that wanted Glasgow as a
firebox of industrialisation, that needed its raw materials and
ships to build and grow an Empire. By the early 20th century
the Clydeside shipyards were making a third of Britain's entire shipping tonnage, a fifth of the world's[11]. They had a
reputation not only for the giant scale of their operations but
the quality of the marine engineering work involved that
meant they could win contracts for the most glorious, state-
ment-making ships of the age, the passenger liners like the
Queen Mary and the *Queen Elizabeth*. For the remainder of the
century, though, shipbuilding in Scotland was an industry
that only flourished as the result of artificial stimulants. The
shipyards were first of all saved by the Second World War —
the destruction being wreaked by German U-boats in the
Atlantic meant new orders for an average of five vessels per
week during 1943. And Bill only grew up to the sound of
steam hammers because the shipbuilding competition from
Germany and Japan had disappeared. Only temporarily. By
1958, Glasgow's contribution to the world's shipping tonnage
had declined to 4.5%[12], and during the Eighties, salmon fishing became more important to the Scottish economy than
the shipyards[13].

While money can drain out of a city like the water in
a river, families and communities cling to their homes and

each other. In 1940 it was estimated that just three square
miles in the centre of Glasgow was home to 700,000 people
(one-third of the entire population of west central
Scotland)[14]. For post-war planners the situation was so bad
they had no choice but to find radical solutions and forget
about the dislocation to people's lives: bulldozing slums; developing new housing schemes around the periphery of the
city; and introducing new satellite towns designed to deliver
modern lifestyles and a fresh start for skilled workers and
their young families: shopping centres, leisure facilities and
open green space. One of those towns would be Cumbernauld. The new estates planned for inside the city
boundaries such as Castlemilk, Drumchapel and Pollok,
were a great deal less utopian in spirit and design. They were
built as cheaply and as quickly as possible, had no local facilities of their own, no public transport, and were ear-marked
for the less wealthy, the unskilled and older populations. But
the re-housing still couldn't happen soon enough for families
sharing their home with creeping mould, faulty plumbing
and rats. By 1958 there were still 100,000 Glasgow families
on the housing waiting list[15], leading to phase three of the
revolution: high-rise flats.

The 1950s were the last years when Glasgow's heavy
industries would be running at full strength, meaning there
was something like full employment in the city. The housing
might have been rain-soaked and raddled, but people's lives
were more comfortable again, warm and frowzy, more likely
to include cupboards containing the solace of cheap pleasures, doled out to the masses in the form of sugar and chem-
ical flavourings. The post-war decade saw a doubling in av-

erage income per head in Scotland, up 25% in real terms. More families were becoming serious consumers, able to buy appliances like vacuum cleaners and washing machines[16], and for a back street grocer, these were the better times, especially when rationing ended in the summer of 1954.

Better than any macro-economic indicator, the grocer's store was a barometer of how things really were for people. The minor tragedies and victories in the histories of households were recorded in the shopping lists of housewives when they made their regular visits to Mr Forsyth: the scrag ends of meat and neeps in the hard weeks; extra sweets and chocolate bars for the weans when the bills were paid. The Forsyths had that penny-pinching realism bred into their bones. It was grocery that had brought William and Martha together in the first place. Martha's shop had run out of onions and she'd been sent out to buy replacement stock from the store where William was working (and this family story was an important reminder of how the workings of romantic love can rely, in reality, on arrangements as morosely practical as the availability of onions). Grocery store-keeping meant long hours of work for the sake of small margins, and each day they both witnessed and felt the need to eke out the value from every shilling. In their son's first film, *That Sinking Feeling*, this ethos was brought to life in the scene where a brisk Glaswegian shop-owner orders only very particular and very small numbers of baked goods that he knows he'll definitely be able to sell that day with no wastage.

Bill remembered a sombre, pessimistic upbringing. His parents were busy with their business and preparing against the day. It was only the family visits for cups of tea and sandwiches that would break the general silence of Sundays. He was expected to entertain himself, keep his neck clean, and his fingers out of the window displays. A happy memory from boyhood was the arrival of gift parcels from Illinois in the USA where his sister had a penpal. Packages would be filled with things they'd never seen before, like Life Savers candy, American comics, and a little farmer's truck with toy spades for him to play with. He had no qualms, though, about the austerity of his parents' outlook, it wasn't a sob story because he felt it was justified.

> "I think it's a much more real way to conduct your life. Because happiness is a very uninformed thing. Because if you're happy, you should be working out what's ahead of that, you know? I'm not saying you shouldn't relish it. But why not be positive about the rest of life, which is apprehension and threat? By embracing it, by admitting it into your consciousness. By volume, there's more of your life spent in unhappiness than in happiness. It seems silly to try to make so much of the one and not the other."[17]

It's a sentiment expressed more famously by a Canadian writer with a Scots heritage, Robertson Davies: "Happiness is always a by-product. It is probably a matter of temperament, and for anything I know it may be glandular. But it is not something that can be demanded from life, and if you are not happy you had better stop worrying about it and see what treasures you can pluck from your own brand of un-happiness."

Bill Forsyth went on to do this very successfully. But at least to begin with, neither happiness nor the treasures of unhappiness were going to be found inside the frowzy, sticky-lipped world of the local cinemas. Glasgow was the working-class 'Cinema City', where cheap tickets to movies were a cultural staple. "I remember as a young kid they had these cinema clubs. I think my mum made me go one Saturday and it was just so noisy, just noisy kids putting the seats up and down. And there were these bossy people. You were herded around like cattle in the theatre."[18] Throughout his life, the experience, and his response was the same. In 2005, after years of staying away, he went to see the Owen Wilson comedy *Wedding Crashers*. "We went to a mall outside Glasgow and had a pretty horrendous experience. We just wanted a night out. But the experience of being with the audience, the stench of popcorn. I objected to the way they were being manipulated, infantilised…The difference between an arthouse film and *Wedding Crashers* is minute. Then after the movie you're herded out, a rat in a maze. Suddenly you're in the car park."[19] He didn't go again for another 14 years. This time it was Quentin Tarantino's *Once Upon a Time in Hollywood* at the Plaza in Truro in 2019 — and he gave the impression of doing so only to avoid having to watch the screening of his own film, *Local Hero*, next-door, just turning up in time to do the Q&A with Mark Kermode. Just being inside a cinema complex meant succumbing to the powers of herd-think and herd-culture.

A quiet boy, not unhappy, just happier by himself. Those Sundays when the Aunties and other relatives descended on the Forsyth household were a mildly painful ritual — needing to be neat and tidy, not fidget, answer adult questions and say the right things, smile at the right times — and he would prefer to stay in his bedroom.

Questions kept coming from everywhere. If anyone at school asked him which football team he supported, expecting either Celtic or Rangers, he would say "Hearts" (Heart of Midlothian, an Edinburgh team) — because that way no-one would ever ask him about football again. He was happier with a book, and even games with friends had a bookish origin. Together they would imitate Richmal Crompton's Just William stories and the gang of Outlaws who scratched around the streets and lanes looking for ways to wangle a slap-up feed, or a few coins to spend on buns and pop; a muddy-kneed troop harried by prissy parents, vicars and older siblings, and always able to bring chaos to any 'respectable' occasion. Compared with the rowdy insistence of Saturday cinema clubs, reading was an occupation that could be carried out on his own terms. In peace. In ways that meant there would be a lucid path between him and the words on the page, a bright channel for forming pictures in the mind. An open space that allowed for a personal response, for different wandering trails of thought and feeling that could be picked up and put down again. So reading wasn't an escape but a means of waking up to reality; a reality made sweeter than the conventions and received wisdom of mass media would recognise or allow for. A lovely kind of truth.

As he grew older, Bill's favourite books would include JD Salinger's *Catcher in the Rye* (1951) and HG Wells' *The History of Mr Polly* (1910). One American and hip, the other an Edwardian antique. But they share (along with the William Brown books) the same sense of grievance at how lives can be strangled by society's expectations; where honesty and decency won't get you anywhere, where there's no point to poetry. Mr Polly is an ordinary man who, in his own clumsy and semi-educated way, is in love with Shakespeare and Rabelais and Gothic architecture but doesn't know why, or what he's going to do about it. All he knows is that he's stumbled into a loveless marriage and a soul-destroying job in a men's outfitters, and that he's sinking quickly into a miserable middle age.

> Deep in the being of Mr Polly, deep in the darkness, like a creature which has been beaten about the head and left for dead but still lives, crawled in a persuasion that over and above the things that are jolly and 'bits of all right', there was beauty, there was delight; that somewhere — magically inaccessible perhaps, but still somewhere — were pure and easy and joyous states of body and mind. He would sneak out on moonless winter nights and stare up at the stars, and afterwards find it difficult to tell his father where he'd been.[20]

Mr Polly runs away from his self-made prison to a simple, drifting life that is blissfully golden. Himself alone.

Salinger's Holden Caulfield is still young enough to do anything, but he's decided to drop out. Everything's "crumby". Underneath Holden's famous teenage angst, his sneering at pretensions, is a disappointed Romantic. He wants desperately to find something real to do, something real to be, something simple and unsullied by modern scheming. He takes inspiration from a Robert Burns poem, "Gin a body meet a body, comin thro' the rye". Holden day-dreams of being a 'catcher' standing by a cliff, stopping the children running and hiding in the thick fields of rye from getting near to the fatal edge. His innocence is twofold: in the ambition to fill his life with such a modest rural duty, but also in how he picks up on none of the raging sexuality in Burns' poem[21].

As an older teenager, Bill's best friend Stu introduced him to the *belles lettres* of Henry James, and via Albert Camus and his existentialism, to a philosophy that was thoroughly sympathetic to Holden and Mr Polly's plight, the value of authenticity, individual responsibility and self-creation. An-other novelist Forsyth kept reading over the years was the Russian émigré Vladimir Nabokov. In 2009, while he was in New York, Forsyth said he was planning a "wee anorak trawl of all his old houses, including the one where he wrote *Lolita.*"[22] Nabokov was "a magician with words and images", he said. And someone who, in an earlier age, had shared Forsyth's response to cinema. In Nabokov's first novel, *Mary* (1925), the narrator sits irritably in a cinema which is "crowded and hot", where people keep whispering all around him. "For a long time, coloured advertisements for grand pianos, dresses, perfumes flocked silently across the screen." The film being shown is one the narrator knows well, because he's been involved, if only very casually, as an extra. Sitting in the cinema he's struck by how much the film-making process has altered the original reality he had been part of: "On the screen that cold barn was now transformed into a comfortable auditorium, sacking became velvet, and a mob of paupers a theatre audience."[23] The deceit involved, it's suggested, is indicative of a bigger trickery, the reign of herd-think and illusions that cheapened people's relationships with the world. Worse, says Nabokov, is how these fantasies are allowed to be preserved on celluloid and projected again and again: "in a fairground barn, where lights seethed with a mystical hiss from the huge facets of lamps that were aimed, like cannon, at a crowd of extras, lit to a deathly brilliance, illumining the painted wax of motionless faces, then expiring with a click — but for a long time yet there would glow, in those elaborate crystals, dying red sunsets — our human shame."[24]

Forsyth's own approach to making films has been shaped by literature: "I get more from reading a novel than from any movie"[25]; "They are so full of ideas and I am very alert to ideas when I'm reading. It is not direct stealing, more the sense of an idea that I can develop and use in my work."[26] Film was his medium technically, as a tool, but the content was so often being formed by a literary sensibility.

*

"My little party piece when I was young and my aunts came to visit was my mother asking what I wanted to be. I'd say a journalist and they would have a wee laugh. I'm not sure why."[27] Bill wasn't totally certain what was involved in journalism — but he did know there had to be alternatives to working in the shipyards or a grocery, even if his years in school had been undistinguished, something of a blank. "I was just kind of shy and introverted and didn't involve myself much in what was happening at school or anything."[28] He was both "not very serious and not very sociable", a member of a small group of friends who would talk philosophy, read "weird books" and — most tellingly of all for us — visit art galleries[29]. Young love wasn't on the agenda: "you really had to be a real cool dude to even get near the girls," said Bill[30]. All he could remember were vague dreams of marrying actress Elizabeth Taylor and becoming captain of the *Queen Elizabeth*, the great ocean liner which had been running between Southampton, Cherbourg and New York since the year of his birth. While Bill didn't feel he'd made an impression at school, that doesn't mean it wasn't a formative time. He was a watcher, attuned to the changing weather of people's moods and the unspoken; the fine, scrawling character of latency in a silence.

Bill completed his studies at Knightswood School, a super-sized, brand new school that had opened up in 1958, a model of Scottish modernism known by pupils as the 'Kollege of Knowledge'. A school in size and newness that was not so dissimilar to Gregory's Abronhill High in Cumbernauld. Bill left the Kollege in 1963, aged 17, with no expectation that he would go on to higher study, and with no particular plans for a career either. There was one idea — a holiday in Greece. None of them, not Bill, Stu or the other friend, had much money, but the plan was to get some temporary jobs, buy a cheap car and go on the road through some sun-baked vistas away from home. At an auction they clubbed together and bought a green Morris Minor van with three gears and a top speed of 40 mph for £10, the kind of van that was used by the post office, for selling ice-creams or as a milk float. It was only after the cash had changed hands that they realised the petrol tank had been drained — and that none of them had passed their driving test anyway. The lads pushed the van five miles to a vacant lot where it would have to stay until they got the money together for driving lessons. The Greek holiday never happened.

Bill took all kinds of jobs to show his parents he was taking life seriously, including going door-to-door selling cleaning products to Glasgow's housewives. He went to an interview to become a pilot but found himself shrivelling among a clique of public schoolboys, slouching elegantly around the waiting room, tall and lean and filled with upper-middle-class certainties. He nearly got the job he really wanted as a writer with the giant IPC magazines (publishing hundreds of magazines, everything from *Woman's Own* to the *New Musical Express*), but only nearly. So he went on "applying for things religiously" and reading the separate 'boys' page of job ads in the Evening Citizen. 'Youth required for film production company', said one. This was a position with the Thames and Clyde Film Company owned and run by Stanley Russell.

Born in Glasgow in 1905, Russell was a pioneer of amateur movie-making who'd gone on to set up the world's first amateur film festival in 1933. He went on to make money directing and producing more than a hundred films for use in classrooms, for promoting businesses and as public information. Carpets, whisky, subsidence, the war effort, policing, as well as all kinds of Scottish industry, were subjects given the chance of reaching more people through film, that new-fangled and eye-catching medium. Making documentary films already had some glamour at this stage, especially in Scotland. John Grierson — who originally came up with the term 'documentary' in 1926 and had a particular interest in the potential of film for mass communications — won an Oscar in 1962 for his exploration of how ships were made on Clydeside, 'Seawards the Great Ships' (not really a 'fly on the wall' piece in the end; the recordings of dockworkers' voices had to be dubbed because of all the rude language). Russell stuck to making short promotional films, but always believed there would eventually be a Scottish film industry, and that the nation would need to keep hold of all the film-making talent it could.

Bill and Stu had interviews with Stanley back-to-back. They waited for each other outside the headquarters of Thames and Clyde, a large Georgian house in Maryhill that looked out over the River Kelvin and the parklands of the Botanic Gardens. Bill was fretting about his application form. He'd filled it out in green ink, and was now wondering whether it might be taken as a sectarian (pro-Celtic) statement. But the meeting in Mr Russell's home was matter-of-fact. Could he handle a broom? What about a lawnmower?

Could he drive? (He had to say no to that one, so Mr Russell
followed up with 'what about washing the car?' instead). The
deciding factor between the two friends turned out to be
brute strength. Bill was happy to grapple with a hefty studio
lamp while Stu thought it was screwed to the floor: "It was
my first professional assassination"[31]. Bill wasn't thinking
about Hollywood or the chance of a vocation. "I think the
first thing was it didn't seem like a job. That was the main
thing. The other thing was that the company operated from
the man's house, so I didn't have to start till half past nine,
till his kids went to school. I was lucky I landed on my feet
like that, because I had friends who went to work at half past
six in the morning."[32]

Monday 10th February 1964 was the start of a new
episode in the history of Thames & Clyde, now a "one man
and a boy outfit". Mr Russell did the filming and the driving
and Bill did everything else, all for £3 a week (or about £55
in today's money). The wizard of film-making — tall and
stocky in his suit, with a bald, bespectacled, kindly face —
included his boy apprentice as a member of the Russell family. After cups of tea and conversation in the kitchen, most of
their days would begin with the duo heading out on the road
to get more scenery in the can. For documentaries without a
screenplay or storyboard, that meant a special effort to give
life to some stolid subject matter, what was mostly inanimate,
prosaic material. "We filmed everything that moved," Bill
recalled. "And if it refused to move we panned across it…or
tilted up it."[33] People themselves were often more a problem
than a focal point. "Say we were filming a scene in a harbour
or something. You'd get all these rubberneckers coming

around and hanging around the camera. So we were forever saying, 'Will you please move away and get out of our shot? We're trying to make a film here.'"[34] Bill learnt the nuts and bolts of film-making, how to be a mechanic of celluloid by heating, cutting and welding film back together: "Back then we manufactured films much as the same way as they built ships"[35]. With Mr Russell, he was undertaking a trade apprenticeship in "old bread-and-butter documentary film-making" that stayed with him as the root of his identity as a director. "I always imagined myself as a guy in a tweed jacket with leather patches and a pipe, that's the kind of film-maker I saw myself as."[36]

With Mr Russell there was the beginning of his script-writing. After a month he was given the task of fleshing out material for a film commissioned by the Bank of Scotland that would encourage customers to open up cheque accounts, *Order to Pay*. The boss was also teaching him the magic of seeing, the poetry of ordinary things. One day when they were due to be picking up some camera equipment from Renfrew airport, Mr Russell decided to take the old ferry across the Clyde rather than use the new tunnel. As a consequence they ended up sitting in a long queue of traffic, watching the rain come down as they waited for the ferry to slowly chug back to their side. Mr Russell pointed to a puddle they could see from the window, glistening with wavy stripes of pale light. If they'd taken the tunnel, he explained to Bill, they would never have had the chance to see that puddle. "I liked that and I liked the job…Ever since I've tried to take the puddle path through life," remembered Bill in a film made in 2009. He regretted the tweeness of the phrase, but it was plainly a moment that had mattered[37].

Bill wasn't the "sorcerer's apprentice" for long. Before the year was out, Stanley Russell had died, suddenly, aged just 59. There were no more Thames & Clyde films, but Bill stayed on as part of the household for another six months to help Stanley's wife work on the editing of unfinished films and deal with the firm's assets and liabilities.

*

I was once a film-maker's apprentice myself. The sorcerer in this case was from the same generation as Stanley Russell, only a lot more sweary. In his suit, tie and braces, a Player's cigarette burning between yellow-brown fingers, my grandad — always known to me and my two older sisters as Dad — had made home movies since the 1940s. His films of sports days, Tulip Parades and May Day processions had been shown to crowds in the village hall in the years before television took over, and even in an age of *Star Wars* those movies were a marvel to me. They were remnants of a lost world, somehow preserved in lozenges of celluloid, a reaction of coloured dyes and chemicals that had somehow, miraculously, stored the light from days long past.

Holiday nights, when the front room was massed with assorted relatives, perched on every last remaining chair arm and pouffe, Dad would put on his show. He'd assemble the tripod and open up the dove-white screen, muttering as it drooped and sagged to one side. He'd drag out the stand for the projector that looked like an oversized ironing board while children ran to and fro, dog yapping, budgie tweeting. There was never any kind of settling or hush. Running commentaries from different parts of the room were expected, along with some giggling. Gossip carried on about who'd come down with an inexplicable illness in the village, who was looking after them, and who was now in the churchyard. We'd be sipping through straws at little bottles of fizzy drink fetched from the pub while boxes of Milk Tray and Twiglets went round. A bitter lemon for Mum. Babycham or Cherry B for the Aunties. For me, sitting on the floor, front and centre to the screen, this would mean staying up late into the night, worryingly late. When curtains were drawn against the night, the old places where death was. What was going to happen if the hands on the clock reached midnight? That was my worry. Because at that time of night, anything in the lamplight shadows could grow teeth.

Finally a reel of film — the recent blazing summer of 76 in Wales, the hula-hula girls at Corton, or Jackie and Brian's wedding — would be found at the back of a cupboard and slotted onto the projector arm, the plastic end threaded painstakingly through wheels and sprockets and fitted past the gate onto an empty reel. Dad would make a few practice rolls back and forth to make sure everything was moving as smoothly and freely as it should. The 1950s-era projector was switched on and we'd see a bloom of light from a bulb that would, very soon, be heating up to temperatures similar to those found in the core of a nuclear reactor. Dad would turn out the living room lights, and there it was on the screen: a bright chamber crusted about the edges. Frames chittering. An almost glamorous smell of hot celluloid and burnt dust. The chamber would fill with blossom trees and seaside fairground rides, old places made vivid and rosy by turquoise skies. Pulsing and flickering. Like ghost-worlds trying with all the strength of light to exist again in our own. We'd see scenes featuring smaller, squashier versions of ourselves at Christmas. Family members looking dressed-up and serious outside the village church for weddings and christenings. Relatives in funny swimming caps. There was less confidence about being watched by the eye of a camera in those days, so not a lot of posing, just the occasional smile and glance at the cameraman — varying from the uncomfortable to the impatient — sometimes a shuffling out of shot or a made-up reason to head indoors.

The titles were hand-made by Dad, some drawn and painted, others put together with letters on a board with a spray of springtime flowers. He would record soundtracks onto a reel-to-reel tape recorder that were meant to fit with each film but mostly didn't. Plinky-plonk piano from Mrs Mills: 'Pennies from Heaven' and 'If I Had A Talking Picture of You'; Bobby Crush playing 'The Entertainer'; new show tunes like 'Chitty Chitty Bang Bang'. What sounded like a requiem for kinder times in the music of Joe Loss and his Orchestra playing 'I'm Getting Sentimental Over You' or Don Estelle and Windsor Davies singing the big hit of 1975, 'Whispering Grass'. His other personal contribution to the performances, their edge of drama, came from all the swearing, mildly outrageous to young ears. The projector would often need tweaks and attention and that would mean touching the metal ("Ach-yah! me bloody fingers!"). Or there'd be a sudden explosion of whiteness ("the bugger's gone and broken!") — because the film was liable to come apart at a join at any time ("Wait a minute. Hang on. Sod it.") Worst of all, a total darkness that meant the end of the programme for the night ("What's it now? That's done it. The bloody bulb's gone!"). It was part of the fun. And beneath the appearance of grumbling, he quite liked to hear everyone laughing when he nipped his fingers, when he trod on a plug or something the cat had left behind the TV ("What have I put my sodding foot in now!?").

I couldn't wait to be part of the home movie operations, their allure and their shambles, and by 1981 (when I was 11) I felt like a co-conspirator. I knew how to fit a new Super 8 film, handle the focus and even light aperture settings for some fancy effects. I could work the splicer and use gum to insert a row of frames, and when the time came for a home movie evening, I'd help set up the kit. Dad would burn his fingers just as often, the films fell apart more regularly than ever, and I must have got in the way with my hovering and questions, but he was a gentle sorcerer, dusted with fag ash, custard spots down his tie. He loved the golden age of mass entertainment, when shows and musicals and their jokes and sentimental tunes were the whistling glamour of life, its trail of sun-sparkle. The films and home-made projects for his model theatre — put together from old bits of cardboard, rubber bands and glue, and decorated with his own evocative drawings, with a biro, felt tips and pastel-shading — were his way of keeping hold of some of that spirit. His *Chu Chin Chow, My Fair Lady, The Mousetrap*. Each of them a little wonder of re-creation.

[1] An artist who generated global attention for Scottish painting, Steven Campbell died in 2007, aged 54, after suffering a ruptured appendix.

[2] 'The Sitter's Tale: From the Scottish National Portrait Gallery: the film-maker has become a character in one of Steven Campbell's stories', *Independent on Sunday*, August 29, 1999.

[3] www.nationalgalleries.org/art-and-artists/39398/bill-forsyth-b-1946-film-producer

[4] Adrienne Atkinson, Email conversation, March 2022.

[5] Ben Lambert, 'Notebook Primer: Bill Forsyth', MUBI, 29 July 2021.

[6] Rita Kempley, 'Everyday of Bill Forsyth', *Washington Post*, 15 October 1989.

[7] Bill Forsyth interview, *Fresh Air with Terry Gross*, 6 October 1989.

[8] John Brown, "A Suitable Job for a Scot", *Sight and Sound*, Spring 1984, p157.

[9] Bill Forsyth interview, Filmwax Radio (New York), 10 October 2019.

[10] Ibid.

[11] T. M. Devine, *The Scottish Nation 1700-2000*, Penguin, 1999, p250.

[12] Ibid., p571.

[13] Graham Stewart, *Bang! A History of Britain in the 1980s*, Atlantic Books, 2013, p429.

[14] T. M. Devine, ibid., p559.

[15] Ibid, p561.

[16] Ibid, p562.

[17] Erica Abeel, 'Bill Forsyth's Rorschach Test', *New York Times*, 22 November 1987.

[18] Abbey Bender, 'From Sponsored Movies to Coming-of-Age Classics: Bill Forsyth Talks About Pioneering Scottish Cinema', MUBI, 3 October 2019.

[19] Tim Teeman, 'Bill Forsyth: the reluctant father of *Gregory's Girl*', *The Times*, 6 February 2008.

[20] HG Wells, *The History of Mr Polly* (1910), JM Dent, 1993 edition, p7.

[21] The original Burns poem included Scots dialect words meaning 'fuck' and 'cunt'.

[22] Gillian Harris, 'Hero of cinema Bill Forsyth ends exile', *The Sunday Times*, 28 June 2009.

[23] Vladimir Nabokov, *Mary*, Penguin (first published in Britain in 1971), 2007 edition, p23.

[24] Ibid, p10.

[25] Kevin Courrier, Interview with film director Bill Forsyth, *Critics at Large*, 1985.

[26] Gillian Harris, ibid.

[27] Ibid.

[28] Lawrence Van Gelder, 'Thoughts While Held Captive By an 'Escapist' Movie', *New York Times*, 23 May 1982.

[29] *Gregory's Girl* DVD, audio commentary — Bill Forsyth and Mark Kermode, 2019.

[30] Jonathan Murray, 'Cornflakes versus Conflict: An Interview with Bill Forsyth', *Journal of British Cinema and Television*, 2015, Vol.12 (2), p.245-264.

[31] Bill Forsyth, Lifetime Achievement Award Film for Scottish BAFTA Awards, 2009.

[32] Lawrence Van Gelder, ibid.

[33] Bill Forsyth, ibid.

[34] Abbey Bender, ibid.

[35] Bill Forsyth, ibid.

[36] Jonathan Murray, ibid.

[37] Bill Forsyth, ibid.

3. Grown-ups

"Look at all these men."
"Boys!"
"What's the difference?"

Bill Forsyth's interest in the possibilities of moving pictures began in the mid-1960s at the Cosmo. Just off the main shopping drag of Sauchiehall Street, the Cosmo (as in 'Cosmopolitan'), a giant art-deco and art-moderne landmark, was the first arts cinema outside of London when it opened in 1939. Once inside, customers became popcorn aristocrats. They entered a world of sweeping staircases, candelabra lights and balconies; a vast auditorium with curving cream walls, a stalls and circle for 850 people. The impression might have been of another movie factory offering shovelfuls of glamour to the masses, but this cinema's marketing was led by Mr Cosmo, a gentleman in a suit and tie (looking a lot like Mr Benn) who tipped his bowler hat to discerning customers[1]. His strapline was 'Entertainment for the Discriminating', backed up by an important point of reassurance: "no knowledge of foreign languages is necessary for the complete enjoyment of superb films". By means of its relationship with the better-known Academy Cinema in London, the Cosmo became the place to see the latest creations from the French New Wave: Jean-Luc Godard, Francois Truffaut, Louis Malle, Alain Resnais, as well as film-makers like Ingmar Bergman and Luis Buñuel.

Bill was a regular at the Cosmo with Stu. This way, cinema suddenly "felt glamorous and cool and interesting. I had this image of crewcuts, baggy trousers, cameras and jazz music". They'd turn up to the Cosmo in their coolest jackets and black roll-necks, smoke Gauloise Bleues cigarettes and sneer at the triviality of commercial cinema[2]. This wasn't 'going to the movies' for Bill, this was being part of a scene where people met in backstreet cafés and talked about jazz and Kerouac. They'd drink black coffee; imagine they were wearing shades; go walking in the rain rather than take the bus; put up their collars and narrow their eyes, draw in another lungful of bitterness from a cigarette. "I wanted to be Louis Malle when I was nineteen because he had made *Le Feu Follet*."[3] Then: "Stu took me to my first Godard, *Pierrot le Fou*, which blew me out of the water. It was another language, a real language. Watching it moved me in every meaning of that word. After it finished...I was waiting for him to say something 'cos I looked up to him. We turned the corner next to the bus stop, he blew out the smoke from his nostrils, and said: 'Fucking great, wasn't it?'"[4]

Jean-Luc Godard's films, and *Pierrot le Fou* in particular, set Forsyth's imagination alight. The connection to Godard was deep-rooted, not just a matter of fashion ("he was my God"[5]), Forsyth saw something — an ethos, a style, a way of talking to the world through film — that changed his life. "After seeing *Pierrot le Fou* five or six times I wanted to be Godard, and I still do," said Forsyth in 1981. "If I had a daughter she wouldn't be allowed to date someone who didn't like *Pierrot*."[6]

When Godard's film was premiered at the Venice Film Festival in 1965 the audience booed. Maybe because they had to. The 34 year-old Frenchman was the *enfant terrible* of the film world and his audiences were meant to be shocked and offended by the way he broke the rules of cinema with silly montages and self-obsession, it was their job. So the Venice audience became irritated and suffered and booed to show they understood their role.

Pierrot le Fou was based, very loosely, on the book *Obsession* (1962) by American thriller writer Lionel White. Godard took the basic idea and played around with the rest, improvising new scenes, putting in jokes, and letting out his anger and bitterness as his mood darkened. Jean-Paul Belmondo played the lead, Ferdinand Griffon, a man frustrated by the emptiness of his life as a bourgeois husband. He runs off with the babysitter Marianne, a wildly romantic and self-destructive character who's become involved with arms dealers and murder. Ferdinand and Marianne go on a madcap holiday. Steal and smash up a car. Sing songs. Tease the tourists. For Griffon, the break from conventional life gives him the space to dream again, to be in love and to write his masterpiece. Godard explained that he had "wanted to tell the story of the last romantic couple, the last descendants of *La Nouvelle Héloïse* [Jean-Jacques Rousseau's novel of doomed love], *Werther* [Goethe's novel of unrequited love], and *Hermann and*

Dorothea [Goethe's novel of love obstructed by class and social ambition]."[7] In other words, to make a film about the dregs of Romanticism and whether it was still possible in the modern age for Romantic idealism to exist, let alone matter. The film concludes with the unreliable Marianne choosing to run off with her arms dealer lover. Sitting on a clifftop by the sea, Ferdinand plans to blow himself up with the strings of fireworks laced around his head. He changes his mind at the last minute, but fails to snuff out the flame. The sweet holiday resort sunshine, the waves lapping onto the shore, only help to emphasise the vicious absurdity of what happens next.

The film was a revelation for Bill Forsyth because of its energy and "airiness"[8], he said. The freewheeling expression of ideas. There was a lack of respect for the cinema canon and its clichés; none of the usual sense of there being a contract with the audience: a build-up, break and resolution in exchange for some entrance money. It showed the possibility of another kind of film-making that was intensely personal, inventive, and intelligent on its own terms (with plenty of room for jokes, like this, one of Ferdinand's diary entries: "We live by hunting and fishing. Tuesday: nothing"). The French New Wave in general would have appealed to Forsyth because of its degree of self-awareness; how its auteurs wanted to strip away layers of surfaces, the pretend realities, to reveal the mechanics and artificiality of what was happening on the screen — a way of encouraging audiences to be actively conscious, not to switch off and just abandon themselves to the ride. This was done through a number of methods. By allowing actors to break the 'fourth wall' and look directly into the camera; using interruptive cuts to avoid deceiving audiences with a smooth reality; mixing up the media with cartoons and pop art; and by getting out of the studio to film something closer to real life than could be found in the controlled environment of a studio.

With its layers of references to art, literature and politics, *Pierrot le Fou* was the kind of film that made the advent of Film Studies degrees possible. On their 'holiday', Ferdinand and Marianne occupy a world given its meaning and sharp romantic reality by the correspondences they see in books.

- A small harbour, as in Conrad.
- A boat, as in Robert Louis Stevenson.
- An old brothel, as in Faulkner.
- A rich steward, as in Jack London.

The journal being written by Ferdinand has a subtlety of observation (without explanation) that goes beyond what would be expected from either a movie script or the attention of cinema audiences: like "POETRY, THE LOSER WINS." Ferdinand and Marianne use their creativity to tell stories and put on a show for tourists that takes pots-shots at American cultural imperialism, the suffering of ordinary people in Vietnam. The terminal flaw in their relationship is the contrast between the different fictions they embrace. Marianne wants to be in a thriller, Ferdinand wants to be surrounded by love and lyricism: "Let's stop pretending to be in a book by Jules Verne," he insists.

Most of all, Godard's film would have drawn a response from a bookish teenage Romantic (just starting to

53

learn about the painful stings of love) because of its bitter pessimism. Ferdinand and Marianne are caught up in a whirlwind romance that's full of everything and nothing. They don't and can't understand each other, and there's an absurd lack of purpose to their time together. She makes a fool of him and so he kills himself, like Romantic heroes do. Bill probably didn't know at the time, but the savagely reckless tone wasn't just *Nouvelle Vague* playfulness. The actress playing Marianne (Anna Karina) was Godard's wife, and the period of filming coincided with their divorce proceedings. Reportedly, Godard's sister was convinced her brother would commit suicide.

*

After Thames & Clyde, Bill was employed by other commercial film production companies in Glasgow, International Film Associates Scotland and Ogam. He worked as an assistant on *Loch Lomond* (1967), a travelogue for the promotional body Films of Scotland; edited a documentary on the life and work of Charles Rennie Mackintosh (1968); and directed his first film, *Still Life with Honesty* (1970) — a beautiful short funded by the Scottish Arts Council on the painter Sir William Gillies. The New Wave spirit is with Forsyth in one particularly effective scene where the camera tracks Sir William walking along a snowy village street. He then spent time working as an assistant film editor for the BBC in London, sometimes helping out on shows like *Z Cars*. Bill was paid £2 10s as an assistant cameraman filming football matches on Wednesday evenings. His attention was less on the game and more on how long the action was taking, because he wanted

54

the leftover 16mm film for his own projects. A friendly cameraman would turn the camera off during any stoppages, meaning there might even be an unopened can of film for Bill at the end of the evening. Working at the BBC also gave him the chance to use its labs to process his films for free. But it was only a brief experiment. "I was back home within a year. I couldn't make it in London — it was no place to be poor. It quite shocks me now, when I think upon it, how short a time I could survive in London."[9]

Forsyth's short films from that period were experimental, the work of a self-conscious 'artist' in the sense of someone exploring the use of a medium and its tools, with not much interest in pleasing anyone but himself: "I was interested in film as a substance, as a material, not to entertain or to tell stories. It was like sculpting with film."[10] They were experiments that resisted the involvement of people like plastic and rainwater. Both *Waterloo* (1968) and *Language* (1969) were about "time, distance and memory"[11]; "Some might call them cold exercises in distanciation," suggested Bill[12]. *Waterloo* was founded on a monologue taken from a sci-fi film where an astronaut wakes up from centuries of stasis to face the ultimate in loneliness: the realisation that everyone on Earth, every familiar face, is now dead. The Edinburgh International Film Festival screened *Waterloo* one Sunday afternoon in 1970. "One person in the middle of a row would stand to leave and rather than adjust in their seats to let him exit, the whole row would file out before him. It was utterly thrilling. Terrifying too, but I loved it…We had literally moved an audience."[13] In those days it really didn't matter to him whether it was in a 'good' way or not. "Lynda

Myles [the Director of the Festival at the time] called me a structuralist in 1970, and I kind of knew what she meant. I played with narrative forms involving montage instead of dramatic action. I thought I was re-inventing cinema, but I was really just like a kid playing in a sandpit."[14] The partner piece *Language* was a wistful, single-take film that opened with his grandfather reading a book about the war (Sir Robert Lockhart's memoir *The Marines Were There: the Story of the Royal Marines in the Second World War* (1950)), before the camera is whisked away and travels by car to a park where a boy and girl are kissing. "The people in the park, perhaps they were the old man's memory? Perhaps the boy was his grandson? I put a Jim Reeves record on the soundtrack, a very sentimental song about 'Today I found your old love letters,' country-and-western music which, like experimental film, makes distances emotional."[15]

This was an age when a young film-maker could still feel a sense of wonder at what might be communicated to others. How moving images could be used to capture and convey those puddle moments through celluloid, moments of seeing, moments of piquant emotion, moments that contained something beyond the ordinariness of surface appearances. Now we can make movies with a smartphone, point and shoot and know the focus and lighting will have been dealt with by an artificial intelligence. No material or substance of any kind to work on. Bill's experience was very different. "I was in love with film itself, the tangible stuff, the celluloid (the smell of it even), the magic it wrought through a projector, the images it could carry; and I loved the tactile experience of manipulating these images in the cutting room."[16]

Another member of the Glasgow documentary community, Jonny Schorstein, was also making shorts in the Sixties, hoping to break into feature film-making. Schorstein managed to get funding from the British Film Institute as well as corporate sponsors like British Rail. The result was two films with a strong French New Wave look and flavour — both of them starring Bill Forsyth. An unwilling actor but a good friend. Bill is (almost) the Scots Jean-Paul Belmondo, handsome and cat-eyed, but a Belmondo hiding behind his fringe. In *KH-4* (1969) Bill plays a painter living in Glasgow. As he walks the streets, witness to a broken civilisation, a post-industrial dustbin, the gloom of his art grows deeper. The fourth wall is broken in the final scene when Bill paints the camera lens black. In the longer film, *Mirror* (1970), Bill gets most of the lines. He's been deserted by his girlfriend Mary and is back on the Glasgow streets to look for signs of her existence. All he finds is an ants nest chaos of people in a modern city: "Where they all goin?" he keeps on muttering to himself, "where they all goin?" *Mirror* included more New Wave novelties: street level filming and sound recording, long tracking shots, a mix of media, and, in the final scene, the microphone and camera are reflected in the mirror as a concluding note of self-awareness.

Forsyth often talked about how alien the idea of acting and actors had been to him, but in none of those interviews did he once mention his own experience, even when he'd put in a very decent shift in both films. He comes across as casual and unmannered, even if he's not altogether a natural. In one scene in *Mirror* in particular, when he lunges into a prolonged kiss with his friend's startled girlfriend, the impression is less Belmondo and more Woody Allen.

*

As a director, his ambition and confidence was growing. In 1971, William Forsyth was chosen to join the first cohort of 25 students at the new National Film School. In other words, he'd been singled out for the kind of professional training that officialdom believed was needed to revive the British film industry (or create a better one from scratch).

It had taken a long time for the state to realise it couldn't rely on market forces and a national history of artistic endeavour alone. The Soviet Union had set up its movie school, the All-Union State Institute of Cinematography, in 1920 (having recognised the power of film in mass communications — for education and re-education). There was CSC in Rome (set up in 1935). France had La Femis in Paris (1944). Even in the USA, where the industry hardly needed any additional fuelling, a School of Cinematic Arts at the University of Southern California had been running since 1929; and, down a few palm-lined boulevards, there was another at UCLA, the University of California Los Angeles (from 1947). Senior figures from the British film industry and government made a fact-finding tour of Europe's top schools and concluded that, yes, perhaps it might be the very thing.

Five years later the School's opening was rushed through in order to prevent the relevant government department withdrawing the funding. The original initiative had come from a Labour Arts Minister now sitting on the Opposition benches since the shock election win for Ted Heath. So what was already a seat-of-the-pants operation had become loaded with further insecurity. With their limited funds, the School's founders had needed help from the Rank Organisation to get a mortgage on a site found in Beaconsfield. Leafy, commuter-town Buckinghamshire and the old premises of the Crown Film Unit, built in 1927 and used most recently as a workshop for converting cookers to run on North Sea gas. For the moment, the National Film School would be an assortment of hangar spaces and offices with buckets to catch dripping water from leaky roofs. Doors left hanging off their hinges, no heating and plumbing that had been written off as unfit for use.

The Director of the School, Colin Young, was a man with a mission — or at least a mission with some if's and but's attached. Colin had a three-year contract to invent his own kind of operation, think big and try out some fresh ideas, knowing there was always his old job waiting for him back in California at UCLA. He probably wouldn't have taken the job at all if his mother hadn't been taken seriously ill at home in Scotland. Young himself had been born in 1927 in Glasgow[17], where his parents owned a chain of three sweet shops called The Sugar Bowl. A career as a film critic had led him to study film at UCLA and then take on work as a tutor. His students included Francis Ford Coppola, Paul Schrader and Barry Levinson (as well as Jim Morrison of The Doors). With this kind of background, Young was listened to as an authority with a serious vision for the role of film in society. In 1965 he went on record to say that Hollywood was inconsequential: "turning out tired material that is irrelevant to what is really going on inside Americans"[18]. Britain's National Film School was going to be based on Young's idea that "filmmakers should be missionaries for a better way of life"[19]. With this in mind, his ideal candidate was going to be "emotionally mature and intellectually lively — and have a feel for putting images together meaningfully and interestingly. In short, they must be publicly-spirited egomaniacs who are terribly talented."[20] These weren't popular views with everyone. For Britain's new Tory Government, the National Film School was ridiculously expensive, its approach to recruitment was unnecessarily élitist, and there were huge costs per student compared with standard university courses. They were also certain that Young's interest in film's social role could only mean one thing when it came to the colour of his politics. The industry itself was also unconvinced: film-making wasn't mean to be an intellectual exercise, it was much more about learning skills on the job. Young had heard it all before, during his upbringing in no-nonsense Scotland, from Hollywood film companies, and in conversations with his state senator Ronald Reagan.

> "This attitude presumes that there is something the matter with somebody who has to go to school to make his way in life [said Young], that it is a sure sign of weakness in an individual if he has to go to school to learn how to do what he would learn in the workplace anyway. But there is a difference in attitude and technique between a person who

has qualified through the industry and one
who has gone through school. The person
who has learned in the industrial environment entirely, will have his or her time directed by others in a workplace which is keyed to
a production of artefacts of somebody else's
requirements. The other type will have their
time directed by themselves in a school environment which is keyed to their development
and will leave within them a spirit of an in-
ner-directed development as opposed to the
industry's outer-directed one...At a film
school the students are given the courage of
their own convictions and they are given time
in which to achieve that."[21]

There was an ongoing struggle over what the School was for
and the funding remained under threat. But the authenticity
of Young and his ideas was demonstrated by his loyalty —
he didn't hurry back to California but remained in charge
until 1992.

The chosen ones turned up in Beaconsfield in
September 1971 to the shell of a possible film school. Musty,
echoing spaces with damp-stained walls; abandoned cutting
rooms; a rushes theatre stripped of its facilities. The only
cameras and equipment they could use had been borrowed
from suppliers on the promise of future business, and, at
least to begin with, films were going to have to be shot on the
cheapest 8mm film and posted off to Kodak for processing.
The shabbiness of some aspects of the institution was

glossed over by the enthusiasm of Colin Young. This wasn't a university for kids looking to have a good time or some kind of executive perk anyway. Together they were going to change cinema — and say something true about the world. At the heart of the School's approach was an open curriculum that would encourage the 25 to become all-round film-makers rather than specialists, to learn via practice and experiment, not a prescribed set of rules. So there would be no written curriculum and no set term dates or hours of attendance. No formal teaching but open-ended conversations: shared sessions huddled together around the Steenbeck editing suite. Students needed to come up with their own ideas for films to make. (This led to one group going down to Devon to make a documentary about stag hunting. Another set up a fake border and customs booth on the main road into Beaconsfield and demanded to see passports. In scenes reminiscent of an Ealing comedy, the Britishers just sighed and turned their cars around to fetch them).

Each of the School's new intake had been given their own canvas Director's chair, on which some of them had etched their name. Among the group though, Bill Forsyth was the only pro. "I was by then an industry veteran, and I lorded it over the Cambridge and Oxford graduates and the Commonwealth countries who hadn't seen an Arri [camera] or a Steenbeck before. My kind of prestige lasted about a week."[22] Young would have been impressed by the 25 year-old's portfolio of work with Stanley Russell and the *Still Life* film in particular, as well as the fact Bill was making money. He'd needed to take time out from new promotional film enterprise he'd set up with a partner, Charlie Gormley.

Young and Forsyth also had that shared connection to Glasgow (who knows, Bill might have been a regular Sugar Bowl customer). Most persuasively of all, it's likely that Lynda Myles would have alerted Young to Bill's radically creative side.

Looking around the room, talent was everywhere. The old-timer in the group was 37 year-old Bill Douglas, about to begin on his remarkable trilogy of films based on his experiences of growing up in the Scottish mining town of New-craighall (*Childhood* (1972), *My Ain Folk* (1973), *My Way Home* (1978)). Mostly silent pieces of work. Stricken, bereft. Black and white photographs with a shivery angst of life to them.

Then there was a young Nick Broomfield, 23: in the right place to try out a new kind of documentary-making where the mechanics were all on show, the mistakes and dead ends and failures (leading to his films about children and crime, *Juvenile Liaison* (1976), and *Soldier Girls* (1981), looking at US army basic training for women).

Michael Radford was only a few months older than Bill, but had been born into a very different milieu. New Delhi. Son to an officer-class father working in Army HQ on plans for the demise of British India. English public school followed by Oxford University. Michael stayed in touch with Bill after Film School and went on to play his own small but important part in the making of *Gregory's Girl*. After years of documentary work, Michael directed his own love story set in Scotland, *Another Time, Another Place* (1983), juxtaposing the passions of Italian prisoners of war with the dour landscape and lives of Scottish farmworkers. Most famously he went on to direct the wonderful arthouse-charmer *Il Postino* (1994), about the relationship between poet-in-exile Pablo Neruda and his postman.

Another Glaswegian in the group, probably already a familiar face for Bill, was Iain Smith. He went on to become Jon Schorstein's business partner in 1976 and teamed up with Bill Douglas to work as the producer for his trilogy. Smith was the location manager for *Chariots of Fire*, and became a Hollywood producer associated with a roster of success over decades[23].

They were only ever a bunch of individuals with different strengths and interests, not any sort of coherent 'generation'. But they had passed the Colin Young test of intelligence and social commitment, they shared an experience of intense thought and debate, and the chance to see each other try out new ideas in practice. And it happened during an important phase for film-making, at the time of the rise of observational documentary and social realism. Films didn't have to be carefully contrived, dramatised and packaged up. There was a belief, instead, in there being a special quality to ordinary lives, if only directors would look in the right places, in the right way. That included an appreciation of people's relationship to places and landscapes. "I think the films I like least are the ones in which the exterior world serves only as a backdrop for dialogue and action," said Michael Radford. "It somehow reduces the film. Sure, you can tell a story that way. But where cinema starts to become magical — and become personal, I think — is when you're aware that the exterior world which you're filming, which has a concrete reality, is nevertheless informed by the inner world of the characters."[24]

Bill dropped out of the National Film School in 1972, just after the Christmas holiday break[25]. Beaconsfield was only a brief interlude for him, but a formative one because of the people he'd met. It had given him a sense of both possibility and direction, a confirmation of what 'good' feature film-making was and how it could be done. The reason for leaving on one level was simple enough. His few months as a student had been constantly interrupted by the need to travel up and down from Glasgow to keep up his day job. There were other reasons for being at home and for clinging to its securities — as Bill admitted in an interview in 1982, he'd left "for one or two personal reasons. I had started to put a home together in Glasgow. I was homebuilding — emotionally."[26]

The city he returned to was changing, some of his roots already gone. His two older sisters had both married Englishmen and moved south. The tenement where he'd been born in Whiteinch had been demolished as part of the development for the Clyde tunnel; familiar landmarks like the local church, bowling greens and allotments had been replaced by a dual carriageway. For Bill though, Glasgow still had its own kind of fond reality. Like those grey clouds and industrial smoke, layer on layer, weaved into one, not dull or grim but swift and feathery, often pearlescent in the morning light. Rain-soaked public parks. Lighted windows in tower blocks. Processions of headlights in the dusk. A mood of sympathy with the ordinary places of home comes across strongly in Forsyth's first film, *That Sinking Feeling* (1979) as well as his most personal, *Comfort & Joy* (1984). There's a sadness in there too. Whatever its limitations as an institution or in its particular philosophy, the National Film School would have been a certain route to recognition, business networks and a career of some kind in films and TV. He'd turned that down in favour of more of the same, the promo films, even when he was bored of making them and the lack of financial returns. What was he doing? Where was he going?

Bill wasn't the rebel who'd agreed to be the Belmondo lead in *KH-4* and *Mirror* anymore. Or the structuralist film-maker excited by the sight of his audience walking out. He needed something else, something more. The kind of work that might mean a new life. Bill didn't want to be Mr Polly stuck in minor jobs, his youthful ability to be part of the gang and enjoy creative adventures leaking away from him as each year passed by. Writing the screenplay for *Gregory's Girl* was what he saw as his big "crossroads" moment[27]. "It was an act of desperation, really. I was at the end of my tether in terms of wanting to make industrial films. I'd done it for six or seven years, and there wasn't even a living in it."[28] Looking back, he saw a feature film as the less risky option. "Either I would... spend the following decades tenaciously developing what was finally manifest as the gallery video-installation genre, or I'd make that slow backwards retreat into conventional cinema. We know what happened. To think that I might now have been the grand old man of international video art (probably with a pad in Berlin)."[29] But a mainstream film surely couldn't have felt easy at the time. He knew something about niche video art and winning the enthusiasm of a cognoscenti; making a film for High Street cinemas was something else.

To start with, Bill needed a hook to sell his film. He found his idea — really more of a reminder than an idea — when he was browsing in a bookshop and picked up a copy of Jack Kerouac's High School novel *Maggie Cassidy*. "I realised I could make a movie about kids falling in love."[30] He wasn't thinking about drawing on his own experiences at school ("that would have been a tragedy not a comedy"[31]) or trying to imitate anything from the high school film genre. There's more of a reaction against *Maggie Cassidy* than imitation in the script itself. It's one of the Kerouac books that does feel more like typing than writing, a 'self-as-hero' book where Jack 'Duluoz' is the dude with hidden depths. He can break hearts, do the 30-yard dash in 3.8 seconds and then stretch out like a hot lazy tiger with his book of Emily Dickinson poems. To the relentless groove of its bebop prose, the novel revolves around whether Duluoz's mighty young soul should be embarking on its journey with Maggie or Pauline. In this context, Forsyth's story looks like a Scots piss-take. Gregory is the unathletic beanpole who doesn't know where to start with girls, who prefers a thrash on his drum kit to much else. The girls are the ones who get to make all the decisions. Most of all, Forsyth is making fun of a modern culture where the biggest problem young people have is not being fancied. "I wanted to show someone in a very luxurious situation," said Forsyth, "growing up in a new town, going to a good school and who was still prepared to whine about the only thing for him to whine about — the fact that he was in love."[32] He had to come up with something more, the screenplay's 'inciting incident', which he decided would be having a girl on the football team. "I was trying to think of some additional problems for the boy, and I was trying to make them modern problems, so it just came from that really."[33]

There are other influences. As Forsyth admitted later in his writing career, he would "just steal little things from novels, you know, here and there and adapt them and change them: this situation, or a word, or a character, or whatever."[34] The relationship between Gregory and his younger sister Madeline — a relationship that's much more important to the film than perhaps comes across immediately — was an idea taken from *Catcher in the Rye* and Holden's dependence on his little sister for understanding and affection.

Then there's Nabokov, popping up in many places in Forsyth's films. *Mary* (or more correctly, in order to make it sound less prim and lavender-scented, *Mashenka* in the original Russian) was first published in English in 1971 — when it would have been a 'new' Nabokov for Bill to read. It was Nabokov's first novel, written when he was 27, and just like *Maggie Cassidy*, it's a novel rooted in autobiography, drawing on Nabokov's experience of first love when he was 16. In *Mary*, Ganin (Nabokov's alter ego) is now aged 25 and living in exile from revolutionary Russia in Berlin. By chance he gets stuck in a lift in his *pension* lodging house with Alfyorov, an overbearing and buffoonish character with a "scraggy neck" — the man who, it turns out from the unwanted confidences he's shared, is the very man who went on to marry Ganin's first love Mary. Without knowing anything of their history, Alfyorov insists Ganin must meet his marvellous wife when she arrives in just a few days' time. Ganin is another of those characters who believe they have lost everything with the end of youth, but with the thought of seeing Mary again his depressed state of mind evaporates, replaced by crystal pools of memory, like blue twilit skies reflected over an autumn lake. Ganin is overtaken by a realisation that sleeping in his past are sacred moments too delicate to even try to remember without taking some care. Mary was the girl in the park with long brown hair tied back with a black bow, the one he thought he'd never get to meet.

> He was a god, re-creating a world that had perished. Gradually he resurrected that world, to please the girl whom he did not dare to place in it until it was absolutely complete. But her image, her presence, the shadow of her memory demanded that in the end he must resurrect her too — and he intentionally thrust away her image, as he wanted to approach it gradually, step by step, just as he had nine years before.[35]

I think *Mary* is where the singular quality of Gregory's summer evening comes from. And maybe also some of the innocence of *Gregory's Girl* as a whole. Ganin had waited for first love to come along, not because he was a cold fish or an idealist, but because he senses that saving himself for romantic love (more than giving in to fumbled teen shagging or just plain wanking) would lead to a heart-stopping fulfilment: "I was simply happy living as I was and waiting. And my schoolmates, the ones who used foul language and panted at

the very word 'woman', were all so spotty and dirty, with
sweaty palms."[36] There's also an idea in the novel of how
awkward teenagers go about talking to girls, how they resort
to irrelevant facts in place of conversation. Sitting on a
"lame bench", Ganin announces that: "Macaroni grows in
Italy. When still small it's called vermicelli. That means
Mike's worms in Italian."[37] ("Thas very interestin, isn't it?"
as Andy would say to the girls).

Nabokov returns to one-off moments of young romanticism again in novels like *Glory* (1932). Martin, another
16 year-old character, sees a cluster of far-off twinkling lights
on a hillside while travelling at night through Provence. Over
time it becomes the symbol of escape from stifling upper-
middle class conventions. Much later Martin runs away and
for a short time gets to live a simple life in that very Provence
village ("a wanderer, alone and lost in a marvellous world"[38]),
but after finally returning to a normal life he is never able to
find the village again. Locals deny the village even exists.
The magical far-off lights ("spilled jewels in the blackness"[39])
are still there, but not the physical place itself.

The film project forced Bill into writing screenplays. "I
asked three different writers if they would do the script for
me and they all said no. They felt I was so close to it that I
should write it myself, so they were trying to point me in the
right direction."[40] But there was no chance he would end up
slaving like a hack writer on a script. It was going to fall into
place, bit by bit, or not happen at all.

> "I know I'm very lazy and if I push myself I
> don't get anywhere. I've just got to take time,

and so I spend a lot of time not doing anything. I delude myself into thinking I'm not
working and that makes me happy because I
know things are happening in my brain and I
spend about six months not writing — taking
notes, thinking things and just structuring
things on bits of paper, not actually sitting
down and writing. I think that's the secret,
not sitting down at the typewriter too early."[41]

The writing, in the end, would become more appealing than
making the films themselves.

*

Everyone remembers Forsyth's films for the jokes. It's even
referred to like it's something he can't help — a Scots
whimsy that keeps bubbling up and over the brim — when
there's a great deal more to the purpose and content of the
Forsyth humour. First and foremost, the jokes in the *Gregory's
Girl* script were there to help him keep writing. Jokes meant
Forsyth had a 'voice' in the script he was happy to put up
with, a way of avoiding accusations of pretension, and an
impetus for stringing together a story. "You hide behind
comedy more easily than you hide behind seriousness," he
admitted[42]. Which is why there are so many jokes in his four
Scottish comedies, the running jokes and sight gags — even
when they're not strictly comedies at all.

Being a first generation TV viewer in the 1950s and
1960s was a practical education in comedy. The program-

ming was a silver stream of cheapo re-runs of Charlie Chaplin, Buster Keaton, Laurel and Hardy. And best of the lot for Bill, the Marx Brothers. These were films that offered lessons in the essential absurdity to human life, and the way in which the little men — the poor, the outcasts, the eccentrics — used their wit and inspired irrationality to win against the odds (heavily stacked odds) to find a way to live in-between the giant, crushing wheels of the modern world, its animus of establishment wealth and power. That also meant learning the difference between the romantic lead (who always got the girl) and the comedians who had to settle for getting the laughs. Not on TV, but also important to mention here is Jacques Tati, who was introduced to a young Bill at the Knightswood School through a surprise screening in the main hall of *Monsieur Hulot's Holiday*. "I didn't even mind that it was in black and white and a foreign language — almost all of the fun in it was visual."[43] Bill was also alert to the niceties of Scots humour, old and new. One example is the scene in *Gregory's Girl* where Gregory is caught getting dressed and he squeaks and covers his nipples with his fingers, a manoeuvre taken from the music hall comedian Lex McLean.

The next TV influence was Preston Sturges, the first screenwriter in Hollywood to also become a director: the first auteur. "[Sturges] was a bit of a hero to us in the 1960s and 1970s, because his movies were coming on TV at that point," said Bill. "You could see that he was…a bit of a maverick and you can see him pushing against the boundaries of the system."[44] Sturges was a scandal. Writers were the lowest life-form in the industry, the manual labour who doled out the raw materials for turning into gold by the actual talent: the producers, directors and actors. The quality of Preston Sturges' work meant he was able to start making demands over how his writing was used, so that none of his original vision was lost in Hollywood's stock trade of fluff and gloss. His screenplays were distinguishable by their natural and believable, spring-bright dialogue; an absence of the smooth blandness of writing by committee, and instead, the oddness and courage of a single imagination. His plots often ran along the ridge of emotions precariously and viewers never felt quite safe from the bumps and falls (is this going to hurt?). Like Bill Forsyth, Sturges allowed everyone to have good lines, not just the leads. He was similarly inimitable as a writer, and went on to be dropped after making a series of four films that lost the studios millions.

For Bill, humour was always going to be part of the formula for getting audiences to stay in their seats. "Film is a universal language because it addresses your emotions. The trick is to learn to speak your own emotional language clearly, and then stick in a couple of jokes," argued Bill just after the release of *Gregory's Girl*[45]. He went on to change his mind soon afterwards. Had audiences really got the meaning of those jokes — or were they getting in the way of understanding what the film was about? "I'm beginning to reach the conclusion that people think comedy is about making us laugh, and if there is nothing more to comedy than laughs, then a lot of effort is going for nothing."[46]

> "It's strange to me that people want humour
> to be in a category all by itself, as pure 'enter-

tainment'. So those who misunderstood *Comfort and Joy* the most were those who thought I was just trying to make a jolly farce. That is a complete misreading of the film. It means that if they misunderstood *Comfort and Joy*, they misunderstood my other films."[47]

Then, in 2021, Forsyth was thinking maybe he was the one at fault, for believing such a gentle web of irony could ever communicate what he wanted to say. "Watching from the wings. It's a very Scottish thing, holding up the kitchen wall at parties, casting comment from the sidelines. Hiding in the wings. I don't know, after all these years, whether that really was the way to have gone."[48]

Forsyth's humour has been a cause for contention among academics. Has the comedy been downplayed in film studies for the sake of concentrating on Forsyth's reputation as a serious auteur, a pillar of Scottish cinema?[49] It's all one really, there's no contradiction because the humour isn't shallow. It's not whimsy, it's purposeful. "Humour," said Forsyth in 1985 after his run of four 'comedies' had been completed, "wasn't invented for entertainment."[50] No — human cultures have used humour as a way of coping with pain and darkness, a darkness that never goes away, no matter what artificial warmth and light the improvements in our material wellbeing have brought. Forsyth has often suggested his comedy comes from Glasgow rather than himself as an individual. A communal sigh, a wipe of the mouth with the back of a hand at the predicament of living in such a place, the industrial grime and low life expectancy; part of the psychology of a blue-collar city ruled by stuffed shirts in Edinburgh and London. "I think that Glaswegian humour is very similar to New York humour, which is really Jewish humour for it is the humour of despair, the humour of the gallows."[51] So, in a way, Forsyth's comedy is not meant to be funny as such, but a means of getting audiences to think. Not jokes but observations of human nature. In a piece written for a showing of *That Sinking Feeling* at the London Film Festival in 1979, Forsyth explained himself like this: "In my city people talk a lot. They even have the unusual habit of saying approximately what they mean. There can be humour and irony in this directness which at first hearing can sound like a beguiling kind of innocence."[52]

There's some Godard in the approach to humour in *Gregory's Girl* too. What's wild in *Pierrot le Fou*, the musical comedy and crazy jokes, is domesticated. Forsyth doesn't want to be seen to working too hard and the delivery is always relaxed. "I'm scared of overemphasising, overdramatising," he said[53]. "The purpose of humour in my work is to defuse any hint of dramatic artifice that might be creeping in."[54] So while the resulting jokes can come across as whimsy, the impulse behind it is still subversion. More than that, Forsyth is saying something about everyday experience. It's odd. We're odd (and maybe the oddness is the best part of us). Asked directly about Forysthian humour, Bill acknowledged how unconventional (and nuanced, in a literary kind of way) it can be.

"I know it when I try and think it up. If I talk about what my ambitions were for it back then, it was something that was slightly magic but isn't corny magic, it was just human magic. It could be something like this sudden midsummer's atmosphere that overtakes people and even the two boys that are wandering around catch it. They say, 'There's something in the atmosphere.' That's almost a kind of solidifying of the idea. That's part of it and it's a kind of a human thing. It was just allowing every individual their eccentricity without taking it to a point where it's just pure comedy. It's trying to capture that little bit of eccentricity that's in everyone without overplaying it. A lot of it was scripted rather than having these things crop up. There was more fun in writing them and playing them rather than trying to hatch them on the wing while we were filming."[55]

*

Hasn't *Gregory's Girl* stayed with us because it's our common story? We all went to school. We all remember the madness of first love — the revelation of it, the unfamiliar, short-lived euphoria, an end to normality — so quickly reduced to the level of all things, an inevitable return to a world of clouds and routine. But a personal drama we wallowed in, shamelessly. So it's a film with a winning formula of nostalgia, one that works by digging into a hoard of once-precious, still-plangent memories. A longing for lost youth? As we've seen though, *Gregory's Girl* was made by a very particular kind of personality. In anything other than the most superficial way, the film doesn't have that formula, it's too individual and un-conventional.

Each of the four 'comedies' was personal, part of a coming-of-age history. "[By the time *Comfort & Joy* was com-pleted] I had taken this character, whoever he was — wheth-er he was me or a version of me — from the age of 16 to around 35 or so. The thing was totally mined."[56] But *Gregory's Girl* is not about youth in itself. There's no sense of the detachment of a writer looking back on childish things, no condescension. The film comes from a perspective where the awkwardness and naivety and romance is not just a memory. Here, I would say, is one of the most important reasons for the longevity of *Gregory's Girl*: it's not just nostal-gia. Bill was still Gregory. We are still Gregory. In itself the film is very simple, but add the dimension of adulthood — what we know, what we've seen and continue to see in our experience of love — then the minor phrasing of *Gregory's Girl* becomes a rhapsody. Like Nabokov's Martin, we're still looking for the lights on the hillside, spilled jewels in the blackness. Because youth never leaves us, as was claimed by another Scot, Robert Louis Stevenson.

> Our boyhood ceased — well, when? — not, I
> think, at twenty; nor perhaps altogether at
> 25, nor yet at 30; and possibly, to be quite
> frank, we are still in the thick of the Arcadian
> period…we advance in years somewhat in
> the manner of an invading army in a barren
> land; the age that we have reached, as the

> phrase goes, we but hold with an outpost, and still keep our communications with the extreme rear and first beginnings of the march. There is our true base; that is not only a beginning, but the perennial spring of our faculties.[57]

The difference between adults and teens was on Forsyth's mind as his plans for the film worked themselves out. "Adolescence is a kind of permanent terminal state," he said.

> "I found myself 30 years old and still an adolescent. I started to look at people about me and found out they were the same. Maybe it was because I had gone back and was beginning to know young people again. I could see there was no difference between their preoccupations and hang-ups and those of my friends and other people — the kind of obsession of working out how one is seen by the rest of the world and how one is presenting oneself and what you think you are and what other people see you as. I think this goes on all your life."[58]

What he says isn't meant to be a criticism of 'adolescent' adults but an acceptance that people don't follow an inevitable or natural curve of progress towards maturity, they gain experience but stay flawed, emotional, deluded. In Forsyth's sober worldview, we don't take on an immaculate state of wisdom over time because knowledge in itself is only ever a limited and limiting thing. As French philosopher Montaigne put it: "the end and beginning of knowledge are equal in stupidity". Gregory was only the first of many Forsyth characters who was a boy-man and man-boy. As one film writer has suggested, they are: "often cases of blithely arrested development"[59]. The school setting is ideal for showing how the supposedly most responsible of adults keep on acting like children, and children like adults. The headteacher enjoys a secret life, tinkling on the piano, sorting out his supply of buns and pastries; the teachers giggle and wink and indulge in their "silly banter" in the staff room. Meanwhile, Gregory's little sister is full of worldly advice, even when she's stirring an ice-cream float: "The nicest part is just before you taste it. Your mouth goes all tingly. But that can't go on forever." A delicate piece of fatalism. Her schoolmate Richard has the suavity and confidence that the much older Gregory obviously lacks; while the teenage writer for the school magazine has the seedy manner of a middle-aged hack ("I mean what do you, and your body, do on a Saturday night for instance?"). No-one changes or 'grows'. Characters stay within a flux of immaturity: unreliable, muddled and stupidly appealing, just as real people tend to be.

The idiosyncrasy of Forsyth's perspective is striking when compared with the version written by Gerald Cole for the film's novelisation. A freelance sub-editor with national newspapers, Cole was a jobbing writer, and given the screenplay to work on he saw a standard high school story about adolescent spots, booze and snogging. This led to a novel where Gregory isn't recognisable as Gregory anymore[60]. Cole tried to fill in the gaps with what we'd ordinarily expect a 16 year-old to be thinking. Like this: "[Gregory] wondered what to do with the evening. *Top of the Pops* at seven-twenty of course. After that he might try the new bar near the motorway where Andy had got away with three pints of McEwan. If a babyface like him could manage it, Gregory should have no trouble."[61] But Forsyth's characters in the final film are child-like in ways that only good-natured adults are child-like. Their behaviours and preoccupations are kind of middle-aged. The contrast is even more clear when it comes to sex. Cole's Gregory is up for it, in a clammy teenage kind of way. "He remembered that party. His first promised orgy, except that all the girls seemed to have sewn their nighties to their underwear…One pecked kiss he'd had, one begrudged peck from a semi-inebriated giggler."[62] Any romance in the final scenes is lost in the novelisation: "The country park: scene of lust, rapine and unfettered snogging — did she realise?"[63] We can see there's nothing very lustful about Gregory, he's dazed by the unexpected magic of the evening, by what's happening to him, the growing reality of Susan and her presence and personality. There's no condom in his pocket.

From Forsyth's (semi-mature) perspective, romantic love isn't a drug that brings happiness, it's complicated; obscure. Other human relationships can be more important, even though they haven't had all the publicity of boy-meets-girl. In the original screenplay there's more emphasis given to the connection between Gregory and Madeline and what they mean to each other, what could be seen as a simpler and more honest kind of love. In trying to explain their relationship, Forsyth goes to the effort of quoting French novelist Christine de Rivoyre in his script notes: "there are all manner of betrothals on earth, and all are blessed if the heart be true."[64]

*

This was Bill Forsyth's movie and not an exercise in genre screenwriting. A personal film by someone who believed that films should be about something. What's not yet clear, from all we've seen so far, is what that might actually be. There's no message — only a kind of genial, irresistible futility. He knew cinema was wrong in encouraging people to think there were happy endings and a natural tendency for good. There were only flashes of something real and true, especially in books and art, if you knew where to look. As Godard's *Pierrot* said on his doomed adventure into the unknown, a hopeless puppet: "Life may be sad but it's also beautiful."

We've found our dreamer. He's in his 30s, living alone in a flat in Glasgow, worryingly low on cash. Bill is looking about his room and out of the window to the city's ashen horizon, wondering whether it was a cool setting or just a lonely one. Not much into socialising in the bars and clubs, he's sitting at his little grey Adler typewriter writing a screenplay for the sort of film he'd never want to see himself. A script with a working title of 'Singles'. Forsyth knew he could subvert cinema conventions. He knew he could.

The truth, though, was that he probably wouldn't have done anything; he would just have been another of those rebels whose rebellion stayed in their head — if it hadn't been for Charlie Gormley.

---

[1] The character of Mr Cosmo was said to be modelled on the cinema's owner, George Singleton.

[2] It's an attitude to mainstream cinema that never seems to have left Forsyth. During the recorded audio commentary for the re-release of the *Gregory's Girl* DVD in 2019, Mark Kermode asked whether the scene in changing room where Dorothy and Gregory are comparing old wounds might have been borrowed from Stephen Spielberg *Jaws* (1975). Bill said he'd not seen *Jaws* until long after *Gregory's Girl* was made. Anyway: "If I was going to steal, I'd steal from Godard or Bresson," he said, "not from Spielberg." He was only half joking, if he was joking at all.

[3] Bill Forsyth, *Sight and Sound*, 1981, Vol. 50 (4) p243.

[4] Tim Teeman, 'Bill Forsyth: the reluctant father of *Gregory's Girl*', *The Times*, 6 February 2008.

[5] Interview with Mark Kermode, The Plaza (Truro), August 2019.

[6] Bill Forsyth, *Sight and Sound*, ibid.

7 Richard Brody, '*Pierrot le fou:* Self-Portrait in a Shattered Lens', SEP 22, 2009.

8 'Morning Discussion with Bill Forsyth', Midnight Sun Film Festival, Finland, June 2016.

9 'Bill Forsyth Takes a Look Back in Laughter', *New York Times*, 2 December 1984.

10 Bill Forsyth interview, Ibiza Film Festival, 2009.

11 Tim Teeman, ibid.

12 Gerald Peary, 'Bill Forsyth', www.geraldpeary.com, September 1985.

13 Tim Teeman, ibid.

14 Bill Forsyth, *Sight and Sound*, ibid.

15 Gerald Peary, ibid.

16 Ibid.

17 Colin Young died in November 2021, aged 94.

18 Ryan Gilbey, Colin Young obituary, *The Observer*, 19 December 2021.

19 Mona Tabbara, *Screen Daily*, 29 November 2021.

20 Ryan Gilbey, ibid.

21 Dominique Joyeux, Interview with Colin Young, *Cahiers du Cinema*, Novembre 1984.

22 Bill Forsyth, *Sight and Sound*, ibid.

23 Such as *Local Hero* (1983), *The Killing Fields* (1984), *The Mission* (1986), *The Fifth Element* (1996), *Seven Years in Tibet* (1997), *Cold Mountain* (2003), *Children of Men* (2006) and *Mad Max: Fury Road* (2013).

24 Andrew J. Rausch ed., *Fifty Filmmakers: Conversations with Directors from Roger Avary to Steven Zaillian*, McFarland & Co, 2008.

25 Bill was awarded an honorary diploma by the National Film School in 1982.

26 Lawrence Van Gelder, ibid.

27 Tim Teeman, ibid.

28 Christopher Connelly, 'The Man Behind *Gregory's Girl*', *Rolling Stone*, 30 September 1982.

29 Tim Teeman, ibid.

30 Lawrence Van Gelder, ibid.

31 Bill Forsyth interview, Film Forum event, October 4 2019.

32 Ian Freer, *Gregory's Girl* review, *Empire*, 1 January 2000.

33 Lawrence Van Gelder, ibid.

34 Jonathan Murray, 'Cornflakes versus Conflict: An Interview with Bill Forsyth', *Journal of British Cinema and Television,*, 2015, Vol.12 (2), p.245-264.

35 Vladimir Nabokov, *Mary*, Penguin, 2007 edition, p39.

36 Ibid., p50.

37 Ibid., p68.

38 Vladimir Nabokov, *Glory*, Penguin, 1974 edition, p150.

39 Ibid., p154.

40 Lawrence Van Gelder, ibid.

41 Allan Hunter and Mark Astaire, *Local Hero: the making of the film*, Polygon Books, 1983.

42 Lawrence Van Gelder, ibid.

43 Nan Robertson, 'Bill Forsyth takes a look back in laughter', *New York Times*, February 12 1984.

44 Jonathan Murray, ibid.

45 Bill Forsyth, *Sight and Sound*, ibid.

46 John Brown, 'A Suitable Job for a Scot', *Sight and Sound*, spring 1984, pp. 157.

47 Gerald Peary, ibid.

48 Euan Ferguson, 'I was quite naive. Probably still am.', *The Observer*, 28 September 2021.

49 David Martin-Jones, *Scotland: Global Cinema: Genres, Modes and Identities*, Edinburgh University Press, 2010.

50 Kevin Courrier, 'Interview with film director Bill Forsyth', *Critics at Large*, 1985.

51 Allan Hunter and Mark Astaire, ibid.

52 Bill Forsyth, Director's Statement, London Film Festival programme, 1979.

53 Kevin Courrier, ibid.

[54] James Park, *Learning to Dream: The New British Cinema*, Faber & Faber, 1984, p109.

[55] Jasper Rees, '10 Questions for Filmmaker Bill Forsyth', *The Arts Desk*, 28 April 2014.

[56] Allan Hunter, 'The Imperfect Anarchist', in: *From Limelight to Satellite: A Scottish Film Book*, ed. Eddie Dick, Scottish Film Council, 1990.

[57] Quoted in Richard Holmes, *Footsteps: Adventures of a Romantic Biographer*, Hodder and Staughton, 1985, p47.

[58] Lawrence Van Gelder, ibid.

[59] James Monaco, *The Encyclopaedia of Film*, Perigee, 1991.

[60] *Gregory's Girl* was Gerard Cole's first novelisation, followed later by Clint Eastwood's *Any Which Way You Can*, punk biopic *Sid and Nancy*, and *Comfort and Joy*.

[61] Gerald Cole, *Gregory's Girl*, Harper Collins, 1983, p8.

[62] Ibid., p14.

[63] Ibid., p120.

[64] Christine de Rivoyre (1921-2009) was also literary editor of *Marie Claire*.

4. Charlie

"Don't stop dancing or you'll fall off."

Bill is pushing at the back of an Austin Maxi.

"Use your shoulder," calls out Charlie from the driver's seat, taking the fag from his mouth. Shoppers in Great Western Street are walking past with their head-scarves and tartan trolleys. Bill gives them a nod and half a smile. Charlie's head appears from the window, little ears poking out from drapes of brown hair. A broad elfin face with a thick knit of eyebrows.

"You use more body weight that way."

The blue, rust-spotted car starts to trundle forward until there's a chokey roar and a lurch. Bill has to run. He needs to ignore the attention he's getting from shoppers and concentrate on the flapping passenger door — the door that keeps on staying some way ahead of him.

"Are y'getting in Bill?"

"Aye."

"Are you sure?"

One leg appears in the Austin, the other leg's still outside, hopping. More of Bill turns up in the car and Charlie's taken hold of his sleeve.

"I thought we'd lost you then. It happens to my business partners all the time. It's tragic really."
They're holding up the afternoon's traffic as they make their way into the West End. Another day of skies like chalk, a dull sun shining whitely on the rooftops.

"Does this thing even have a third gear?"

"Don't talk like that. She doesn't like it, do you?"
Charlie pats the gauges.

"Anyway, we don't need a third gear where we're going."

"Where are we going?" Bill asks.

"To celebrate."

"Oh aye. We're celebrating making a film about tin cans are we then?"
Bill grimaces dramatically. Charlie squints back at him, the fag clamped between his teeth. Bill shrugs and looks away.

"Don't just think tin cans," says Charlie. "Look. We're talking about stuff that keeps the modern world alive. Right there in that canning factory is a bit of human history, the stuff that actually matters. Treasure from the earth. Harnessed by man to protect and hold the tender produce of the soil. And yeah, think about it Bill — it's what sees us through the winter isn't it? It's tin cans that makes sure food is always on the table, what keeps the tears from a wee bairn's face. With your pictures and my words we'll make a symphony out of this, you'll see. It can be done — hey, look, it's Eddie — Eddie!"

He works the handle to roll down the window. A young crowd in the street are milling around clothes shops, taking no notice of Charlie and his shouting. There's music from one of the doorways, something with a country and western twang that's full of loss and longing.

"Maybe it wasn't Eddie."

Cars start hooting behind them. A bus swings round the side, with a rattle and a grind and a guff of carbon monoxide fumes and dust.

"Tinned minds, tinned breath. Tinned cars too," says Bill.

"Exactly. Tins are really in demand aren't they? So, come friendly tins and fall on us. This is just the beginning Bill, isn't it, of being film-makers? Once we show our lovely films to someone who knows what they're looking at, one of the big people, the money people, they'll see. Your pictures, my words, and they'll see!"

"Let's hope they're really interested in soup preservation in Hollywood eh?"

"We'll soon be film-makers making commercial films. Thrillers. Not big budget but a whole series of them, so we get a bit of volume going. Thrillers about real life round here, real Scottish people. Not your Agatha Christie thing or heroes always wearing their suits."

"So there'll be arsenic in the Highland Toffee you mean?"

"Look. We can do this. Like I've said before Bill, all we have to do is learn from the best. We've got a cassette re-corder — we need to keep on taping the classics from the telly and then we can play them back and learn how they're put together. The structure of them, the timings. When to release the tension and put in a gag."

"Mibbe."

"I tell you there's a formula for these things, you just have to get the secret of it. Get the workings right, the right levers for hooking people in. A script, you see, has to be like a machine. With intrigue. Excitement."

The Austin pulls into Woodlands Road coughing like a jakey, and rolls along the kerb, reduced to something closer to its natural state: a metal box on wheels. Entering the Halt Bar is like finding a night-time in the day. A Victorian night made from velvet winter-curtains, a fug of smoke and the sombre gleam of wood panelling in lamp-light. Charlie and Bill join the drinkers around the Halt's famous U-shaped bar like they've only been out for a minute or two to fetch a paper and a pint of milk. Old conversations start up again without the need for formalities. Peter[1] is there for the architects' gang, holding up their end as part of the Bohemian set with a pint and a fag in his hand: "You have to change the way people live first — if you want to change how they think," he reminds Charlie, winking, taking hold of his lapel and giving it a tug. "And none of your porn's going to help."[2] Mike and Mark[3] want to talk to Charlie about who to speak with at the city council. They had cash to spend up there, and surely now was the perfect time for a documentary on the joy of the indoor toilet?

Bill orders them a half and a dram and finds himself watching Charlie as he waits. There was still something compelling about the sight of his partner working a room, like an elaborate piece of clockwork and all of its moving parts slotting into one place and then nudging onto another; those wide, full lips and the words that caught at people's attention; his hands confirming another point. The confidence of a polymath combined with boyish enthusiasm; an easy enthusiasm delivered via the softest of Glaswegian accents. It meant Charlie could keep a straight face and say anything, claim anything at all, and you felt bad if you didn't believe every word. Sitting with Oscar[4] and Pat[5], Bill knew Charlie would be trying to get them to share some of their new kit, or ideas on how to get in with another tourist board. "How's your epic about the metal smelter coming on?" he hears Charlie ask. The waves of charm were as warm and palpable as the trickles and curls of cigarette smoke over the bar. A natural businessman. Or he would be, if he could only think a bit smaller.

Peter's wife Rita[6] comes in to fetch her husband home, a sketchbook still under her arm, says hello to Bill and then gets caught up in conversation with the rest of the gang. She can't stop. "Watch yourself," warns Peter, putting an arm round Bill's shoulder, "she always has her needles with her. Stand in one place too long and you'll be crocheted." Rita blithely hits him with her bag. Drinks are supped and offers of lifts are going round. No-one's keen to go with Charlie and Bill in the Tree-mobile and they leave alone, blinking at the sudden light. Bill's going home to his flat, Charlie's out for dinner.

"Where shall I drop you?" asks Bill.

"Sunset Strip."

"Oh aye."

"Anywhere in Santa Monica will do kid."

"Somewhere back of the uni okay 'til then? Where y'goin — the Chip?"
Charlie's leaning back in his seat, getting comfortable, wiping his fringe away from his eyes.

"Take me to Musso's for martinis with the guys. We'll crack wise. Ciro's for dancing. Then it'll just be me and my lonesome typewriter working through 'til dawn."

"You want palm trees with that?"

"Keep driving Bill, keep driving and we'll get there in the end. We'll be film-makers."

"In our open top Duesenberg. Me, you and Gatsby."
Charlie sings:

"Oh chicks and ducks and geese better hurry —"
He digs Bill in the ribs until he's joining in.

"When I tek you out in the surrey —"
Their heads tilted back, mouths open wide, they chug their way up Great George Street.

"When I tek you out in the surrey — with a frrriii— nnge on top!"

*

Bill first met Charles Gormley at International Film Associates (IFA), the firm set up by Laurence Henson and Eddie McConnell (the cameraman for John Grierson on *Seawards the Great Ships*). It was just another day, in another "damp Glasgow basement" and the low-rent world of promo shorts for 23 year-old Bill. This time he was hunched over the Steenback working on Eddie's film about Harris Tweed: *Island of the Big Cloth* (1971), funded by the Harris Tweed Association, the Highlands and Islands Development Board and the British Wool Marketing Board. A colleague was introduced who'd provided the seductive script he was going to be working with (written from the perspective of a poised Outer Hebridean gentleman: "At first it was hard for us men to understand the interest visitors took in our Tweed, and that the simple cloth we carried on our backs had caught the world's imagination."). Nine years older but a Puckish, smooth and knowing presence about the place.

Another book-minded boy from a working-class family, Charlie had been expected to concentrate on making sure of a steady and sensible income. His father, a sheet metal worker, had made it clear that films could be a hobby and nothing more. So Charlie travelled each day from his home in Motherwell to a Further Education institution in Glasgow known for its specialism in engineering, Stow College, and studied to be an optician (what was, after all, the mechanics of seeing). After three years in the profession, and with enough money behind him to do his own thing, Charlie ditched the opticians' practice to join the IFA. This might have been the dog-end of the industry, what Forsyth called "low, low film-making", but other doors could open. By the time he met Bill, Charlie had already co-written a Children's Film Foundation film with his boss Laurence, *The Big Catch* (1968), about Ullapool tykes trying to catch a wild pony in order to raise money to fix their boat. As Bill was soon to find out, Charlie knew he belonged in Hollywood. It was (almost) in his blood: "he claimed the status of 'second-generation', since his mum, when young, had been an usherette at the Rutherglen Odeon." The golden age of Hollywood studios was a temple, a fortress and the gilding to Charlie's mental landscape. More than a career ambition, feature films were a creed and a lifestyle: "his language, his associations, verbal rhythms, were pure folklore Hollywood," said Bill. Charlie loved to play the part of the hack writer. The red-eyed, juiced-up talent like a Sturges or a Wilder, a Chandler or a Mankiewicz. Cigarette in hand, a casual tilt of the head: "Do you want it good or do you want it Thursday?"[7]

Together, they were Tree Films: Charlie the family man, with a wife and two sons to support, the salesman, the smart wordsmith; and Bill, the lone wolf with loads of technical know-how and New Wave ambitions. They had a letterhead that said 'Branches Everywhere', a HQ that was basically a shed at the back of Bill's place in Park Circus, and a whole lot of excitement about what they could achieve. Meanwhile, the sponsored films themselves were starting to feel mechanical: "I assembled the shots, Charlie sprayed on the commentary and then some music was welded to the mixture. Hey presto, a sponsored film."[8] And as a start-up, competing with three or more established businesses in Glasgow alone, they weren't pulling out the plum jobs. Company employees couldn't expect much of a salary package, and Tree relied on family and friends. Cameraman Michael Coulter was Charlie's brother-in-law, not long out of his teens and looking for experience; Iain Smith, from the Beaconsfield days, was the clear-headed numbers man who helped to keep a muddled and financially leaky operation afloat; Jon Schorstein and Eddie McConnell took on some of the camerawork jobs. The Highlands and Islands Development Board — obviously happy with the Bill and Charlie team from *Island of the Big Cloth* — were an important client. They funded Tree's first creation, *Islands of the West* (1972), a film selling the windswept charms of the Hebrides. This was the first credit for Coulter, the cinematographer who would go on to film *Four Weddings and a Funeral* (1994), *Sense and Sensibility* (1995), *Notting Hill* (1999) and *Love Actually* (2003) — as well as working on each of Bill's films. Other Highlands and Islands' funded ventures included *Shapes in the Water* (1974), about the craft of boat-making (narrated by Fulton Mackay, the prison warder Mr Mackay in *Porridge*, later to play the beachcombing Ben Knox in *Local Hero*); *Connections* (1977), where Charlie had a great time playing a jet-setter exploring the evolution of transport, part-presenter, part-comedy act (oops, where's his trousers!?). Other creations saw the team explaining how to get a home improvement grant to improve your Glasgow tenement in *If Only We Had the Space* (1974); how schools were changing in *Educational Provision in Midlothian* (1975); and how eco-friendly measures were being used to look after migrating seabirds in *The Cromarty Bridge* (1979).

A more curious and exotic venture, the very last Tree film, was *The Legend of Los Tayos* (1979) for Thames Television. In his internationally successful book *Chariots of the Gods? Unsolved Mysteries of the Past* (1968), Erich von Däniken (a Swiss hotel manager cum amateur archaeologist cum publicity-seeker) had argued that a secret 'library' of drawings and gold artefacts found in the Los Tayos caves in Ecuador was evidence of extra-terrestrial intelligence. Here was ancient knowledge of astronauts, helicopters and space-age technologies[9]. Bill and Charlie were persuaded to travel to the upper reaches of the Amazonian rainforest and the

'Cave of the Oilbirds' by Stan Hall, a civil engineer from East Lothian who'd read von Däniken's books and wanted to explore the caves for himself. Stan knew the best way to rally support for an expedition was to involve a celebrity. He wrote a letter to Neil Armstrong to invite him along, and it was his unexpectedly positive response that made the resulting cavalcade possible. In 1976 a Royal Air Force cargo plane delivered a band of geologists, biologists, cavers, archaeologists, along with members of the Royal Highland Fusiliers, the Black Watch, our documentary film-makers — and a world-famous astronaut — to the foothills of the Andes. Bill, Charlie and cameraman David Peat, spent a month living in a jungle camp and its mud, shooting in the streets of the nearest city Quito as well as inside the mysterious caves themselves: a watery chasm of birds and bats; chambers ribbed with shale, cathedral-like in their giant arched spaces; a labyrinth of tunnels made stranger by their chaos, by the spouts of waterfalls and coloured pools, rods and curtains of light from cracks in the rock overhead. "Yes — people are actually journeying down the Amazon looking for flying saucers," said Charlie's intro. The film was completed but Tree's final payment of £15,000 for the project was never received.

Bill downplayed their efforts later, but at the time, these films were an opportunity to get noticed. They'd take any chance to add some Hollywood vim. Looking for a different way to film workers on a building site, Charlie once borrowed a pram so that Mick could attempt a home-made tracking shot. Tree documentaries could be accomplished pieces with a stamp of wit and artistry to them. A film like

Islands of the West, as one example, contains a gorgeously skaldic melancholy: dizzy views over unpopulated landscapes; tracking shots around the coast to reveal another white-and-blue-smashed shoreline. Charlie mixes myth and Hebridean folk songs into the narration, and alongside the necessary tourist information there's a lacing of poetry: "The men sing to their boats and pretend the sea does not exist. As though its name was terrible, like an old and angry god."

*

Every participant in the little pool of the Scottish film world was desperate to make 'real' films. "It was where everyone was aiming. It was the end of the rainbow," recalled Bill in 2020[10]. But many of them were feeling the decline of their youthful confidence, still in their flats and bedsits with books and a typewriter, jazz records on the floor. Not really 'artists' like they thought they would be. They'd been doing conventional jobs too long to believe that anymore. They still had plenty to say but no way of saying it. Making a mainstream film was a dream that saturated serious afternoons in cafés, talking script ideas as the dregs of coffee grew colder, swapping copies of Pynchon and Vonnegut, talking Polanski and Bertolucci; the hazy, booze-soaked nights in bars that ended with walks home under a Gothic moon and its only friends, the ragged clouds; possessed by a dream that had ended up feeling more like the throb of a long, dull hangover. All they wanted was an audience, and an audience that wouldn't presume, even before the first screenings and reviews, that a low-budget film from Scotland had to be terrible.

There's another window onto that kind of life, that battle, in the film *Long Shot* (1978), a mockumentary that stares upwards to the high walls faced by all the chancers looking for their big break in the movies: the unreturned phone calls, the hard truths, false promises and broken appointments. Set around the 1977 Edinburgh International Film Festival and its circle of directors, actors, producers, film writers, assorted hangers-on and eccentrics, *Long Shot* — naturally — stars Charlie Gormley playing himself. Absolutely no acting involved. The irrepressible charmer blags his way into gala parties and off-diary art gallery events, getting himself in front of Wim Wenders and John Boorman. There's no limit to his belief in the script for *Gulf & Western* (about the Aberdeen oil boom and the influx of American money[11]) — even if it's not really been written yet. He's got heavyweight backing in the bag ("I can have my choice of director" he says, and "Vanessa Redgrave has already said yes"). There are many pleasures to be had from watching Team Charlie chase around a silkily-textured, black and white Edinburgh for its one big chance of meeting up with American director Sam Fuller, the man who can guarantee them investor cash. (Besides being a cult, low-budget maker of war and western films, Fuller would have been a hero because of his connection with Godard and appearance in *Pierrot Le Fou*: Ferdinand bumps into Fuller while he's making a film based on the poet Baudelaire's *Fleurs du Mal*. Ferdinand asks Fuller what cinema is. It's like a battleground, says Fuller, it's love, hate, action, violence and death).

Alongside the comedy of *Long Shot* — which includes a turn by Alan Bennett as a very unsympathetic doctor — is a sense of frustration and despair. For Charlie's character the only reality is making movies. Being among people who are thinking or worrying about anything else, is a waste of time. The pursuit of the pitch that will unlock the big money is an obsession; so there's agonising over what will work, and in the end, a rock-bottom question: was having to make a bad, low-budget film better than not making a film at all? The hopefuls are buzzing and manic in their black and white limbo, living off fags and cans of McEwan's bitter, singing snatches from Hollywood musicals. No cars and no money for taxis, begging lifts. The *Gulf & Western* script itself is a fickle and fluctuating thing ("I thought it was about sheep?" argues one latecomer to the project). Charlie wants to make it about something 'real', but in the end it'll be whatever the money wants it to be, and far more time is invested into the schmooze than the writing. "Who do I have to talk to?" is the continual refrain from Charlie, "So I talk to who?" Stuck in a Kafkaesque nightmare of offices filled with secretaries and runners and marketing people who know very little and can do even less. The meeting with Fuller never happens.

Long Shot is an honest reflection of the situation in the Seventies when the British film industry was valued by imperial Hollywood only for its technical expertise and cheap studio space. *Star Wars* (1976) was made at the dog-eared Elstree studios, *Superman* (1977) at Pinewood, *Alien* (1978) at Shepperton. Film-makers like Charlie's character were anything but 'independent' because they depended entirely on access to a tiny network of production companies, funders and distributors for their financing. Those doors had to open — or you'd have a film like *Long Shot* itself, made on a micro-budget by a bunch of friends with no pretensions of reaching anything other than a niche audience[12]: a fun piece of navel-gazing that was made from leftover short ends and expired film stock (some from communist East Germany).

Bill's in there too. In what must be one of the most discreet screen performances in history, Bill appears as a silhouette (on a busman's holiday, editing *The Legend of Los Tayos*). He's not sure. Maybe the images aren't up to the words, suggests Bill. Was it really enough to show pictures of people getting out of helicopters when the voiceover was talking about alien visitation?

*

Oil executives sit round a boardroom table watching a TV screen with serious, dutiful faces. All except one. The chief man at the top of the table has fallen asleep. Forsyth knew just how he felt.

This early scene in *Local Hero* was based on the showing of a cheesy sponsored film of shimmering deserts and oil pipelines with a perfectly bland corporate voiceover. Ersatz inspiration for men in suits.

"By [1977], the company had become quite moribund," said Forsyth. "We really weren't very good at making these kinds of films. It's very hard work, you know, trying to make things like marine engines interesting."[13] And if he and Charlie were going to eventually make feature films then it wouldn't be as a partnership anyway. "The simple truth was that we both wanted to direct, and even to write and direct, and that intent involves journeys that are inevitably solitary ones."[14] The end of Tree Films, though, didn't come until after Bill had released his first film in 1979 and received some recognition for what he'd achieved and was capable of. "I doubt very much I would have mustered the personal chutzpah to climb that mountain and try to emulate [the feature film-makers] without the constant example of Charlie during our heady decade together."[15] Charlie had taught him many things about the practicalities involved with selling ideas, about producing loose, easy rhythms of writing, and most of all, the importance to commercial screenplays of humour. So wanting to make a feature film wasn't even necessarily a conscious decision, it didn't happen as a result of sudden possibility. It was absurdly inevitable.

> "I wasn't alone. I was with people who
> wanted to do the same thing, so we sustained
> each other's dreams and talked about the fea-
> ture film at the end of the rainbow. It slowly
> got to the stage where we'd talked about it so
> much and dreamed it so much, that there was
> no point in not doing it. We were just ready."

*

There wasn't a Scottish movie scene in the Seventies, only rumours. That's what happens when any substantial money is missing. The character of the film-makers as a group be-comes something much less than a movement, or even a sloppy network. It just happens. People bump into one an-other on the corner of Argyle Street or on the top deck of the bus, they escape from the rain and sit in bars talking about their plans. It's civil and unassuming. Family get involved if they can; friends turn up over the summer, short of work for a while, and want to pitch in. So Charlie's brother-in-law became the cinematographer for Bill's films. Paddy Higson from the Halt Bar picked up on production jobs, in an unpaid voluntary capacity to begin with. The actors from the Glasgow Youth Theatre who appear in *Gregory's Girl* were called up for other bits and bobs parts. The Youth Theatre's production designer and stage manager, Adrienne Atkinson, went on to work on all three of Bill's 'comedies' as well as *Housekeeping* (1987) — and became Bill's partner, the mother of Sam and Doone[16].

Charlie went on to make two of his own feature films. *Living Apart Together* (1982) stars BA Robertson, recruited to play the part of a mixed-up singer/songwriter around the time when he was still at the height of his pop career (shades on, jacket sleeves rolled up, big blow-dried hair)[17]. Glasgow's Kingston Bridge turns up in the film along with some Forsythian traits: a low-key mood, naturalism and humour mixed with some darker underlying themes of human fallibility and self-destruction. The producer was Paddy Higson. Charlie was the first of the pair to work with Peter Capaldi (before *Local Hero*), here chosen to play Robertson's slimy love rival. John Gordon Sinclair and Jake D'Arcy (PE teacher Phil Menzies) turn up serving drinks in bars; Billy Greenlees (Gregory's pal Steve) plays 'First Heavy', taking part in a carjacking; Douglas Sannachan (Billy the window cleaner) appears in a music shop. *Heavenly Pursuits* (1986) was Charlie's own schooldays film, this time centred around the lives of the teachers and a plot that explores the nature of miracles. Mick Coulter was cinematographer. Gregory's Dad is cast as the headmaster; Jake D'Arcy is there again, getting argumentative in a pub. Gordon Urquhart's wife Stella plays a nurse; the Italian boss Mr MacCool from *Comfort & Joy* has a part as a Vatican priest.

Both films suffer from overly-busy plots. Tensions between characters appear and disappear before they have had a chance to become interesting, the plot's already moved on. There's also a distracting sense of how carefully the lines have been scripted, and maybe sometimes in too smart a way. As John Boorman says of *Gulf & Western* in *Long Shot*, a screenplay can feel desperate to be made into a movie. And that could be why Charlie made less of an impression on cinema history than his Tree Films' partner. All that confidence and charm meant he believed he could do everything solo, and would do everything he thought was needed to make a film work for the industry. Bill, meanwhile, was always uncertain about movies and his place in that realm, looking for ideas on how things could be done differently, absorbing as many examples of real-life experiences into his writing and approach as possible.

In *Long Shot*, Charlie was willing to hand over the whole project to Boorman in order for *Gulf & Western* to be made, to step back and have no real say on anything as long as he at least got a credit as 'Producer': "well, you know," he says, "I have been the producer — the producer of the script up to this stage." The end of the film sees Charlie breaking out of the inhibiting black and white reality of Glasgow and arrive in the technicolour land of California. He's basking in the dusty-blue radiance of Sunset Strip and its palm trees.

He's not a player there — the industry doesn't want him, not yet — he's just a tourist taking in sights. The Chinese Theatre and the prints of movie stars in the cement of the nearby boulevard like archaeological evidence of a remote, mostly mythical civilisation. As close to the fantasy as Charlie (and we) can get.

Charlie Gormley died of cancer in 2005, aged 67. His last words were a quote from the Edward G Robinson gangster movie *Little Caesar* (1931): "Is this the end of Rico?". Proudly, he'd seen his son Tommy become a sought-after talent in British film production following a string of assistant director roles and work with Ken Loach on films like *Riff-Raff* (1991) and *Raining Stones* (1993); Terence Davies on *The Long Day Closes* (1992) — and Forsyth on *Gregory's Two Girls* (1999). What Charlie didn't get to see was Tommy's subsequent rise to mega-heavyweight status. As JJ Abram's go-to assistant, Tommy Gormley has been an essential, hands-on presence in the making of many of the most successful blockbuster movies of the past 15 years: the re-booted *Star Wars* franchise; the *Star Trek* re-boot; *Mission Impossible* films; *Wonder Woman* (2017 and 2020). Films made with exactly that formula for mass enchantment that Charlie had always been trying to find, in his own amateur, hopeful kind of way.

It's maybe not a world with much starlight or romance to it anymore. Not when failure is no longer an option, when the commercial formulae are so well established, and when the riches involved have become so inhuman (*Star Wars: the Force Awakens* generated more than $1.5 billion in profit from ticket sales alone). The financiers won't stand for it. Each element to the algorithm must be correct.

[1] Peter McGurn, an architect involved with urban regeneration projects across Glasgow and the west of Scotland. He was often joined in the Halt by Andy Macmillan and Isi Metzstein, responsible for many modernist church and education buildings, such as St Bride's Church in East Kilbride, Cumbernauld Technical College and Robinson College in Cambridge.

[2] Charlie had been recruited by Dutch film-makers to write the English script for *Blue Movie* (1971), one of the most commercially successful films from the Netherlands ever.

[3] Mike Alexander and Mark Littlewood ran Pelicula Films from 1971 making documentary shorts like *Dunfermline* (1974) and *A Town Called Ayr* (1974); and a Children's Film Foundation film, *Nosey Dobson* (1976).

[4] Oscar Marzaroli was a photographer (one of his images of Glasgow was used for the cover of Deacon Blue's *Raintown* LP), as well as being a cameraman; he worked on *Seawards the Great Ships)*. Oscar died in 1988 aged 55.

[5] Patrick Higson, an editor and producer married to Paddy, who would go on to be producer for *That Sinking Feeling*, *Gregory's Girl* and *Comfort & Joy*. Paddy would often join her husband and the Halt gang on Friday evenings, sometimes with the children left outside in the car with pop and bags of crisps.

[6] Rita McGurn, a talented artist working with ceramics and textiles who also worked as a designer on Charlie Gormley's two feature films in the 1980s and *Restless Natives*.

[7] Bill Forsyth, 'Charlie Gormley: Long Shot to Hollywood', *Long Shot* DVD notes.

[8] Ibid.

[9] Von Däniken's book sold more than 70 million copies. He went on to design his own theme park based around the world's unsolved mysteries in Interlaken, Switzerland. One Swiss commentator described the Mystery Park (opened in 2003, closed in 2006) as a "cultural Chernobyl".

[10] Gerry Clark, Interview with Bill Forsyth for the Glasgow Youth Theatre, 2020.

[11] Sometimes said to the the inspiration for *Local Hero*, but wrongly. The idea for *Gulf and Western* was a Western-style thriller, with guns and cowboy hats on the streets of Aberdeen. David Puttnam had the original idea for the 1983 film which took Bill Forsyth in a very different direction.

[12] The writer/director was Maurice Hatton (1938-1997). 'Maury' was known for writing and directing thrillers: working with John Thaw in *Praise Marx and Pass the Ammunition* (1970); Eileen Atkins in *Nelly's Version* (1983) and Andy Garcia in *American Roulette* (1988).

[13] Lawrence Van Gelder, 'Thoughts While Held Captive By an "Escapist" Movie', *New York Times*, 23 May 1982.

[14] Bill Forsyth, ibid.

[15] Ibid.

[16] Adrienne settled in a suburb to the north of Glasgow but was before that living in Italy, working on her painting. It's interesting to read her reflections on the nature and value of paintings as 'handmade' works as a glimpse of the kinds of conversations she and Bill may have had about mainstream art. Most of all, the importance of ideas. "Crude, accessible sentiment dominates [most works of art] and although pleasing to the eye, the vast majority of this ubiquitous fare has no real bearing on our lives or intellect on any profound level. Henry Miller amusingly described the hordes of hobbyist painters he encountered in Paris in the 1950's as, *'Cunts with paintboxes strapped to their backs. A little talent and a fat wallet.'* But mere decoration or skilful draughtsmanship alone should never be confused with art."

[17] BA Robertson was known for his chart hit 'Bang Bang' (1979), but wrote bigger-selling songs for Cliff Richard: 'Carrie' and 'Wired for Sound' (1979); and Mike + the Mechanics' 'The Living Years' (1990). He also wrote the song for Scotland's World Cup campaign in 1982, 'We Have a Dream' — sung by John Gordon Sinclair.

5. Kids

"Seducing people's sisters at your age — go and break some windows...demolish some phone boxes."

The community hall looks like it's been opened up to refugees for the night. Sleeping bags are all over the floor and a flotsam of makeshift living has washed up around the hall's edges: holdalls and plastic bags, grubby trainers and towels, some discarded Irn-Bru bar wrappers and packets of Golden Wonder crisps. Some orange, ceiling-length curtains have been drawn together and the lights are all on, making a cosy night-time space, thick with the smell of bodies, socks and orange peel after a long day of rehearsing the *The Auld Alliance*[1]. No-one's going to bed just yet. It's summer and a holiday for the Glasgow Youth Theatre, not just a tour. Many of the kids have never left Glasgow or spent a night away from family. This is an escape to a Highlands fantasy of underage drinking, dope, fags and anarchy — or as much as they could get away with,

and only after the big stushie of unloading and setting up the
stage rig was done.

Sanny's still on stage in his costume.

"Am no fuckin wearin it."

Puff runs on in a wig, mincing round like he's holding up the
ends of an imaginary dress.

"O Sanny, ma wee bawbag —"

"Is no right, I'm tellin you. Is manky!"

"Ohhh, yer took the words right outta ma mouth —
" sings Puff. Big John and Maggie[2] join in, sitting on the edge
of the stage with their legs swinging.

More kids are coming from the hall's toilets changed
into pyjamas and dressing gowns, already lining up for their
bedtime ritual. The youth theatre's John and Adrienne,
alongside the black-bearded figure of Bill-the-driver, are getting the spoons and bottles of Night Nurse ready. They'd
bought up a load of bottles when so many of the group had
come down with colds. Now, they realised, it was their only
real chance of getting some sleep whether the kids had colds
or not.

A stocky figure with wavy shoulder-length hair,
Eichmann appears.

"This the spankin queue then?"

"Naw Eich. Ye jus need to take yer trousers down.
For checkin."

"Can see my meat and veg any-time."

"All veg pal, I seen it already."

"Shut the fuck up Sanny."

*

Gordon, Rab, Caroline (and dog) on tour. Courtesy of Caroline Guthrie.

Bill Forsyth was used to the peace of the cutting room, where he would sit with the gentle hum and warmth of his editing equipment; conversations about the ins and outs of documentary funding. Not this, two weeks of driving a minibus for the GYT as it bundled on from one village to another, taking urban theatre to the provinces. Not the company of a troupe of excited teens and hours at the wheel with wet pac-a-macs, condensation and BO. They were polite and earnest enough if you were talking to them on their own, still wee ones away from home chewing on their Hubba-Bubba; but together, after they'd been in the pub? Still. Bill was learning, learning about actors as if they were another resource, like

getting to know his way around a new splicing rig. Otherwise, if he didn't, he believed his shyness was going to keep
him out of the 'real' film universe. "I felt that if I'd ever have
a career I'd have to do something about it. I'd made these
experimental films but I thought the major chore of a film-
maker was to relate to actors."[3] There was no instruction
manual, and he'd needed to just force himself into their society. Working with inexperienced young people seemed to
him to mean the least risk ("I wouldn't feel like a fool; they
wouldn't know more about making a film than I did."[4])

It had been done before — maybe not in a way that
was a direct inspiration for Forsyth, but out there in the
movie aether of possibility. Barney Platts-Mill made *Bronco
Bullfrog* (1969) with young people recruited from London's
East End, like his main character, Del Walker, an apprentice
plumber with Newham council. Only two years older than
Forsyth, Platts-Mill went on to make a film with members of
a Glasgow gang around the same time as *Gregory's Girl*, the
Gaelic language *Hero* (1982). They were both interested in
cinema verité, but had different ideas of how that realism
could, or should, be conveyed. For Platts-Mill it meant dealing with active forces: angst and violence and crime surfacing
as a product of simmering social problems; while Forsyth
found his own kind of reality, equally convincing, in the pass-
ive and watchful, with a still small voice. They were much
closer when it came to humour. In one scene in *Bullfrog*,
wideboy Del buys just the one cinema ticket then saunters
round to the fire exit to let in his mates; right in front of
them all is an old lady in a fluffy hat who's keener than anyone to get inside for a freebie.

In 1977, Forsyth approached the head of drama at the Arts Council to ask whether he could be introduced to the Scottish Youth Theatre. They suggested he should try the Glasgow Youth Theatre instead. Maybe because it was smaller and less structured than the SYT and a film-maker couldn't upset the formal rhythms of a place that didn't have any. Or maybe they knew John Baraldi and what a little miracle the GYT was becoming. The GYT had been in the news for representing Scotland at the Festival of Young People's Theatre at the Royal Court Theatre in London, and for its flamboyant, tartan takeover of Sloane Square, hosting a Glasgow Ceilidh with bagpipes, dancing and a Scots Olympics featuring kipper tossing, haggis putting and an Irn-Bru drinking competition.

Gerry, Rab and Gordon. Courtesy of Rab Buchanan.

The Dolphin Arts Centre was based in an old nursing training college, a frowning bulk of Victorian Gothic sandstone in the East End: in Bridgeton, a district synonymous with 'multiple social deprivation', having the lowest life expectancy and the highest levels of poverty in the city. The name of Bridgeton was infamous because of its razor gang of the 1920s, Glasgow's own Peaky Blinders, the Bridgeton Billy Boys[5]. Bridgeton was also known for being a base for the Orange Order in the city, the Protestant fraternity and its annual Orangemen street marches.

Among John Baraldi's friends in theatre, even those with stalwart left-wing credentials, none could understand why he'd want to be in Bridgeton. A gently-spoken, round-cheeked young man from Connecticut, John had taken his degree in Drama and English at the University of Manchester in the late Sixties, and had stayed in England for his first job as assistant manager at Chesterfield's Civic Theatre. Here, living among Derbyshire's coal-mining communities, John came to know much more about English working-class life, the consequences of unemployment and pay strikes and fighting over political principles for families when it came to staying warm and clothed and fed. Theatre, he could see, should have a role to play in allowing people to express themselves and have a voice. Rather than high-class entertainment — the fancies and fun, the air of hauteur — theatre could say something about life as it actually was. John turned away from the expected career route among the red velvet drapes and brass fixtures of London's West End and took a job with Strathclyde Regional Council to run the Dolphin. With skeleton-funding from the Arts Council there was enough, at least, to offer something for the local community around the building's sprawl, its old lecture spaces and classrooms, by re-arranging the furniture and heating one more room at a time as the Dolphin's activities grew.

The Glasgow Youth Theatre was one more addition to a busy community arts centre already offering weaving, pottery, sculpture, knitting and music. It was the product of a bottle of wine and a late night conversation between John and Adrienne Atkinson in one of the Dolphin's under-heated work-rooms. Facing "another lone all-nighter", Adrienne was fed up. She'd seen enough of the Glasgow Citizens Theatre's new offshoot, a community and schools touring venture (Theatre Around Glasgow), and all the different hats she'd been expected to wear.

> "I was made designer, but sadly, that little company never showed even a glimmer of the thrilling creativity the main company was so famous for. Designer is also too grand a term for what I actually did, which included everything bar acting (except for one show when the cast insisted I come on stage to join in the final song... something I resented intensely at the time). I built and painted the sets, got the props, made the costumes, drove the van, did the sound and lighting, and stage managed the shows. No wonder they were crap."[6]

John came to the rescue that night, with his booze, support and eventually, a big idea. Why couldn't they start their own theatre company, one where they could make the rules themselves? "I was too green to imagine such a thing was possible," remembers Adrienne, "but John was a terrific instigator and he felt confident he could source initial funding."[7]

Here come the kids. The new Glasgow Youth Theatre was a club open to any 15 to 18 year-olds who wanted to turn up on a Friday evening to theatre studio space converted from the college's old gymnasium. Some would hang around the Dolphin more often, even six days a week in the holidays, morning to night. Because the alternatives in the East End of the Seventies, in a landscape of tenement demolition, rubble and wasteland, weren't great. "The only extracurricular activities available were football or gang fighting," said one of the Dolphin's regulars, Alan Love[8] (who'd been known as 'Puff' since primary school because of what chlorine in the public swimming baths used to do to his eyelids — on top of the effects of pre-teen smoking[9]). "The Bridgeton area was a dark, foreboding, dangerous place to be. Local works and industries were in rapid decline or gone altogether, and the area itself was steeped in sectarianism and gang violence. Money was an absolute stranger to us back then, and any fun we had needed to be manufactured from scratch."[10] Sanny (Douglas Sannachan) was born in the neighbouring Catholic district of Calton where the Calton Tongs drugs gang ruled. When his family moved to Barrowfields it was a case of the same problems/new faces, and Sanny would

Left to right (kind of): Big John, Gordon, Sanny, Caroline, Anne, Claire, Puff and Janette. Courtesy of Margaret Hughes.

come across members of the Torch and Spur gangs in his local streets, sometimes fighting each other with swords[11]. The threat of violence, getting a kicking for no reason, the odd punch or slap, was always a real one, and school didn't provide a safe haven. "There wasn't a lot of learning going on. It was a riot," said Sanny[12]. Even for those with a warm family home to return to, children would know about the effects of poverty, alcoholism, glue-sniffing and heroin, would have seen the signs of them about the neighbourhood and known their lingering look and smell.

The Dolphin was a place where the kids could just be kids. "It was viewed with deep suspicion on the whole," explained Alan. "But the locals were happy to exempt us from their lifestyle, and we were even given the nod in the local drinking establishments."[13] "There was a whole lot of

folk running about the Dolphin Centre," said Rab
(Buchanan)[14], another of the East Enders along with Puff
and Sanny. "Youngsters, my age, teenagers. A strange bunch.
We tried to keep well away from them."[15] Rab had arrived at
the Dolphin via his love of music. Growing up in the
Gorbals ("we didn't have a bath indoors until I was nine or
so"), the kids were left to find their own fun. "We would col-
lect old mattresses and drag them to the back of disused
tenements where the stairwell was. We'd go up the first floor
and jump out of the window, up to the second floor, jump
out — then the third floor. Really stupid."[16] Rab found safer
entertainment with his radio, getting into stuff that no-one
else had heard of. "Things like *The Who By Numbers* and
Santana blew me away. Jazz stuff like The Nice." His music
teacher got him to sign up with a junior choir that met at the
Dolphin, a few years before the youth theatre even existed.
Sunday nights to begin with, then extra days on Wednesdays
and Fridays working on musicals, until he got to hear about
the GYT and made the switch. "The people in the choir
were older than me — came from places that were a bit better off. Posher. It felt like the guys in the youth theatre were
just as rough and ready as I was."

There was plenty of fun to be had in the Dolphin, a
draughty old wonderland. A little side room upstairs in that
dark, rambling Gothic building was known as the 'Coffin
Room'. Sanny once climbed into the coffin — left over from
some arts project — and waited until a bunch of visiting
school kids came past so he could, very slowly, push open the
lid and get to enjoy every one of the screams of terror he'd
caused. "It was a great place," he said, "because you could

actually get away with stuff."[17]. One evening there'd be the City of Glasgow Military Band tuning up, the next the puppetry club, coffee mornings going on during the day. The kind of free-wheeling arts centre where bee hives were kept on the roof[18]. From the age of 14 when their school offered them the choice of getting kicked on the sports field on a Friday or going to the Dolphin, Puff and Sanny had a go at every art and craft on offer: "Pretty soon we were there every spare moment and it basically became our lives," recalled Alan. "While we were there of course, we became aware of the GYT and knew John Baraldi well. We were perhaps not John's ideal candidates for the theatre — but we eventually grew on him and were accepted into that little world. Only a few of the GYT members actually came from the East End. Quite a few came from quite affluent areas, but we never held that against them; they obviously had their own demons to contend with. The warmth and friendship and fun that Sanny and I were immediately part of was all consuming."[19]

Friday nights were special. Rehearsing for plays and getting ready for the tours could be hard work, but mostly the GYT would feel less like a youth theatre and more of a social get-together, a chance to chat and hang out. A lot of the formal part of Fridays was taken up with exercises designed to build trust and confidence; like crowd surfing (being lifted up and passed overhead from one person to the next); falling backwards and hoping to be caught in someone's arms; allowing yourself to be pushed around while your feet stayed rigid. And there were exercises to improve breathing and relaxation, find ways to keep a 'clear mind', or have a go at acting out abstract ideas in a physical form. "They'd say something like 'be a fried egg' and we'd end up lying on the floor and sizzling," said Sanny. 'Be an Apple Pie' is remembered in particular because of Gordon Sinclair's take on it: holding his balance with one leg lifted off the ground then leaning forward with an arm raised to the sky. ("How's that an apple pie?"/"Well it's more of an apple pie than what youse doin lying on the floor!") And it was Friday after all, so the GYT would make their way together to a bar at Bridgeton Cross — The Keystane[20], a flat-roof, single-storey place with a wood-panelled front and lattice windows — or at least, those who looked old enough. Sanny knew he was a "no-no". "Hey you. Oot. That's what they'd say when I tried to sneak in."[21] It didn't help that many of the regulars were teachers from his school.

Caroline Guthrie[22] was one of the later arrivals to the party. She'd wanted to be a film star from the age of five when she'd heard the working-class accent of a child actor from Yorkshire in *Whistle Down the Wind* (1961). It hadn't taken long to realise that film stardom (or even being an actor at all) was something that probably only happened to other people, and she'd been working in Marks & Spencer and thinking about a future in retail management when her mum saw an ad in the local paper for the GYT. For a girl from East Kilbride, Bridgeton was "like another planet," she said, "it was so rough", and she only went because her boyfriend's cousin promised to go with her. At first sight, the Dolphin was just some "broken building", but the people inside changed her life. "I loved it as soon as I walked in," said Caroline. "There was such a mix of people: some people who'd come from places with no bath, others might

117

be living in a posh bungalow. It was always such a laugh —
and nothing to do with acting, the acting was incidental."
Outside though, Bridgeton itself lost none of its menace. "I
turned up one evening wearing these white jeans and a green
top [Celtic FC colours]. They said to me: how the hell did
you get here alive?"[23]

While being at the heart of everything, John Baraldi
(as one of the "grown-ups") stayed a mystery to the group.
What was an American doing there anyway? John was only
in his mid-20s but seemed much older, an unexpectedly wise
and benevolent presence. Their Cat Stevens — exotic, funny,
patient, a Bridgeton mystic — someone willing to listen
rather than push his own ideas, his agenda or even authority.
The GYT wasn't about the acting in itself, there were never
any auditions, and if things got out of hand John would step
in with a quiet, level and purposeful intervention: "Sanny.
Fucking stop that." The much bigger problem was getting
acknowledgement and funding from the regional arts funders. There was a right kind of worthy, and an outsider
theatre group in Bridgeton wasn't it. John also felt that being
an American didn't help: "our faces didn't fit"[24]. It made
him sick to attend arts body jollies and see the great and
good drinking quantities of free wine worth more than the
sums he was asking for (and being refused). When the world-
renowned Ballet Rambert company was persuaded to do
outreach work at the Dolphin centre, and when the GYT got
to work on an operetta with Alasdair Gray[25], it was only be
cause John raised his own funds. He tried everyone, including Jimmy Boyle, the famous gangster, convicted murderer

Rab demonstrates the Apple Pie. Courtesy of Gerry Clark.

and inmate of the Special Unit at Barlinnie Prison in Glasgow — 'The Big Hoose' — that was reserved for dangerous and psychologically disturbed prisoners. Boyle had set up a fund for East End community projects with the money he'd generated from writing his memoirs, *A Sense of Freedom* (1977)[26]. To complete the frustration for John, the GYT only became accepted as a 'good thing' among Scottish funders after that week at the Royal Court, when it had been given validation by a London institution.

So Bill talked to John: "he was a very cool guy…and very accessible too"[27] and the laid-back vibe encouraged Bill to begin his plan, swallow hard and cycle over to Bridgeton on Friday nights. He sat in on improv sessions and rehearsals for the next production, an observer at the back of the room watching John and Adrienne with the actors to get a sense of what was involved: "it was a pretty deprived area so the kids were quite lively."[28] A nice piece of understatement. The Friday routine could have gone on for months ("I sat around quivering with inadequacy"[29]), if John hadn't stepped in and told Bill it was time to explain his plans. "You know," John had said, "the kids are starting to wonder who you are. Who is this weirdo that doesn't say anything? You have to talk to them."[30] It was normal enough for the GYT to have visitors from the council or one arts body or another. "What was unusual was that one guy began showing up every week and would hardly say a word," said Gerry. "Bill would just stay in the background and keep to himself, occasionally talking to John."[31] The next Friday, Bill took the train from Partick into Bridgeton, but found himself getting off early, at Charing Cross. He really didn't want to do it. Not really. What was he doing writing feature films anyway? Sitting on a station bench, he wrestled with himself and his worries as the trains came and went through the city; bustle all around him, people going home, people heading into the centre for their nights out. "I sat there and imagined what my life would be like with the film and what it'd be like without the film."

Bill survived. He talked about his plans for what would eventually become *Gregory's Girl*, and in order to demonstrate the kind of work he'd done he set up a screen

Bill and Ann. Courtesy of Margaret Hughes.

and projector and showed the group *The Legend of Los Tayos*. "We were immediately impressed that: 1. He'd made a film. 2. He'd been up the Amazon," said Gerry[32]. But it was only the start of getting to know his actors. They were naturally sceptical (make a feature film, in Glasgow? Oh aye.) They'd make fun of him and his black baseball cap: "Look — there's the guy who thinks he's an internationally recognised film director."[33] Especially when they found out he'd been going round the local girls' schools looking for a female lead (oh aye). But they were all good signs. He wasn't treated as different or aloof from them, and there was no stiffening on Bill's side from a threatened ego. "He was a very quiet man," remembered Caroline. "He just hung about. Another of the grown-ups that we didn't take that much notice of — there was so much else going on."[34] Bill was just Bill, someone who

121

would win their lasting respect and affection. Puff got to know Bill better than most: he would spend a day at week at Tree Films running errands for them in exchange for a chance to learn about the editing suite equipment. "Slowly, Bill came round and started to trust us and have fun," said Puff. "We soon got to know him for the incredibly fun person he is. No-one had a clue about Bill's film-making background to begin with, but what shone through, apart from his excellent sense of humour, was his sheer intelligence. There was a real sense of deep trust that we shared with each other, of pure love, and Bill was right in there with all of those feelings."[35] Sanny remembers one time on their summer tour sitting in the front seat with Puff while Bill was driving them on to the next stop. They'd been chatting together and only after some time did they notice that after all the hours on the road, Bill's eyes were closed. He'd nodded off. It was only after they'd started shouting and shaking Bill's shoulder that they realised it was his party trick: just the one eye had been shut[36].

The 15 year-old Gordon Sinclair[37] first gave the GYT a go as a way to avoid double English on Friday afternoons. A big prog rock fan, when he turned up and saw Rab in a Rush t-shirt he knew he'd be okay. The first session he attended involved working with a script telling the story of a girl joining the boys' football team, trying out improvisations around some plot situations and writing their own sketches to perform. That was how the GYT always worked

Gordon's first formal stage appearance (*The Auld Alliance*, 1978). Courtesy of Rab Buchanan.

in putting together their own revues, with bits and pieces of ideas and real experiences — like the piece from Sanny who came up with 'First Date' for an upcoming summer tour, where a nervous teenager waits under a clock for their date.

About a year on from when he first turned up at the Dolphin, Bill's script was done.

*

I wanted to work in theatre, on the stage, backstage or in the box office, anything; because of Dad, but also because of the experience of being in school plays; what seemed to be a short-cut to the more earnest places of adulthood, where Kim, the Goth with the piercings, turned out in a taffeta frock for a Regency comedy; Deano did Shakespeare with a leotard and a face full of make-up; almost grown-up in the way we were on each other's side, with no jeering, no hard gleaming eyes looking for weakness, no-one caring about my baggy corduroy trousers.

The long road to opening night would start with the cast getting together for rehearsals at lunchtimes, still a bunch of schoolchildren carrying our scripts like any other textbook, wary and sheepish. We'd be regretting having signed up for something that was going to take so much effort, learning lines, getting lifts over to school in the evenings, and some of us didn't seem like actors at all — we knew were going to make a mess of it. The lead parts would have been taken by members of the year above. You could tell who they were straight away. They had louder voices and didn't mind sounding posh. They were the ones already willing to take on the persona of being an 'actor', who let their confidence on stage all hang out, loose and limber doing their scenes, or slumped round the piano playing ad hoc versions of chart tunes for sing-a-longs.

Overnight, a set would appear in the school hall and there was the realisation that a public performance was actually going to happen. Costumes had been made and tickets were being sold (if only to parents who couldn't say no). There it was, the wicked spell of theatre: a masochistic mix of excitement and terror.

I did Plautus' *Pot of Gold;* Farquhar's *Beaux' Stratagem; Strife* by John Galsworthy; *Arsenic and Old Lace.* I was the Chocolate Soldier in *Arms and the Man.* Then Genghis, Dracula's deformed servant in *Dracula Spectacular.* I liked the comic parts best. The times when the world seemed to stop — a feeling of tension and rapt attention hanging in the rich darkness of a cave, a darkness that's visibly tense against the hot shimmer of stage lights; in the columns of dust and the shadows in the wings — and you knew the next line, the next facial expression was going to break the tension with a big laugh.

For that reason I was miserable as Lysander, one of the romantic leads in *A Midsummer Night's Dream*. I'd wanted to be Bottom and nothing else. Instead I went out each night alongside a Hermia who couldn't help but sigh with despair whenever she saw me arrive on stage, the untrendy hair and general state of podge. Her great love. There were going to be no laughs for Lysander, not unless his toga fell off.

*

Bill knew what the next steps would be in making a little low-budget film like this: the bulk of the money would come from the British Film Institute (in this case he'd worked out they'd need £29,000), topped up with money from private and corporate sponsors to make life more comfortable.

The GYT worked with him on the application pitch. John had raised money from the Gulbenkian Foundation, a super-wealthy arts funder, to buy a reel-to-reel video recorder, camera and monitor, which meant they could film some sample scenes for the BFI to see. In these clips, Gregory was played by Danny Benson, a member of the GYT who was also training as a police cadet[38]. Rather than entering the realms of film legend, Danny went on to become a chief constable with Strathclyde Police. When the BFI went up to Bridgeton, the young actors performed some scenes on the

Danny Benson is pictured (centre), above Rab (Cousin Itt-style), being pointed out by Gerry. Courtesy of Janette Benson.

spot and took the visitors out to the pub. Everyone enjoyed themselves, and the BFI's verdict was that they were onto a winner. Bill himself felt that he and the GYT were the right package. He had plenty of practical experience; he'd (nearly) been through the National Film School; and the proposal was an opportunity for the BFI to show its support for the provinces and an area of (multiple social) deprivation. But the BFI cycle took time, four to six months to critique the script and overall proposals, which was followed by more meetings and efforts to position the film as supportable by the BFI. "I remember one torment of a meeting when I tried to explain that *Gregory's Girl* was really a structuralist comedy."[39] Even when the final decision was meant to be announced it was delayed. The BFI were due to call on the Thursday and they didn't. There was no answer when Bill phoned up their offices the next day. Finally the call came on Monday to say it was a no. The BFI's committee of writers and film professionals agreed that *Gregory's Girl* was too commercial, it didn't need public money. That year the funding went to a film adaptation of Dennis Potter's disturbing morality play *Brimstone and Treacle* (1982), starring pop star Sting as a demon, the anti-Mary Poppins. He arrives from nowhere and uses his uncanny charms to win the trust of the exhausted parents of a young woman left in a vegetative state after a car accident, subsequently taking his chance to sexually abuse her. Certainly uncommercial.

"I spent a good year with the kids and then suddenly I had to go to them and say, 'Look, this isn't going to happen.' And that's what really stimulated the idea for *That Sinking Feeling*," said Forsyth, "because I had all this energy with the kids and also the people in the film business like the crew and the cameraman that I'd been egging on to help me out."[40] And he really wanted to show the BFI he didn't need them. He'd make a film about the world the GYT kids knew. They'd scrape some money together and take the film on tour, just like one of their plays, go round Scotland's community centres and church halls with their own projector. Yeah. Fuck 'em — because by this time, Bill had been infused by the outsider spirit of John and the GYT. More soberly, he was also interested in the work of the Association of Independent Producers, a pressure group which believed in the need for a proliferation of indies as a self-supporting community and the possibilities of indie film-making as a counter-cultural and political force. By 1981 Forsyth was calling for there to be "at least twelve half-million pound films every year. I volunteer to make two of them."[41]

The core of the film's story came from gossip over-heard at the Dolphin. Some friends the group knew had decided to break into a bowls club to see what cash they could find, but all they'd managed to steal was a bowls trophy. What could they do with it, something so useless? This was a bit of real Bridgeton life. Street adventures. What happened when you had nothing to look forward to except a bowl of cornflakes for dinner, and the original script was subtitled: "A film comedy in one illegal act". Other ideas for *That Sinking Feeling* came from the sketches the GYT had been rehearsing for its summer show, *One for the Album*, a series of observational coming-of-age pieces. Bill called the resulting film a "fairytale for the unemployed"[42]. Rab plays Ronnie, who's come up with a plan to raid a factory and pinch its stock of stainless steel sinks. He's "supposed to be the leader of the gang but is pretty hapless and hopeless at it, it's a dream that he has when he falls asleep in the park one day eating his cornflakes"[43]. It was familiar stuff to the kids, and also in tune with the faltering mood of a film director who now had very little money in the bank himself — who was basically just another member of the unemployed, no longer able to afford to run his car. There was something bracing and purging about the whole desperate thing, and in spite of all the project's limitations, they were going to do it. Again, fuck 'em, they weren't going to be in the pockets of the film establishment. "It felt good," said Bill, "being on the streets with no money."[44]

Forsyth started by writing "begging letters" to companies about the GYT and their dream of making a movie, pitched originally as a short for UNESCO's International Year of the Child. "I wrote to all the unions and got a letter back from a secretary at one of them [the Amalgamated Electrical Workers Union] — I swear you could see tear stains on the paper — saying her boss had told her to write saying they couldn't contribute. So she'd enclosed a Postal Order for two pounds of her own money."[45] There was £250 from the Scottish Film Council, £50 from Shell Oil, £25 each from William Hill bookies and Marks & Spencer. It all helped, and in the end *That Sinking Feeling* was made without the impetus of any particular funding money at all[46]. Production crew from Bill's documentary days gave up three weeks of their time for free, including Paddy Higson from the Halt Bar gang and Tree Film's Mick Coulter, and they all chipped in to provide food to keep everyone going (Anne Marie Macdonald appears in the credits as 'Assistant Director' when her actual job was making the bacon rolls). As a 'youth project' they managed to get a 30% discount on the lab bill, and 10 cans of cheap 16mm film stock from Fuji (just enough to persuade Mick that they were serious).

Compared with the time and attention already lavished on *Gregory's Girl*, *That Sinking Feeling* was thrown together. "A down and dirty film," according to Bill. "Reasonably straightforward, street-level filming."[47] In line with the New

Wave handbook then, and well-suited to the sketch-driven approach of the GYT, how they would chuck some often inspired ideas into the air to see how they would land. Many of the scenes were filmed in and around the Dolphin in the March and April of 1979. The plumber's yard with the sinks, Thomas Graham's, was just round the corner (and was also the place where Sanny was working as an apprentice). Paddy managed to persuade the owners to allow them to film for a whole weekend (a big leap of faith, thought Bill, because the film could have easily been the front for an actual heist). This was the hardest part of the filming. Time in the factory was strictly limited and Eichmann and Big John in particular had taken to disappearing off to the Bridgeton pubs. Eich wasn't really up for dressing up as a woman for his part. He had a reputation in the East End to protect, and would always draw the line at anything he thought was "daft"[48]. "I was convinced that he would just walk out," said Gerry[49]. The minibus had to be used to check on the circuit of drinking places to round up the GYT and lure them back to the filming with hamburgers. Somehow they got it done. "When the workers were coming back to work on Monday morning," said Bill, "we were coming out like dead rats."[50] They ran out of film stock before the end of the actual screenplay. Rab was there on set: "Mick said 'right, we're all finished', and Bill said 'okay, but mibbe we can get one more take of that scene'. 'No' says Mick, 'I mean that's really it, there's no more film.'"[51]

Through his friendship with Lynda Miles, Bill managed to get *That Sinking Feeling* a premiere at the Edinburgh Film Festival in the August of that year. The Festival guaranteed them an audience of national journalists, many of which were taken aback by the quality of the film, its — very Glaswegian — gusts of wit, and unassuming social commentary[52]. That week, Glasgow's *Evening Times* included two items on Bill Forsyth. One near the front reported on the "triumph" of his debut film; and another, at the back, gave notice of the impounding of his furniture because of unpaid council rates[53]. In his review in *The Observer*, Philip French wrote how *That Sinking Feeling* brought back "happy memories of Ealing in its heyday and Ealing's resident Scot, Alexander Mackendrick. A delightful comedy, it does for present-day Glasgow what *Hue and Cry* did for postwar London — it gives a gang of lively, unemployed working-class teenagers the freedom of the city. This time, however, they're the crooks, and the objective of their elaborate heist is a warehouse full of stainless steel sinks." Elation at the reception from critics was followed by disappointment. The number of Scottish people prepared to pay to see the film turned out to be very small: because "they didn't want to be disappointed with something local," said Bill. "I grew up that week I can tell you."[54]

John Baraldi moved on to head up the youth theatre in Cumbernauld (of all places)[55]. No matter how hard it was to tell the kids, he "didn't want to be a Mr Chips."[56] Without him the GYT fell apart, the enthusiasm and buzz receded as John's replacement looked to focus on more 'serious' theatre, beginning with an attempt at the German expressionist play 'Gas' (1917) set in a gas production plant during the First World War.

The end of the GYT after just three exciting, mould-breaking years — which included an invitation from the BBC to create their own one-off TV programme[57] — has been felt by its members ever since. "We had no expectations about anything except for having a good time and a good laugh," said Caroline. "We just took it as something normal that the BBC would let us make our own show, that we could choose what we wanted it to be like. We took it in our stride — no big deal. The GYT is something that will never be re-peated."[58]

Bill stayed in touch with the GYT, always planning to re-pay the loyalty of his young actors with paid work when there was money for it. And they stayed in touch with Bill, if not always in the way he wanted. One evening he returned to his Park Circus Lane flat at the top of the city to find his home had been broken into. A body-shaped hole "like a Looney Tunes cartoon" had been left in his kitchen window and a camera and a pen-knife were missing. In the kitchen was a major clue. The intruder had spread ketchup onto an onion and taken a big bite from it. It could only be Eich-mann, "off his head on something". After his adventure in Bill's flat, Eich rang to apologise properly, and did his best to explain what had happened: "I think I was just seeking your attention," he told him[59].

Billy Greenlees was a much-loved member of the GYT, because of his easy humour, his big singing voice, and because he was a rebel who combined a hard man persona with decency and a good heart. Eich was the one, out of all of them, expected to become the 'star'. But he'd had a crazy life, a "difficult childhood"[60], and was capable of slipping off the rails. For a short period, Billy had been a member of the Blue Angels — Scotland's version of the Hell's Angels — which was where the nickname 'Eichmann' had come from. Its members were named after history's super-villains: so Billy was Adolf Eichmann, the senior Nazi responsible for devising the 'Final Solution'. Billy detached himself from the Angels, not wanting any part of the slide into violence and crime that seemed to have become part of its way of doing things.

Puff (with Eich). Courtesy of Caroline Guthrie.

There had been years of persuasion from schoolmates Sanny and Puff to get Eich to join in the fun at the Dolphin, but eventually he came to love performing on stage, either with the GYT or singing with a rock band at the Nationalist Bar in Calton. Eich's new hobbies didn't mean the local characters could afford to forget who he was.

"I was blissfully unaware of Eich and his family's reputation in the East End until one night I was queuing in a Bridgeton chippy [said Gerry]. The guy in front of me was giving me dirty looks from a face full of scars, as if someone had been practicing Chinese writing on him. When I came out of the chippy he was waiting for me, aggressively wanting to know why I had been standing so close to him. I knew that no matter what answer or apology I offered, I was going to get a kicking. Just as I was beginning to explain the concept of a 'queue', Eich appeared out of nowhere — and the guy's attitude immediately changed. 'Awright Gerry?' Eich asked me. 'Eh, aye, mibbe,' I said. Eich turned to the scary, scarry guy. 'Any problem here Bean Man?' 'Naw, nae problem here,' is all he could say. After a brief conversation where the Bean Man agreed that he had no grievance with either me or Eich, he disappeared off down the road. I thanked Eich for his intervention and explained that I thought I was

about to get a doing. 'Naw', says Eich. 'That's
the Bean Man. He's shite at fighting. That's
why he's got a face full of second prizes.'"[61]

Eich didn't take acting too seriously. It needed to fit into his
life and not the other way around. When he was picked out
for a part in a prime-time episode of *Play for Today* in 1979,
Eich's big scene was to be filmed at Greenock Docks. The
BBC had paid through the nose to hire the entire dock location, time was tight and they couldn't afford for anything to
go wrong. Then Eich didn't turn up. BBC producers were
frantic, running round Glasgow, hitting the phones, chasing
down anyone who might know where he was — like Sanny,
who knew exactly where Eich was: he'd had gone to see the
band Bad Company play at the Apollo, but he wasn't going
to grass him up[62]. The only reason Eich was found was because his hair had been coloured bright red for the part of a
knife gang leader, and he was eventually seen in the crowd.
The BBC's dash to the docks with their young actor was giv-
en a police escort to clear the way.

Being a public figure didn't work out for Eich. After
Gregory's Girl he became even more well-known for fronting a
TV beer advert with the catchline of "D'ye want a pint. The
usual?". "Eich was so recognisable," said Sanny. "Wherever
he went there'd be people shouting out to him — aye, the
usual! the usual! He was tormented by it, the poor guy. By
then I was down in London doing plays and I kept telling
him he was just too good not to come back to acting, but he
was on a downer about it all."[63] "He was probably the most
talented of any of us," agreed Alan[64]. "His career was going

from strength to strength when fate intervened. He developed an overactive thyroid gland which so affected his facial features and confidence, that it brought that chapter of his life to an end. For those who knew him though, his character shines through on screen like no other." Billy died in 2009, aged 47.

That Sinking Feeling was picked up for the London Film Festival and plans to get back on the road in the minibus could be scrapped. With some help from David Puttnam, the film got a wider distribution deal — and as per the pattern that so frustrated John Baraldi, Scottish audiences were now duly interested. Consequently, Bill was approached by two up-and-coming producers, Davina Belling and Clive Parsons, about making another film[65]. Without a stock of new ideas waiting on the shelf, he turned back to *Gregory's Girl*. Why not? Between them they secured a pot of £180,000 — around the minimum needed to make a 'proper' film — with support from the UK's funding body, the National Film Finance Corporation, and another, more unusual source. For the first time, a TV company was going to pitch in to make a feature film. STV (Scottish Television) was the pioneer for what was to come in a bigger way from Channel 4[66].

Maybe, after all, being turned down by the BFI had been the best possible thing to happen to Bill. "It was fortuitous," says Rab. "He made *TSF* instead, and that meant there were professional producers and more money to make *Gregory's Girl* — it would have been a different film without that."[67]

[1] A play written by Glasgow-based Edward Boyd about the 13th century alliance made between the kingdoms of Scotland and France. Originally meant for the BBC, it was considered to contain too much swearing, and Boyd offered the script to the GYT instead. He was best known for his 1960s and early 70s crime dramas, including *The View from Daniel Pike*.

[2] John Hughes (who played Vic in *That Sinking Feeling*) and Margaret Mctear (a nurse in *TSF*) would go on to be one of the GYT's married couples, along with Janette and Danny Benson.

[3] Gerald Peary, Interview, Toronto Festival of Festivals, September 1985.

[4] *Fresh Air with Terry Gross*, 6 October 1989.

[5] The Bridgeton Billy Boys made their own suitably brutal appearance in the BBC TV programme (series 5). The 'Billy Boys' chant, used as a war cry by Protestants, continues to cause controversy by being sung by Rangers FC fans.

[6] Adrienne Atkinson, Email conversation, March 2022.

[7] Ibid.

[8] Gerry Clark, *One for the Album: the story of the Glasgow Youth Theatre*, Glasgow Youth Theatre documentary film, 2020. An entertaining, must-watch history of the GYT featuring interviews with Bill Forsyth, John Baraldi and many of the group members about their memories.

[9] "My absolutely detested nickname," said Alan of 'Puff'. "It stuck and cuts me deep to this day." Alan was Eric the photographer (as well as being Alec, one of the sink-stealing gang, in *That Sinking Feeling*). He'd hoped for a career in theatre, but was always wary of the lack of acting work going, and went on to have a career as a senior social work professional in North Lanarkshire. "Trying to recreate life post-GYT was extremely difficult and I didn't have the staying power. My love of theatre has remained with me, and I'm actually in the latter stages of a stage work which I really think has all the right elements. If I had some of my old crew to bounce off, I'd have it done in a week. But I don't. I should have it done by the end of the year [2022] and then I'll just need a couple of kids, director and stage manager. Sound familiar?"

[10] Alan Love, Email interview, June 2022.

[11] Sanny's life as a 16 year-old in Calton was documented in a chapter of a book by the *Daily Mail* journalist Bel Mooney in 1978, *Year of the Child*. "His home is an old tenement building above some shops: a three-room flat on the fifth floor. He panted as he reached the top. His mother Nancy, his father William and his granny sat by the fire in the warm living room, with the television on." Mooney had been put in touch with Sanny via convicted murderer and gang leader Jimmy Boyle, who'd become aware of the work of the GYT while he was still in prison. Even at that stage, Sanny was talking about the GYT as having changed his life. His final quote was: "I'm not going to be like the rest round here. I'm going to do something with my life!"

[12] Douglas Sannachan, Telephone interview, 9 August 2022. Sanny was window-cleaner Billy; Simmy in *That Sinking Feeling* and turned up in *Comfort & Joy* ("Hello folks!"). He kept up his acting career with parts in *Taggart* and *Rebus* and as a regular in performances at the Pavilion Theatre in Glasgow, as well as honing an expertise in stained glass window repairs. He was the writer/director of comedy horror *Starcache* (2018), which premiered to an audience that included Bill Forsyth. Bill folded up the paper marking his 'reserved' seat in order to make a crown he presented to Sanny. Most recently, Sanny has been working alongside Gerry Clark on the *Rhinoman* project with young actors and film directors (artisannie.com).

[13] Ibid.

[14] Rab Buchanan was working as a stage manager at the Dundee Repertory Theatre when he was given the part of Andy. Besides his lead role as Ronnie in *That Sinking Feeling* and an appearance in *Comfort & Joy*, Rab has been involved with stage management at a number of Scottish theatres, including the Tolbooth Theatre in Stirling — most recently working as a sound and lighting engineer.

[15] Gerry Clark, ibid.

[16] Rab Buchanan, Telephone Conversation, 10 August 2022.

[17] Ibid.

[18] A quirky location used for a scene in *That Sinking Feeling*.

[19] Ibid.

[20] In Landressy Street until the bar was demolished and replaced with housing in 2009.

[21] Douglas Sannachan, ibid.

[22] Caroline Guthrie played Carol, the girl who terrifies Gregory by coming out of phone box in a skimpy miniskirt and off-the-shoulder top. Caroline also appeared in *Local Hero* (as wee punk Pauline, John Gordon Sinclair's girlfriend who chases after Peter Capaldi) and *Comfort & Joy*; had a part in *Chaplin* (1992) as half of a 'courting couple', and has made a string of TV and radio appearances since, including the series *Glasgow Kiss* (2000), *Ghosts* (2018) and *Casualty* (2019), as well as being a regularly used voice actor.

[23] Caroline Guthrie, Telephone interview, 27 June 2022.

[24] Ibid.

[25] Gray was soon to become renowned for his extraordinary novel *Lanark* (1981).

[26] A success story for the Special Unit, Boyle was released from his life sentence after serving 14 years in 1980 and went on to marry his psychiatrist and become a noted sculptor and novelist.

[27] Ibid.

[28] Film Forum, Q&A with Bill Forsyth ahead of a showing of *Gregory's Girl*, October 4 2019.

[29] '*That Sinking Feeling*: The film that put Scotland on the map', *The Herald*, 5 October 2019.

[30] Jasper Rees, '10 Questions for Filmmaker Bill Forsyth', *The Arts Desk*, 28 April 2014.

[31] Gerry Clark, Email conversation, 15 July 2022.

[32] Ibid.

[33] British Film Institute, Q&A with John Gordon Sinclair ahead of a *Gregory's Girl* screening, 5 December 2015.

[34] Caroline Guthrie, ibid.

[35] Alan Love, Email conversation, June 2022.

[36] Douglas Sannachan, ibid.

---

[37] John Gordon Sinclair moved to London in the early 80s and went on to be a film, TV and West End theatre star (performing as a lead in the musical *She Loves Me* in the 1990s; playing a Navy SEAL alongside Brad Pitt in *World War Z* (2013); and appearing in 2019/20 in the cast of crime drama *Traces*).

[38] Danny went on to play the part of Dave the Policeman in *That Sinking Feeling*. He had the costume already after all (although he drew the line at wearing the police helmet without official sanction).

[39] Bill Forsyth, *Sight and Sound*, Vol.50 (4), 1981, p243. Forsyth was making a point about needing to conform to the intellectual conventions of the time — but it's also a reasonable position to take: it is a kind of structuralist film. Structuralism as a theory gained in popularity in the 1960s in the wake of existentialism — what was known as the 'linguistic turn' in film studies, and gained a foothold in academia (structuralist ideas would have been meat and drink at National Film School seminars). Essentially it meant the way we rely on cultural codes, a shared language of meanings and assumptions (that may not be an accurate reflection of reality). A structuralist film know this, and plays with or subverts this idea: we see a football match (but there's a girl), there's cookery going on (led by a boy). Cinema itself is just a set of codes: people go to a darkened room together, buy popcorn and nachos, expect to be entertained by heroes and villains.

[40] Abbey Bender, 'From Sponsored Movies to Coming-of-Age Classics: Bill Forsyth Talks About Pioneering Scottish Cinema', MUBI, 3 October 2019.

[41] Bill Forsyth, *Sight and Sound*, ibid.

[42] 'Bill Forsyth raises a tartan cheer', *The Guardian*, 13 June 1981.

[43] Jonathan Murray, 'Cornflakes versus Conflict: An Interview with Bill Forsyth', *Journal of British Cinema and Television*, Edinburgh University Press, Vol.12 (2), 2019.

[44] Bill Forsyth interview, Filmwax Radio, New York, 10 October 2019.

[45] Claire Walker, '*That Sinking Feeling*: The film that put Scotland on the map', *The Herald*, 5 October 2019.

[46] With an official budget of £5,000, the film was included in the Guinness Book of Records as the cheapest feature film with a general release ever made. A large proportion of that budget was needed for the film stock and processing.

[47] Bill Forsyth interview, Filmwax Radio, ibid.

[48] Eichmann (Billy Greenlees) was Steve, Gregory's pal with the white jacket and a baking prodigy. He was Wal in *That Sinking Feeling*, the nightwatchman's lady for choice; knife gang leader Dunky McAfferty in a 1979 *Play for Today*, 'Just a Boy's Game'; and was due to play Chancer in the long-running sitcom *City Lights*, but only appeared in the pilot episode before deciding to step back from acting.

[49] Gerry Clark, ibid.

[50] Gerry Clark, ibid.

[51] Rab Buchanan, ibid.

[52] Reportedly, seeing *That Sinking Feeling* was an inspiration to the 17 year-old Armando Iannucci, who realised the possibilities of writing Glaswegian comedy.

[53] Bill Forsyth interview, Filmwax Radio, ibid.

[54] Kevin Courrier, 'Interview with film director Bill Forsyth', *Critics at Large*, 1985.

[55] John Baraldi kept moving and challenging himself in a series of arts sector and cultural fund-raising jobs, including a Russian exchange scheme for ballet, film, circus and theatre; Manchester tourism; acting schools and a multi-cultural arts centre in London. He's now based in Malta, the director of a programme setting up arts projects internationally as means of "encouraging leadership, social cohesion and economic well-being".

[56] Gerry Clark, ibid.

[57] The BBC allowed the GYT to produce and star in their own episode of *Something Else*. The show aired on BBC Two on Saturday 22 December 1979 (5.10pm to 5.50pm) and included performances from The Skids and The Revillos as well as an interview with up and coming director Bill Forsyth, who talked about the issues being faced by Glasgow and the need for more future-looking development plans. There were also some sketches involving new things to do with an old Coke can, and the problems caused by pencil skirts.

[58] Caroline Guthrie, Telephone interview, 27 June 2022.

[59] Ibid.

[60] Gerry Clark, ibid.

[61] Ibid.

[62] Douglas Sannachan, ibid.

[63] Ibid.

[64] Alan Love, ibid.

[65] They'd worked together as a team on some typical 70s British films: the X-rated *Rosie Dixon, Night Nurse* (1978), with Ray Winstone causing borstal mayhem in *Scum* (1979), but had stepped up a level in terms of industry attention by producing the new film vehicle for post-punk singer Hazel O'Connor, *Breaking Glass* (1980).

[66] Jonathan Murray, in his book *Discomfort & Joy* (p68), describes *Gregory's Girl* as "a paradigmatic Channel 4 feature before the advent of Channel 4". From its beginnings in 1981, Channel 4 Films became a key part of British film-making, investing in around a third of all films being made in the UK by 1984.

[67] Rab Buchanan, ibid.

6. Actors

"Oh *that* Dorothy. The hair, the teeth and the smell."

The patter of rain on tree canopies, a mass of green, is finally slowing; water drips its way down a stairway of branches. Somewhere a bird sings under the umbrellas of leaves, a solitary rain song like a trickle of brightness in Abronhill. Mist is clearing, moment by moment, to show the Campsie hills in the distance and a far-off patchwork of clouds, whites and greys on the pale blue horizon.

Even on an afternoon in June the lights have had to be switched on inside Abronhill High School. Filming is cancelled for the day and Mick is wiping down his camera. Bill is sitting on boxes talking about tomorrow with Clive and Davina. Paddy is busy going round to make sure actors are sticking around for some rehearsals, not heading straight back into Glasgow on the bus. In comes Gordon, a tall lad in a Patti Smith t-shirt and flared jeans who's arrived with another box of stuff from home for Adrienne. Gives her a little thumbs-up.

"Do your folks know about this?"

She's pulled out a tray of pot plants.

"Oh aye."

"Okay. Don't suppose they have a battery toothbrush do they?"

Gordon's already gone. He's seen Dee sitting on a chair in the school foyer reading her script. They'd been introduced but not spent any real time together yet. During the actual filming wasn't a good time, and anyway, he knew the guys were watching his every move from behind the camera. He waves to her but it's no good.

"Ah, you know," he says, to get her attention, "this is kinda my holiday from a real job. I really could be in Rimini right now."

"Oh — right."

Gives her his best smile. But she's still looking at the script. Was this what it was going to be like? They were going to be together a lot over the next few weeks, and wouldn't it be better to — you know — get to know each other. She had nice eyes. Everyone said so.

Gordon didn't know he was going to play Gregory until Bill turned up at his house one Monday night in the spring of 1980. It was raining outside and his Mum was cross with him for leaving their guest out on the doorstep. Gordon was stuck in a teenage daze — what was 'Bill the director' doing in his home anyway? He belonged at the Dolphin. There and only there. Gordon had settled into a routine as an apprentice electrician, got used to having some cash in his pocket for the weekends and kind of forgotten about acting. They'd expected Rab to get the main role, but no, said Bill. Seeing Gordy raiding for sinks, clambering out of the van like a Ninja in a balaclava, had started him thinking. That long-limbed awkwardness. How it looked like his arms and legs would never be in the right place. Unavoidable comedy. So Gordon would take time off for *Gregory's Girl*? Of course he would. It was going to be the perfect summer, back together again like the GYT tours, but this time making a film that was going to end up in lots of cinemas. And when he read the script he knew it was right for him: "Gregory's life experience was much the same as mine. I used to be dragged through life by the hair."[1]

"I should be working on my tan," says Gordon. Dee looks 'Gregory' up and down, from the big layered hair to his denim flares and back again.

"There's plenty o'work to do isn't there? Look. A few white bits y'have there."
She's pointing at his face and every part of him that's showing round his t-shirt. Encouraged, he sits down with her on the stairs. She'd have been in the school year above him, but why not. He'd play it smooth. Show some maturity. After all, he'd been around a bit already — and they could be friends whatever happened. Maybe some kind of kissing might be needed after all.

Dorothy had been the hardest role to cast and Dee was brought in very late. There were relatively few girls in the GYT and Bill didn't see any of them as being quite right. He'd not had much fun telling them so. All the GYT gang knew Dee Hepburn was a pro, having played the role of

145

Maggie in a BBC series alongside Geraldine McEwan in *The Prime of Miss Jean Brodie* (1978) when she was just 15[2]. Paddy though, had come across Dee personally while they were both working on a TV advert. The retail giant Goldbergs was launching a new chain of fashion outlets, Wrygges, aimed at 15 to 24 year-old women. Its advert involved girls pretending to be dancing at a disco. Paddy could see that here was an attractive young Scots actress with stamina, who could maybe look convincing on a football pitch, running at boys with a ball at her feet.

Dee thought the audition was the most laidback she had ever had. So casual in fact that it took months before Dee realised she'd got the part. She'd met with Bill and Paddy at his office, 'Lake Films', and chatted about this and that regarding the film. "Bill then just said 'Great. Fine. Okay. Shall we go for a drink then?'" said Dee. "I thought he just meant the two of them, but he wanted me to come along with them as well. We went to a bar somewhere in the West End and Bill ordered this bottle of champagne. I was happy to join them in toasting the success of the film, and I just thought, well, good luck to them. I didn't really think I was going to be Dorothy."[3] They'd speak by phone sometimes. Bill would give Dee a lift to get-togethers for the film and drop her back home in East Kilbride, when he'd be ushered in by Dee's mum for a cup of tea and biscuits, sat down and coaxed into conversation. As it turned out, he and Dee's mum had more in common than they'd expected, having both been born in the very same street in Whiteinch. And another coincidence that would have pleased Bill's sense of felicity: Dee's mum was a Madeline, the name of Bill's epitome of a wise and affectionate femininity in the script. In the end, with mum's prompting, Dee just came out with it and asked the director straight. Was she Dorothy then? Well of course, said Bill, unaware of the consequences of his reticence, didn't she know?

Bill sent Dee to Partick Thistle for both an initial screen test and a six-week training course ("We thought we would get her the best," commented Bill, drily.[4]) The first day, Dee was so nervous about her one-to-one footballing lessons she was sick at the bus stop and needed to telephone Bill to make an excuse[5]. She'd played football before, but only kickabouts with friends for fun. Dee turned up the next day to find herself with Scotland goalie Alan Rough and Partick player-turned-physio Donnie McKinnon (brother of more famous twin Ronnie), learning some skills, and most importantly, how to look like a natural player, with strength and flair. An "ungirlish" presence. By the end of the six weeks, Dee could do 40 minutes straight of keepie-uppies — she'd been doing so much practice in the evenings at home that her dog, a collie-cross called Bonnie, had learnt how to juggle the ball herself. Bill was talking about trying to include Bonnie's performance in the film, but scheduling turned out to be too tight.

"I'm not really a professional y'know," said Gordon, trying again.

"Oh. You'll be fine though."

She's looking out at him from underneath her fringe. Half-expectantly.

"I'm just an electrician really. Y'know, wiring up school bells and alarms and things like that. So you'll have to — y'know. Be gentle with me."

"Sounds like an okay job to me," she says. "While youse been having fun round here, I've been playing football at the sports centre with nine year-old kids who wanna take big lumps out o'me."

"Well, could be worse," he says, leaning in confidentially and waving his script at her. "At least you don't have to kiss me eh?"

She gives him a look like he's her little brother, then looks away and down. Clare would have laughed at that line, Gordon knew she would. And where was Clare anyway?

"Well. You know, better go see the guys."

It's only then he notices that Dee has hidden her smile. That lovely toothy smile.

The oldies appear with a big waft of Brut, and Jake has already taken Gordon's place next to Dee to catch up, whistle round his neck[6]. They knew each other from the filming of *Jean Brodie* (Eich was going round saying they'd been snogging in it). Gordon gives each of them a nod and a grin. Really good guys who'd been on the telly.

"Alright there Gordon. Y'hear about Chic?" asks Alex[7].

"Thas right — is he here?" wonders Dave[8]. "I've not met him before. Looking forward to it."

"Ah Paddy, is Chic Murray[9] in today? Wanted to say hello."

The production supervisor flies past:

"Next week, we think, next week — you seen Rab anywheres?"

Lots of shrugging.

"Y'know Alex I was goin to ask you," Gordon begins, "you bein a real actor an' all. Why are you doin this anyways?"

The oldies are laughing.

"Well Gordon. If you're thinking about a career in acting there's a little thing called money you'll be needing," says Alex.

"Can't be much, not for this? Not with us lot eh?" Alex puts an arm round his shoulder and steers him to the school's entrance doors, wide open to Abronhill's estates.

"Look out there son. Can you see much acting work out there? Naw. I cannae either."

Rab's upstairs in one of the empty classrooms with Caroline and Puff sharing a can of Top Deck Shandy. They're leaning out one of windows that looks out over the front entrance. Rab tries to flick the ring pull down onto Eich's head, standing outside with a fag.

"Eh Rab," he calls up.

"Y'all right there Eich?"

"Fuck off."

"That's nice isn't it?" says Rab to his fellow drinkers. They're laughing and looking for something else to lob out the window.

"He's just pissed off because he missed lunch," says Caroline.

She's dancing up and down the landing, an excitable pixie. Caroline had given up on her chances of becoming a trainee manager at Marks & Sparks for this. They wouldn't give her any days off. And she really doesn't care.

"Hey look — they're paying me for doing this."

"Then you go home afters," says Puff. "Not even a star on my bedroom door. Don't think they believe there's gonna be a proper Scottish film at all, and definitely not with me in it."

"My Dad still hasn't forgiven me for the last one. He walks past the Classic Grand, the place they show the dirty movies, the ones for perverts, and there's *my name* in lights. His son starring at the Grand. I'm top o'the bill. His mates have seen it up there on the board: Robert Buchanan. Now I'm taking time off from the Rep for another film and he's thinking, oh aye, right. Better take a change of pants son, y'know what I mean?"

Caroline's bent double, tears in her eyes.

"S'jus brilliant."

"Now you're a porn star Rab, what you gonna do with all that money?" asks Puff.

"Like loadsa pants now?"

"I know exactly what I'm goan to do, I'm goan straight down music shop and I'm buying a synth, a really good one —"

Paddy's found them for rehearsals. She's brought her son Christopher with her, carrying a fluffy penguin head under his arm. Puff shakes his hand and they exchange serious looks: "You're gonna be a star too wee man."[10]

Paddy's already moved on to her next job.

"Where's Clare?"

"Oh. She went down to London yesterday for her singing and stuff. She was coming back though," Caroline adds quietly, worried she might have put her foot in it.

Outside, Eich and Sanny are smoking on the school steps, not bothered by the rain now it's easing off.

"So you doin any actual cooking in this?" Eich's taking no notice, more interested in the big plume of smoke he's made. Pat's joined them, looking for a light[11].

"You're making those buns right?" Sanny keeps on going. "Y'naw, forget the film, I'd pay jus to see that."

"And I'd pay jus to see you clean some fuckin windaes pal."

"Naw naw Eich, thas no right. What you need to say is, clean some fuck-ing 'wind-owes' young man."

"Aye. Right. What does she want from me anyways?"

"Eh, what's that?" asks Pat.

"It's Davina. She says no-one's gonnae understand Eich's accent."

"Too 'brawd' she says. Wha'ever the fuck that means."

"Hold yerself. Here's company."
A girl with a bob haircut is trotting towards them, struggling with a bag that keeps on slipping off her shoulder. Biting her lip. The bottled essence of girlish femininity.

"Piece o'work, eh boys," mutters Eich.

"Y'all right there Clare."

"I must be late — am I late?"

"Naw — naw matter anyways. Calm yerself."

"I was comin in then I remembered I had to wash my hair. They've been complaining about my dirty hair!"

151

Eich and Sanny smoke their cigarettes and exchange a look.

Courtesy of Clare Grogan.

Clare Grogan's family lived in smart Bellahouston on the south side of Glasgow[12]. She was one of three sisters who all went to the Notre Dame Convent School (the last Scottish all-girls state school until 2019). When she met Bill Forsyth she was a pupil in the sixth-form, a member of the more Arts Council-friendly Scottish Youth Theatre, and in a New Wave band she'd set up with college friends, Altered Images[13]. Clare wasn't that impressed when some old guy called her over while she was working as a waitress and started talking about being in his films. It was Halloween and Clare had dressed up as a Latin ballroom-dancer in pink and black silks[14]. "I was 17 and in my head I was thinking, 'It's a guy in his pants with a camcorder, so I think I will just say no to that one'."[15] That wasn't Bill, he didn't have the nerve. The old guy was Mike Radford, his friend from the National Film School. They were catching up over dinner at the Spaghetti Factory — a cool kind of place known for its live gigs that was popular with undergrads — when Bill pointed out Clare and mentioned, casually enough, that she was the kind of girl he was looking for to play Susan. He sat there, cringing, making the occasional smile and nod of agreement while Mike did the talking and the young woman in front of them twisted around on one foot, pleased and embarrassed by the attention. She was still a young girl. Asked later to write a short piece about herself for the film's publicity[16], Clare explained that she most liked "reading *Mandy* comic", "sleeping, eating and being generally lazy"; going on to say how she wanted to be "Mr Cadbury's daughter", and had recently come up with a new name for herself: 'Tullulah Gosh'[17]. It was only months later, when Bill got the restaurant manager to vouch for him as a genuine film-maker, that Clare was finally signed up for the summer filming and promotional tour that followed — jobs she would have to juggle with band rehearsals and meetings with record companies.

Gordon sees Clare coming and pretends to be going her way.

"Oh hi."

"Hi."

"You managed to avoid hitting anyone today then? Good girl eh. No teeth falling out, no stitches 'cross your

Courtesy of Clare Grogan[18]

forehead. Always the sign of a classy lady."

"Okay Gordy, that's enough o' the funny. Nice flares by the way."

"Oh right, thanks."

"Did you not get the memo about straights then?"

A good pal but — nah — not boyfriend material, thinks Clare, clutching her bag to herself. Too much like a stork directing traffic[19].

*

Hollywood legend Billy Wilder once said a director had to be "a policeman, a midwife, a psychoanalyst, a sycophant and a bastard." It was just this kind of movie biz quotation that made Forsyth anxious about what was expected from him. He hated being The Director. His hero Nabokov (again in *Mary*) described the director character as "standing on a platform between floodlights and yelling himself to insanity through a megaphone."[20] It was an impossibly "time-consuming" role, complained Forsyth, endlessly messy and demanding, and what did he know anyway? With this in mind he purposely tried to write a script that limited the director's input. "I couldn't deal with more than three people in a scene at any one time…I was just recording their acting. I didn't have any cinematic ambition."[21] Bill would stay behind the camera as much as possible, always self-conscious, just checking to make sure the right shots were in the can. There was always more pressure on the acting when supplies of film were limited, with less scope for one re-take after another, and Bill had become used to counting every second as the physical material rolled along and was used up. The production team would take on the job of organising operations, who was doing what and when, keeping the crew and other actors quiet during filming, and even doing the calls of 'action' and 'cut'. "When I'm standing around on a shoot looking pre-occupied, I'm actually just whistling to myself, hoping people will think I'm looking pre-occupied."[22]

That Sinking Feeling had led him to discover a basic truth of movie-making, that the director didn't need to teach actors how to act. Which was a relief. But he still felt like he should be doing something more with them. "I don't know what to do with actors," admitted Bill during the *Local Hero* filming. "I tend to talk too little or too much."[23] There wasn't any choice though. He'd needed to become an auteur out of necessity, to save what he'd written from the mainstream cinema machine. "I think something better happens, in the sense that there is one custodian of the original idea. When you're directing a film that you've written, all you're doing is trying to maintain the integrity of the original idea, and so you become a kind of defender of the idea against everything that happens."[24] Forsyth was an auteur "by default" he said, as the only way to keep himself separate and unexamined. "If you write and direct, people tend to leave you alone. Producers think you've got all the answers so you're an auteur whether you want to be or not."[25]

A lack of knowledge (and interest) in the laws of moviemaking and a detachment from its process led to an unusually liberated approach. The best kind of amateurism. He'd learnt from observing and talking to other directors that it was a myth that a movie director had to be loud and brash, stomping around their little empire ("a lot of film-makers are fairly retarded people.") Because of the time he'd spent with the GYT there was a familiar atmosphere. "He was the kind of director who allowed you to bring your own ideas onto the set," said Caroline. "He'd say 'I'd quite like to see this happen — how do you think you'd do it?' He was brilliant that way."[26] Actors who'd spent less time with Bill could find him more of an enigma. "I knew Bill as a quiet man," said Dee. "He wasn't assertive like other directors I've known; I'd have to try and get from him what he wanted. A

nice man. Unusual. I was intrigued by him as much anything. That very dry sense of humour."[27]

"There were lots of laughs off camera and on
camera," recalled Rab[28]. "Loads of stuff going on. We were
quite often standing behind the camera trying to corpse
people." Bill was "dead easy" to work with, "one of us"[29].
"You knew you were getting it right because you'd see Bill's
shoulders shaking with laughter behind the camera," said
Gordon. "I had to ask him to move out of my eyeline, because it would get quite distracting."[30].

An indie producer friend of Bill's was called up to appear as the TV cook, the one who's way too heavy-handed
with the sugar, after the BBC refused permission for a clip
from *Delia Smith's Cookery Course*[31] (Delia's use of sugar being
beyond reproach). The unit runner David Brown got to have
a cameo as the referee of the football match at the start of
the film, and went on to have the job of location manager on
Local Hero and production manager for *Comfort & Joy*[32]. The
cat impressions were by Mr B Forsyth. Young members of
the Coulter family were given jobs: Louise Coulter as the
film's accountant; Eric Coulter as a runner[33]. Forsyth would
try to recreate the same family feel in his future productions.
For the bigger budget *Local Hero*, for example, he brought in
his own Scottish team to work alongside the more experienced professionals demanded by the film's financiers.

"Film-making is a mature activity," observed Forsyth
in 1981[34]. It had taken time — 15 years — to learn the
mechanics and art of film and then go on to understand and
make the best of actors. Forsyth was bookish enough to
know the importance of authentic voices over 'lines'. He had

listened to the kids, their stories and jokes and manner. How they dealt with the business of love. "The scripts were formed by Bill sitting in rehearsals as a kind of dramaturg," remembers Adrienne, "editing the young people's ideas as he went along. He's a good and unsentimental observer of human traits (and I believe he'd learned a great deal about humour from Charlie Gormley)."[35] Bill always kept his notebook with him, said Gordon: "watching us, writing things down we said. Then later things would turn up in the script and we'd think, 'Ah, that's one of our stories.'"[36] And he wrote the dialogue with particular actors in mind. "I think Bill knew what a show-off I was," said Sanny. "Trying to be one of the older ones and not quite making it. All mouth about the girls. Even if I didn't know anything I'd have to tell you how it was done."[37] The relationships Bill had made and the non-corporate environment for film-making meant the kids were able to be themselves: the camera could record the truth of young relationships and emotions.

Even with limited budget and time he was always happy to give actors the opportunity to get to know each other. In order to find the right girl to play Gregory's little sister Madeline, he and Gordon went down to the Cottage Theatre in Cumbernauld and sat in on an exercise where the girls were asked to give advice to the boys about girlfriends. The 12 year-old Allison Forster was picked out as one of the best (and eventually got the part because she looked more like she might be related to Gordon), and they spent time together chatting before the filming started, to recreate the kind of natural connection that already existed inside the GYT[38]. Gordon and Clare met up at the huge country park in Pollok. "He was lovely and funny from the word go. We both loved acting — and we also knew we had to make it work," said Clare, adding that they got to know each other much better on the promotional tour to the US[39]. It was in Pollok park that Bill picked up on an idea that turned into one of the film's most famous scenes. The two of them were lying down on a couple of park benches, chatting, mucking about, when they started doing some daft horizontal dancing.

There were "lots of little interpersonal things going on," said Bill. When the school magazine reporter pops into the changing room to interview and flirt with Dorothy, Gordon wasn't happy. "When we were filming, Gordon was actually getting on with Dee. And during that scene, Gordon became jealous because between takes, the other guy was chatting her up. And he had a car he could really drive. So the whole thing became real. He was really mad, you know!"[40] The result was a uniquely accomplished naturalism. The faint flush and awkwardness to Gregory's face when he asks out Dorothy for a date is something other than acting. The same applies to when Gregory is kissing Susan goodnight at the end of the film. "At that age, snogging and being filmed. That was awkward."[41] The shyness is real (a glass of wine, in the end, was a necessary supplement, as both claimed not to feel any attraction to the other).

There was a felicity to the chemistry between people. And this is another reason for the singularity of *Gregory's Girl*: how natural talent and a lack of 'professionalism', even some gaps and limitations, combined together. Most importantly the chemistry allowed the film to not just be about formal acting skills: "they kind of set the template for the acting in my kind of film-making, because I kind of worked out that actors in my films, they don't have to act, they have to just behave, you know? And, if they act it kind of shows. These kids taught me the difference between what acting and behaving is on the screen."[42] "If I have any theory about film," said Forsyth, "then to me film is about *being,* not performing."[43] From his perspective, young people were already used to 'acting' anyway. That's what teenagers did. They tried on different masks, pretended to be one kind of person or another. Forsyth wanted the awkwardness, it became his default mode: "I used to equate the awkwardness with reality."[44] And anyway, a focus on performance would have meant artificially creating an effect, pushing through a plot, working on the manipulation of an audience.

Being was something else — and it's no coincidence he gave his most thoughtful, ambitious film the title *Being Human.* The novelist Milan Kundera explained the larger importance of 'being' like this: "Living, there is no happiness in that. Living: carrying one's painful self through the world. But being, being is happiness. Being: becoming a fountain, a fountain on which the universe falls like warm rain."[45] So there was a method there. A conscious effort to offer a new realism, a Scottish realism, an alternative to a carefully constructed artifice that had been fussed over by artisans. "A reaction against what you could call the traditional English dramatically structured film, and also, especially, the English form of film acting...I'm doing that because of the relationship that Scotland has with England."[46] Instead the film follows a simple story told by people who are mostly being themselves, living through momentary, disconnected experiences; an unforced kind of story that could change as easily as the weather. Reality and acting come together in ways that may not always be as fluent or smooth as other, more micromanaged films, but it's a reason why *Gregory's Girl* continues to contain a fresh cinematic reality.

One of the remarkable qualities of the GYT, maybe something that was unparalleled in the world of film and theatre, was the lack of competition. No one was pushy. No one was trying to be cute. "People would say: 'Oh you'd be brilliant at that', 'You should definitely be the one to play that part'," said Caroline[47]. And that was different. The GYT was a space for people to be themselves in, people who maybe wouldn't normally have gone anywhere near a theatre, and not solely a means of being 'seen' and making a career.

None of this means *Gregory's Girl* was an improvised film, or that it was somehow written by the GYT. It comes with the sound of Bill's writing, and actors stuck to the script during filming. In 2019, he explained how the script was his "safety net". "Maybe having come to actors late, as it were, I was a bit of a dictator. And so we would talk and rehearse and I would let the kids blow off steam in that way. But when it came to [*That Sinking Feeling* and *Gregory's Girl*], I was pretty well insistent on the dialogue. For my own sake, I didn't know any better, I wasn't an improvisatory filmmaker, so I thought, 'Well, I better not start having them improvise or I'll end up who knows where.' So it was a nice rigid machine. I kind of regret that sometimes, but you know, it's the way that I ended up working."[48] The cast would try and throw in their own bits of improv, but they wouldn't make the cut. One outtake involved Alex Norton and Chic Murray walking along a school corridor. The headteacher is worried about staffing for 2A and 2B, what could they do? Alec offers some sensible advice, then mentions another teacher (this bit wasn't in the script), and says she's not feeling well either. Chic throws him an apple and says "Give her that. That'll do it" and struts off. Alec pulls silly faces behind his back.

Forsyth protested too much about his abilities as a director. He might have disliked the process, but the actors themselves appreciated his patient, good-natured, swan-like efforts — because the thrashing of doubts and insecurities, the struggle to cling to ideas and intentions, was certainly going on under the surface. Bill Paterson, the lead in *Comfort & Joy*, felt it was solely modesty on Forsyth's part. "He was a lovely director and never had any difficulty talking through what he had in mind. He was also good at doing the important thing of saying when he thought something wouldn't work. So no, never any tentativeness, in fact quite the reverse."[49]

*

"I especially remember the scene after our date in the park, where there's a shot of us walking off into the sunset," said Gordon. "Clare Grogan and I were both in tears. It was the last day of filming. It was all over. This magical bubble we'd been in was about to burst."[50] People had come together in unlikely ways to make *Gregory's Girl*, and become involved in a series of moments in time that few of them would ever forget — a swan song for the GYT, a realisation of improbable hopes that had resulted in a one-off alchemy. And whether he liked it or not, Bill Forsyth was at the heart of everything, with his ideas, his radical principles, his cussedness, his reticence and uncertainty.

When the final shots were being finished up, when Mick was urging them to get a move on before the last of the light was gone, what mattered most to the director? Was it the people, or was it the place and what he saw there? Was he looking at Gordon and Clare and the evanescent moment they were sharing together, or was it the quality of the sunset? The place and the landscape. The ochre tinge to the summer haze, a crepuscular oddness that had fallen over the grey new-build sprawl of Cumbernauld.

---

[1] Siobhan Synnot, 'Still Bella after all these years: Cast and creator share behind-the-scenes secrets as *Gregory's Girl* turns 40', *Sunday Post*, 26 April 2021.

[2] Dee Hepburn went on to appear in the TV series *Maggie*, presenting *It's a Knockout* and then playing Anne-Marie Wade in the soap *Crossroads* between 1985 and 1988 (followed eventually, after time spent with her children, by a swan song film role with Oliver Reed in *The Bruce* in 1996). She had a career in sales and business development, on the road selling patient-lifting equipment for an East Kilbride company.

---

3 Dee Hepburn, Telephone interview, 16 January 2023.

4 *Scotland on Screen*, BBC4, 2009.

5 *Gregory's Girl* 30th anniversary Q&A, 2010.

6 Jake D'Arcy was PE teacher Phil Menzies (Bill's first choice had been Bill Paterson). Cast as boyfriend to the young Dee Hepburn in *Prime of Miss Jean Brodie*, she'd been taken aback that she was expected to kiss such an 'old' actor (he was 32). Jake went on to feature in many of the most successful Scottish TV exports: *Rab C Nesbitt*, *Tutti Frutti*, *Taggart*, *Hamish Macbeth* and *Still Game*. He died in 2015 aged 69.

7 Alex Norton, 30 at the time, played teacher Alec. Bill saw Alex and Bill Paterson in a 7:84 Theatre production of *The Cheviot, the Stag and the Black, Black Oil*, and wanted them both to be in his new film. Alex had already been in films and TV from the age of 16 and has been on screens ever since, with a key role in *Taggart* between 2002 and 2010, parts in *Patriot Games* (1992), *Braveheart (1995)*, and most recently, *Waterloo Road* and *Two Doors Down* (as well as being in *Local Hero* playing embattled ice-cream seller Trevor in *Comfort & Joy*).

8 Dave Anderson, 34 during filming, played Gregory's Dad, Mike. He'd already been seen in *Doctor Who* and *The Avengers*. He was a villager in *Local Hero* (and appeared in both of Charlie Gormley's films) and went on to long-standing parts in *Taggart* and *City Lights*.

9 Charles 'Chic' Murray (1919-1985) was a comedy legend known for his stand-up routines as well as TV appearances on the *Sykes* and *Dick Emery* shows in the 1970s. A hero to, and friend of, Billy Connolly, he was famous for his one-liners such as: "It's a small world, but I wouldn't want to have to paint it" and "after I told my wife that black underwear turned me on, she didn't wash my Y-fronts for a month". The 61 year-old played the headteacher with great skill and comic timing.

[10] Chris Higson went on to a career in films as a carpenter and construction manager (working on everything from *The Crow Road* (1996) TV series to Peter Mullan's *The Magdalene Sisters* (2002) and Ken Loach's *Jimmy's Hall* (2014)). Chris is now said to be working as part of Peter Jackson's film operations in New Zealand, often in the workshops helping to build full-size replicas of World War I aircraft, not for films but Jackson's own collection.

[11] Patrick Lewsley was Billy's boss, Mr Hall. He'd had minor parts on TV before (*The View from Daniel Pike*, *Scotch on the Rocks*), but at the time he was working at Cumbernauld council in the housing department. More work came his way afterwards as Mr Henderson in *Maggie* (1981), a removal man in *Comfort & Joy*, and, of course, in *Taggart*.

[12] Claire Grogan took the part of Susan (credited as C. P. Grogan and then 'Clare' Grogan because there was a Claire Grogan with an Equity card already). After her pop career with Altered Images (who split in 1983), and playing the Mr Bunny ice-cream girl with the mysterious smile in *Comfort & Joy*, she went on to become the object of schoolboy desire for a new generation by appearing as Kristine Kochanski in *Red Dwarf*. She also tormented Ian Beale in *EastEnders* in the late 90s. Altered Images re-formed to release a new album and tour in 2022/3.

[13] Inspired by Pete Shelley of Buzzcocks and how he used to play about with their single covers.

[14] Clare still has the dress: "I always like to go for the sparkle option."

[15] Patricia Kane, Clare Grogan interview, *The Mail on Sunday*, 14 June 2020.

[16] *Gregory's Girl* production notes, Moving Image Archive, National Library of Scotland.

[17] Clare didn't adopt the name after all — but the idea was picked up by an indie band in 1986 who called themselves Talulah Gosh.

[18] One of the few remaining copies of the film's script. Clare only came across hers in a box under her parent's bed when her mum died. "Usually with a script there'd be notes to myself — in this one there's just doodles."

[19] Clare and Gordon stayed close friends. They were the partnership who took on much of the promotional interview work for the *Gregory's Girl* launch, including the tour of the US (where they spurned the chance to attend the Golden Globe ceremony because they didn't think they should have to work on their day off). They appeared together in the video for Altered Images' 'Bring Me Closer' single in 1983. John Gordon is the smooth James Bond character in another white jacket, wearing almost as much make-up as Clare. There's more kissing.

[20] Vladimir Nabokov, *Mary*, Penguin, 2007 edition, p25.

[21] Tim Teeman, 'Bill Forsyth: the reluctant father of Gregory's Girl', *The Times*, 6 February 2008.

[22] Jonathan Hacker and David Price, *Take Ten: Contemporary British Film Directors*, Clarendon Press, 1991, p107.

[23] *The Making of* Local Hero, documentary film, 1983.

[24] Lawrence Van Gelder, 'Thoughts While Held Captive By an "Escapist" Movie', *New York Times*, 23 May 1982.

[25] Radio interview with Bill Forsyth, The Leonard Leopate Show, 2010.

[26] The Ross Owen Show, interview with Caroline Guthrie, 2016.

[27] Dee Hepburn, Telephone interview, 16 January 2023.

[28] Rab has recommended watching *That Sinking Feeling* with the sound turned up full so you can hear cast and crew laughing in the background. Standards had been tightened up for *Gregory's Girl*.

[29] Rab Buchanan interview with Darren Collins, Robert Burns Theatre, 1 November 2010.

[30] Tim Robey interview with John Gordon Sinclair, *Daily Telegraph*, 4 April 2021.

[31] Penny Thomson went on to become Director of the Edinburgh Film Festival in the 90s.

[32] David Brown was assistant director of *The Killing Fields*, production manager on *Star Wars: the Phantom Menace*, and more recently the producer of the *Outlander* series filmed in Scotland (close to Forsyth's home).

[33] Eric went on to a career as a TV producer and Head of Drama at STV: responsible for the re-boot of *Taggart* and working as producer on the *Bodyguard* (2018) mini-series, *Our Girl* and *Shetland*.

[34] Bill Forsyth, *Sight and Sound*, ibid.

[35] Adrienne Atkinson, ibid.

[36] Brian Beacom, *Gregory's Girl*, *The Herald* Magazine, 17 April 2021.

[37] Douglas Sannachan, ibid.

[38] Allison Forster emigrated with her family to Toronto in January 1981, missing out on the limelight. She only realised the film had been a success when it appeared on Canadian TV. Allison did no more acting, lost any trace of her Scottish accent, and worked for many years as a waitress.

[39] Clare Grogan, Telephone interview, 27 February 2023.

[40] Christopher Connelly, The Man Behind 'Gregory's Girl', *Rolling Stone*, 30 September 1982.

[41] Clare Grogan, ibid.

[42] Jonathan Murray, 'Cornflakes versus Conflict: An Interview with Bill Forsyth', ibid.

[43] *When Bill Paterson met Bill Forsyth*, BBC Scotland, 2011.

[44] *Gregory's Girl* DVD, audio commentary — Bill Forsyth and Mark Kermode, 2019.

[45] Milan Kundera, *Immortality*, Faber & Faber, 1991, p288.

[46] Scott Malcomson, 'Modernism Comes to the Cabbage Patch: Bill Forsyth and the Scottish Cinema', *University of California Press Film Quarterly*, Vol.38 (3), 1985.

[47] Caroline Guthrie, ibid.

[48] Abbey Bender, ibid.

[49] Jonathan Melville, 'Interview: Bill Paterson on When Bill Paterson Met Bill Forsyth', *ReelScotland*, 1 March 2011.

[50] Jack Watkins, 'How we made *Gregory's Girl*', *The Guardian*, 3 November 2015.

7. Cumbernauld

"It's modern Andy, it's good — modern girls — modern boys — it's tremendous — look."

On a Thursday afternoon in June, I took the bus from Glasgow to Cumbernauld: a dual carriageway into the countryside, a succession of slip roads, roundabouts and ring roads.

Wherever we stopped there were groups of school kids on their way home. All of them teenagers, 14 or 15, but they might have been from different species. Boys, either alone or with one friend; lank hair and spots; their heads tilted down as they spoke with a soft Glaswegian burr about football and computer games. Girls bunched together in chatty gangs, their eyes straight and level; every one of them in a short skirt or hot pants with black tights. "I knaw. She's not gonnae put up with him," said one.

I'd imagined making a proper arrival in Cumbernauld, seeing the signpost and then a vista over housing estates or at least the top of the town centre. But the bus

168

hurried in via a back door, making it impossible to tell whether we were really there or not. We followed a road through Condarrat and its neat village bungalows and local stores; then more junctions and what might have been Cumbernauld, some houses hidden behind high grassy banks and trees. Was I meant be getting off? The teenagers with school bags were, not bothering with any coats or jumpers even though it had been raining most of the afternoon. I was more than ready for the reliably bland comforts of a Premier

Inn, to set up camp on a king-sized bed with my notebook, street maps, and a tea bought from the supermarket. The sleeper train had delivered me up at Glasgow Central at 7am after a night of rattle and roll (and a mysterious sloshing). There'd been some exploration of the city's peaceable early morning streets and the grey riverside in a drizzle. Then a day spent with my head in the archive at Kelvin Hall.

Forty two years to the day since the first scheduled filming for *Gregory's Girl* had taken place and I was finally going to be in those Cumbernauld places that I'd longed for, that strange, entirely irrational longing. But now I was starting to wonder why. Maybe I was going to discover a certain quality of magic in the air, something that might explain why Bill Forsyth wanted to film there. Get some movie tourism thrills at least. Or was I just doing it to be workmanlike and pick up on some first-hand atmosphere to add to the book? I'd been loaded up with expectations, and then realised, as the bus made its way onto another ring road, that I'd left those expectations, or at least the meaning of them, behind me. In a DVD box.

The sky was porcelain white, but summer had arrived in Cumbernauld. You could tell from the sight of two boys rolling down a grassy hill. They were home from school and out to play on a warmish afternoon. I couldn't hear them over the noise of the bus but you could tell they were laughing, rolling through the newly mown piles of grass, going on and on. They were looking over at each other and cracking up, enjoying themselves too much to notice they were getting ever closer and closer to the big roundabout and its speeding traffic. Falling and laughing.

I got off, uncertainly, at the Asda superstore.

*

Cumbernauld was the product of mother Glasgow's exhaustion. She had been an heroic eighteenth-century innovator, a Victorian super-power, a city that had grown with the reckless gusto of an imperial adventurer, with the riches to turn its fantasies into monuments of stone: the neo-classical fortress of the Royal Bank of Scotland in Exchange Square; the baronial turrets, tourelles and battlements of the City of Glasgow Bank; the Venetian splendour of the City Chambers; the Moorish fantasy of the Templeton carpet factory. Glasgow wasn't made so much from the cool financial returns of industry as a towering confidence in what the future would bring to those who were deserving. An architecture of moral conviction, of how a sense of mission and duty — whether it was rooted in any formal religious doctrine or not — had been rewarded. Each pointed arch, pillar, statued figure, wreath, fresco and ornament was a reflection of God's rich mystery. A mystery that had become more lucid and more manageable through the achievements of the great and good.

For a suitably fine style of living in the age of Empire there were fashionable villas, fortified by iron railings and gaslight, radiating out in streets far from the noise and foul air of the river and its factories. Sauchiehall Street stretched out with them, offering more of its grand 'warehouses', dressed and lit for the newly-respectable occupation of shopping, the forerunners of the soon-to-come department stores. It was an ultra-modern lifestyle that depended on a colossal human machinery to make any of it possible, meaning a grotesque contrast between the limelight of the city's theatre stage and an accretion of slum-living round the back. Such a weight of life lying thick and slab around the Clyde. Tenements and terraces that were leaky with everything, heat and cold, birth and death. A separate micro-culture with its own unsavoury little grocery stores, public houses and dram shops; its own environment and atmosphere: corridors of smoke and other unbreathable airs; dunghills, typhoid and cholera; and crime (at least for those with the health for it). By the 20th century, Glasgow had become buried and blackened, cramped both physically and in spirit by the pent realities of an old city made from a history of extremes.

Above the rooftops and chimneys, looking to the horizon and the not-so distant fields, there were draughts of clean, wind-blown Scottish air. The impetus for the actual building of new towns didn't come until after the Second World War and political consensus over the need to reform and somehow soften the impact of runaway capitalism. Along with welfare payments and the nationalisation of hospitals, utilities and railways — all intended to create a more equal society and better living conditions for low-income families — there came the New Towns Act. This cleared the way for publicly-funded Development Corporations to work outside the Town and Country Planning rules and get on with the urgent job of building more houses. Lord Reith, chair of the New Towns Committee said the new towns would be like "essays in civilisation", allowing more people to enjoy "a happy and gracious way of life". On the southern outskirts of Glasgow, East Kilbride was begun in 1947; Glenrothes across the water from Edinburgh in 1948; Cumbernauld in 1955, 13 miles north-east of Glasgow; followed by Livingston (west of Edinburgh) in 1962, and Irvine on the Firth of Clyde in 1966.

It was a moorland ridge, a hilltop looking out to a ring of green vales and meadows. There were stone remnants of the military defences the Romans had prepared against raiders from the wilderness in the north, and nearby, a windswept village close to the site of what had been a castle. A few small farms and their crops and grazing animals. Between them ran the burns and lowland peat bogs that gave the place its name, *Comer-nan-allt*, meaning 'the meeting of the waters'. With a budget of £70 million, a 900 acre site was sketched out, centred around a wide oval area that would sit along the hogs' back of Cumbernauld Hill — because the Chief Architect, Sir Hugh Wilson[1], had a romantic notion in mind: a fond recreation of the Italian hilltop town of San Gimignano in Tuscany. The new Cumbernauld would be a Renaissance citadel where the centre, a truly civic zone, would be at the heart of everything for its citizens: their workplace, where they would shop, where they'd go to find a hospital, a library, schools and other public buildings, a centre that would be alive with people and their comings and goings through the day and night. The rest of the development land, falling gently away from the hillside centre, would be dedicated to a tumble of closely-packed homes and landscaped pathways, a web of winding passages, little steps and squares that would offer a new vista around each corner. Any citizen of Cumbernauld would be able to walk into the thick of the town's centre and its piazzas within 20 minutes from wherever they lived — and not need to cross a single road. Like San Gimignano, Cumbernauld would also have its towers, small groups of mid-rise tower blocks (rather than church towers or a campanile).

All of this was radically contrary to the 'Mark I' designs for new towns, still inspired by the ideal of an English village, and their grid-like arrays of small community cells with their own village green and low-rise centres. Instead, this was urban medieval. There was going to be a population of 50,000 people (with 40,000 of those coming from Glasgow's waiting list for housing)[2], living in homes that were uniform and classless rather than separated into districts of affluence, and more densely concentrated than somewhere like East Kilbride. The traffic plan was another departure, this time taken from American cities where there had been a premonition of a future of personal motor cars rather than public transport. There would be a single spinal road running straight into (and under) the town centre linked to vaults for underground parking and as few intersections as possible; a complete separation of motorised vehicles and pedestrians, who had their own system of footpaths, underpasses and overpasses, for the sake of safety and a principle of free flowing movement, like a well-engineered machine[3].

It was a toss up between Geoff Copcutt[4] and Derek Lyddon[5] over who'd get to design Cumbernauld's crowning glory, the hilltop centre, and who'd work on the housing estates. Housing was easy — it was always the aim to make homes as indistinguishable as possible anyway, encouraging residents to look to the communal heart of the place for their everyday business and identity. Copcutt was the man expected to do something different. In 1957 he'd been picked out by the bible of contemporary architecture *Zodiac* as "one of Britain's promising young architects". A member of the *avant garde*, a visionary eccentric: "wild in every way: wild beard, wild hair… suits like carpets"[6]. Part of his method included drawing on 10 yard-long rolls of paper with a bamboo stick brush and Indian ink, with the instinctive manner and 'beginner's mind' of a Zen Buddhist monk. When a group of visiting Russian dignitaries came to see the model of the new town centre he'd designed, Copcutt had placed plastic toy rockets (taken from cornflakes packets) around its perimeter. "I'm almost sure that immediately Cumbernauld became some red dot on a target chart in Moscow," said another member of the town's planning department, Brian Miller[7]. "[Copcutt] was basically a loose cannon. There were always shouts from Hugh Wilson going 'oh god have you not done this….' He had very strange ideas."[8]

After three years of design work, Copcutt's vision was ready for the builders. Even then they "had to do a caesarian" to get the final drawings out of him[9] — and there it was, the world's first indoor town centre, an icon of brutalist architecture and one of the most controversial structures in Britain: an attenuated, multi-layered viaduct made from rough grey concrete; decks of functionality connected by ramps and walkways into different-sized open and closed spaces: a bus station, shopping mall, town hall, offices, a hotel, even an outstretched prong of penthouse apartments on concrete stilts; bulging pods topped with sleek fins and antennae, corridors of tiling streaked with exposed wires and pipework. Explaining his thinking in the *Architectural Design* journal, Copcutt described the megastructure he'd created as "a drive-in centre", "a giant vending machine through which the motorised user drives to return revictualled"[10].

For the world's architectural establishment, Copcutt's Cumbernauld design was a daring success and proof of the power of its professionals to change human behaviour and experience. Futurism had been delivered at last: "the dreams of the 1920s and 1930s are being built on a hill near Glasgow," said the American Institute of Architects in 1967, bestowing the town with the R.S. Reynolds Memorial Award for Commercial Architecture. This was the "future of community architecture for the West". *The Washington Post*'s architecture critic Wolf von Eckardt proclaimed: "Leonardo da Vinci, nearly five hundred years ago, envisioned a city where all the vehicles move underground, leaving man to move freely in the sun. Leonardo might also have sketched Cumbernauld's town centre, a soaring citadel surrounded by meadow."[11] Princess Margaret was more casual in her praise, but expressed something of the hopeful mood of the times on her visit in 1967 when she described the Centre as "fabulous".

The problem for Cumbernauld's Development Corporation (the CDC) was how they were going to sell the dream to businesses and families — not just tourists and dignitaries visiting to see some space-age design porn, or those simply desperate to get out of Glasgow. There was a national marketing campaign that depicted a place offering new kinds of work (hi-tech); new kinds of fun (golf! windsurfing! snooker!), for a whole "New Generation" of modern people, the cool young consumers. "What's it called?" asked the ads, and before long Scotland knew very well that it was "Cumbernauld". The CDC, of course, also commissioned a documentary film: *Cumbernauld, Town for Tomorrow* (1970)[12] narrated by Magnus Magnusson. To 21st century eyes the film is a delightful anachronism, redolent of that peculiarly Seventies meld of the melancholy and the cod-modern. There are speeding cars on empty roads, looping around perfect channels and curves of concrete. Wistful strings are heard playing over shots of green meadows. It was the safest town in Britain, claimed Magnusson, with an accident rate one-fifth of the national average because of its "perfectly logical solution to the conflict of cars and people", the "engineering for pedestrians; conveyor-belt walking". The houses are small and sturdy and cottage-like, as if they've "grown up from the ground". Every 400 homes has its own cornershop. The film worked hard to stress how the concrete spaces were filling with an influx of young people, "young pioneers breaking out of city life for the first time". A third of the population was under 15. People were "giving it personality" it said, lingering over girls in crop-top jumpers, mini-skirts and pointy bras doing the Twist and the Mashed Potato. Magnus admitted there might be a shortage of commercial forms of entertainment for the moment, but Cumbernauld folk knew how to make their own fun: like the teenage hops organised by the local church (known, brilliantly, as 'Kirk-a-Go-Go'). All in all, said the film, the new town was a controversial one-off, yes it was "a challenging social experiment", but

whatever people thought of Cumbernauld, it was at least
"impossible to feel indifferent".

And they came: there was a population of 43,000 by
1975. US-owned businesses overall were the biggest source
of jobs. There was the Burroughs Corporation (what would
become part of Unisys in 1986) manufacturing computer
equipment for banks; an outpost of the Atlanta-based Lov-
able Bra Company; and Avery, making self-adhesive labelling
machines. The single largest employer though, would be
British, the administrative offices of the Inland Revenue.
178

After Glasgow, moving to Cumbernauld was like arriving among the Hobbits of the Shire. Mostly low-lying groups of new houses dotted over a gentle, green and undulating landscape, little sweeps and corners of raised cobbles and sculpture. In 2012, Owen Hatherley in his book on Britain's urban landscape, *A New Kind of Bleak*, called Cumbernauld's landscaper G.P. Youngman[13] the "Gaudi of pavements". "A winding pedestrian path weaves through what you abruptly realise is not a park at all, but what Cumbernauld has instead of streets — hillocks on each side, a wooden walkway, thickets of trees. You could be in a nature reserve…but you definitely couldn't be on a street."[14] Half of Cumbernauld was green space. And the shopping could be done indoors, out of the rain.

But Cumbernauld wasn't a dusty blue Tuscan hilltop; it wasn't a place that would be lapped by the cooling passage of a summer zephyr; its population couldn't look forward to being warmed by Sirocco winds from the Sahara throughout the winter. Having to keep walking up the hill into Cumbernauld's Centre, the point most likely to be lashed with winds (those rain-bearing winds), was unappealing, and even treacherous for people with both prams and shopping bags. The Centre was ugly. Residents saw that from the beginning, long before its decline had begun. Renaissance brutalism was never going to be a 'thing'. Instead, a feature that had been embraced by the architectural *cognoscenti* like the luxury penthouse protrusion, became known locally as the "alien's head", and no-one ever chose to live in the apartments, they had to be converted into offices. In the end, Cumbernaulders didn't want to go into the Centre at all. There wasn't much marketplace bustle, sometimes just an eerie stillness: empty approach roads and pedestrian corridors and squares. Concrete corridors oozing damp. Soggy old newspapers. Drifts of plastic bags and empty drinks cans rattling into corners. A hinterland. No bars or restaurants or arts facilities open at night — but anyone could make their way into the Centre any time, meaning broken fixtures and glass left for the mornings, big daubs of graffiti, the odd pile of sick, discarded clothing. Eventually glazed roofing and side panels had to be erected to protect visitors from the weather. Great expanses of concrete themselves were left exposed and the percolation of water run-off led to structural damage in many places. A large section of the shopping centre had to be demolished, as did the entire Golden Eagle Hotel, a business that had never been profitable and was left empty for many years until it was knocked down. When he visited in 2012, Owen Hatherley described the Centre as being "like a concrete shanty town, with a series of seemingly random cubic volumes 'plugged in' to the larger structure, all of them in a drastic state, their concrete frames with brick infill looking half-finished, which alarmingly may have been intentional."[15]

The modest residential areas of Cumbernauld weren't much compensation. There were no real 'streets' to wander anywhere. The underpasses that joined the town together had turned into traps for wind-blown litter, and could become threatening places at night, used as shelters from the rain by teenagers with nowhere else to go, as well as impromptu toilets. The promo film had boasted of how each estate had its own 'community room' that could be used for groups and their activities. They could have been, but they mostly weren't, not without constant, concerted effort from volunteers, and Cumbernauld's population slipped into a different mode of living instead: smart new homes, wall-to-wall carpeting and appliances, driving to work, watching TV, and driving into the city if they wanted entertainment. This was a modern life, but atomised, a wrench away from the Glasgow communities where people had lived, worked, shopped and drank in one locality, all within the radius of a few adjacent streets. In Cumbernauld, even the new social facilities like a cinema, ten pin bowling and an ice rink came and went because of a lack of trade. All those pathways for sallies into town were really only being used by children. Around the empty plazas and meandering pathways came the mournful refrain of the New Town Blues.

Cumbernauld is now synonymous with architectural disaster. In 2005 Channel 4's *Demolition* programme asked for nominations for places deserving obliteration — and Cumbernauld's town centre came top. It won *Urban Realm* magazine's 'Plook on a Plinth' award in 2001 and 2005 (plook being a Scots word for pimple or zit) and keeps on being nominated. In 2022, an attempt to have the original megastructure listed as a site of special architectural interest was overturned.

It had been the wrong site. The new town was meant for Renfrewshire, not Cumbernauld — but that didn't suit the nearby residents of Houston, the constituents of Viscount Muirshel, John Maclay, the Secretary of State for Scotland at the time. If it had to be Cumbernauld, critics have argued, then the centre of the site should have been

more protected from winds, placed somewhere on the lower-lying ground where the train station was built. Only phase one and the first part of phase two of Copcutt's plan was ever realised, and they were built with cheap materials and in ways he'd never intended, leaving his vision seriously mangled. He'd always seen the Centre as plastic and constantly evolving anyway, an "urban morphology" with plug-in modules to meet different needs and uses. Copcutt had been left deflated by what he saw: "This fragment — still big enough to define a future — was shorn not only of its second

182

row of pylons and penthouses, with a host of functional and spatial consequences, but also of the mosaic of sites I had tucked in for flea-markets, the winter-garden front to the tiers of offices, the tube roof illuminating the chapel, the glistening 'airplane wing' which was to have tilted open over the library, and even the wall of dwellings with upper promenade designed to curtain the parkland…countless minor delights clothing the concept were not so much 'simplified' as simply missed."[16] A business mistake was made in only allowing retailers to rent their premises, putting off the biggest High Street names. Most commentators blamed the town's state on neglect by local authorities after the CDC was disbanded. They didn't understand the idea of a civic centre, had lost sympathy with ideas of modern architecture, and saw it solely as a (struggling) shopping mall, leading to a dismal form of inattention: cheap, bodged attempts at upgrades and "a spiral of decline, public stigma and disrepair"[17]. To top it all, in April 2022 Cumbernauld's biggest employer, the tax office, was closed down.

New towns were never intended to become museum pieces, curiosities of Sixties' optimism, they were a seed of energy that needed to keep on being nurtured, encouraged to grow and change. Like Milton Keynes. What began as a joke of a town has kept on trying to re-invent itself, to offer more of what people want from their home town. Now it's a city with a population that has grown from 40,000 in the late 1960s to more than 260,000.

Cumbernauld has lived on for many residents as a place to draw the curtains and sleep in, to be half-embarrassed or forgetful about what lies outside. That doesn't

mean people don't love the place and its patchwork of design
and greenery. Recounting a history and calling on the verdict
of experts who have only been professionally engaged with
somewhere is one thing, but it doesn't lay a finger on the actual experience of those who have lived in a place, what they
have seen and felt and kept as memories. The subjectivity of
it all is a mess, temporary and unreliable. Wherever we arrive for the first time, whatever is new, can seem strange and
unfriendly; and, in time, just become over-familiar and unin-
spiring. Even the golden plains of Tuscany can become a
dreary sight. It's only a lot of dry soil, villas and the black
spears of cypress trees after all. Places become stamped over
with a palimpsest of memories and moods, turning them
into a bank of moments that have meant something. And so
places take on both character and sympathy, become a
source of a sparse, everyday poetry; a consolation; even another kind of reality. Like that spring evening when you'd
had to stay late at work. The boss has been 'concerned'
about how things are going. So you'd ended up missing the
bus and had to stand there alone in the cold, waiting for another hour with nothing to do but watch the sun go down,
tinting the concrete flyover and the walls of the multi-storey
car park with twilight shades of orange. Growing paler as the
minutes pass. In one of the flats opposite, a blue flicker of
TV in the window. The air is high and thin and the trees are
coming into leaf. Or, that winter night when you'd met
someone, unexpectedly, someone you were going to see
again. Walking back home the long way, watching the streetlights and the stillness of things. Where every piece of
crooked pavement, every rooftop, is part of the theatre of

the moment. It's in these moments and not the work of strategic planning committees, architects or developers that places are made.

*

From the beginning, Milton Keynes was Cumbernauld with extra money. It was in the orbit of London and Home Counties employers looking to expand to bigger, cheaper office space. It meant Milton Keynes Development Corporation was a true animal of the Eighties, comfortable in its sprawling lair on Saxon Gate, not much different in size than the entirety of Cumbernauld's shopping centre. MKDC was in a position to build an American city for a new era in British life. Roads were set out on a strict grid, along with a hardwired network of concrete avenues, boulevards and walkways, leaving clear rectangles of development opportunity. Even if the city was the subject of ridicule — the gimmick of the concrete cows was the main thing everyone remembered about Milton Keynes — it was modern, and stayed modern. It had Britain's first US-style multiplex cinema, The Point, a glass-panelled monument to affluent leisure that glowed at night on the city's skyline with a tacky but somehow still romantic allure; and a shopping mall that was opened by Margaret Thatcher in 1979, with 130 shops, six department stores. A true temple of consumerism in marble, glass and steel, flooded by natural light and blooming with tropical plants and trees. MK was a proper Eighties day out.

I came to know the MKDC well in the late Eighties, towards the end of its reign when big business was king and deals for commercial and residential development were falling into their lap in ways that left its executives "excited" and "delighted" on a weekly basis. Triples all round. I was a trainee reporter on the outer reaches of the radar of MKDC's PR department, someone to coax or bully, depending on the occasion. Even at a time when local newspapers still had some influence, MKDC knew that withdrawing co-operation would be a problem for a newspaper worried about competition from other local papers and missing out on stories. When MKDC called about another of their exciting announcements, you jumped.

The Herald & Post was housed in a mirrored-glass office block on Upper Fifth Street. We had a big advertising department, some clapped out word processors and a bunch of journos on fancy swivel chairs, smoking fags in-between phone calls. We were expected to be out on the streets of MK to find stories most of the time, out in what was sold to us during interviews as a 'company car', a crappy old-style Mini. Each district had its own look, personality and roster of 'types'. The traditional, subsumed village of Woughton-on-the-Green was olde English posh, the place you rarely went, and if you did it was to be told about a charity gymkhana. More often I would find myself in Netherfield, less than a mile away from Woughton, where I'd be hearing about personal tragedies and disasters, the missing relatives, the shock illnesses and young deaths, the prison sentences, that — shamefully — were just another week's copy. The MK police had a favourite joke about Netherfield. Did I know there was actually a zero crime rate in that neighbour-

hood? Because people were only nicking back what'd been taken from them in the first place.

These were the estates that made me think of *Gregory's Girl*. The look of little Sixties homes and the patterns of lawns and pathways that criss-crossed the communal spaces. Mundane lives, filled with ordinary feelings and ordinary moments of romance, played out in those scruffy cul-de-sacs and play parks. I didn't know it at the time, but there was a logical reason for the feelings of *de ja vu*. The softly rolling contours of the landscaping, the knots of trees and wedges of greenery, were designed by the same man, GP Youngman.

Why is it that places like these have such an affecting look to them? No matter how dreary the location; just a load of cheap housing imposed on a rural wasteland; the takeover of some greyish-green scrub of hinterland by bricks and tiles and asphalt. Those homes, whatever their shape and size or how tightly they have been packed together, immediately take on an aspect of pathos. Little homes carry this kind of weight from being symbols, like an open fire or a steaming pot, they convey a pang of the mix of happiness and unhappiness that people always know. And when a certain light is cast over the face of them and their windows, like a morning blue or an autumn twilight, they can easily become the source of a speechless romance. Even in Milton Keynes.

*

Gregory's Girl was made in the honeymoon years when Cumbernauld still constituted an exciting prospect of modernity. At the same time, Bill Forsyth was unfailingly kind in the way the town was filmed, making sure the scenery was mostly Youngman and the country park. No Copcutt in sight. But why choose a new town in the first place? Forsyth's response has usually been that Cumbernauld was a suitably "adolescent town"; "Even the trees in Cumbernauld are teenagers so everything fits."[18] It would be a departure from the standard depictions of Scottish life on film — either Highland crofts or hard-boiled urban decay — to something new, a fresh green piece of growth from the grizzled stump of Glasgow. Virgin fields. And it was a development he knew about from the beginning and felt some attachment to as a local venture:

> "one of the very first jobs that I had, way back in 1964 when I started, I remember going out with the cameraman and filming, when they were making that road just past Cumbernauld – the big diggers were out and all that – so I was in on the New Town thing, you know? It made me feel like it was mine to use, because we had spent most of the 1960s and 1970s doing our duty making these propaganda films…I wasn't like someone kind of dropping in from outer space and saying: 'Oh, how do we present this thing called a New Town?' I was on the same level as it, and I think it made it easy for me to use it in a subtler way: it's there and it gradually reveals itself…I wanted teenage trees, you know? Because it was kind of raw, it was a raw landscape."[19]

Forsyth also knew it was going to be an easier place to film in than Glasgow. He would have heard about the opportunity from Mick Coulter, Patrick Higson, Murray Gregor and Jon Schorstein, who'd all been part of the making of *Cumbernauld HIT* (1977), a daft crime comedy funded by the CDC for its promotional campaign. In the movie, evil Fenella Fielding attempts to hold the town to ransom for £100 million with her 'pineapple bombs' — what really turns out to be a side issue amid the rash of opportunities to randomly feature hi-tech employers and — hey, look, some attractive transport and shopping features[20].

Cumbernauld was interesting in other ways for Forsyth. The New Town phenomenon was nagging at him. What it was, what it meant for people. Whether it could be a 'good thing' or was just a folly. One suggestion has been that the new town, as a centrally-planned community, is used as a mirror to the way in which Gregory gets organised by the girls; another that Cumbernauld is a "modernist re-imagining of the boundaries between public and private space comparable with, and sympathetic to, what the movie attempts."[21] These are interesting and sparkly patterns of thought, but it doesn't feel like they have any firm relation to the world outside of a seminar room. What does appear to be important to Forsyth, though, is Cumbernauld's combination of modernity and marginality. Looking at the portrait painted of him by Steven Campbell, Forsyth immediately noticed the setting and what it suggested. He's on that green hill above Glasgow: "me peeking out from behind the tree — that feeling of being at the margins of a city, what Apollinaire called 'the Zone' — is a real preoccupation of mine, it's something quite personal, and I'm always going back to it in my own work. I don't remember ever talking to Steven about it, but he seemed to know about it anyway."[22]

Guillaume Apollinaire (1880-1918) was a modernist poet; a haunter of libraries, a flâneur and socialite. His poem 'Zone' (1913) is set on the streets of Paris and describes a long walk he took into the city in the early hours of the morning, returning afterwards to his home in the suburbs of

Auteuil. It was a route filled with the familiar sights of shops and people he knew, but also inherently and irremediably altered; charged with strangeness. Because the modern world had begun to move at a hurtling rate. Dynamic, fascinating, but also chaotic. It left Apollinaire feeling disturbed by the way the past had been dumped, people left disconnected; in a state of quiet anxiety at the sight of the hurry and charge of science and technology, industry and consumerism. The Zone is a place where you can never quite belong. A relentlessly modern, in-between kind of place. More nowhere than somewhere. A Cumbernauld kind of place.

*

When Bill wanted to buy a souvenir for the cast, he chose a silver referee's whistle hung on a dark-blue ribbon. Engraved on each of them was the wry, unsentimental inscription: "The worst summer since 1907". Weather reports from June and July 1980 tell the story of drizzle, fog, light rain, heavy rain, thunderstorms, and how there was one or more of them happening each and every day of filming. "It would be impossible to make films in Scotland without thermal underwear," concluded Forsyth[23]. They only had seven weeks (compared with the standard average of 14 weeks) so they could keep a lid on costs; which meant every delay and run for cover was another painful knock on the bruise of lost time. The frustrations kept on coming. Like when it came to filming against the background of red ash football pitches rather than grass. Red ash (or 'blaes') made from burnt colliery waste, was used for Scotland's playing fields as a cheap, hard-wearing surface[24] — character-building for anyone brave enough to try a slide tackle or diving header. "It was totally awful," said Forsyth. "It changed colour in the rain. It would rain for two hours and then the sun would come out and it would dry up and go from deep orange to pink in about half an hour. The cameraman was going crazy."[25] The crew had to resort to using arc lamps when urgent pitch-drying was needed, and at one point a make-up girl had to step in and stop the match underway. "It was so cold that my knees had turned blue," explained Dee[26]. While the rain would sometimes stop, the winds kept on blowing in from the surrounding hills and valleys, buffeting cast and crew on Cumbernauld's bridges, whistling through the tunnels, causing problems for the sound recording — as well as the condition of those big feathered hairdos.

Given the length of Scottish summer days, the crew would wait around until conditions were right for each scene. Adrienne's memory, like that of many others in the cast and crew, was of sweet summer days. Because later in the evenings the weather would often clear, leading to golden splashes of illumination to what was already an excited holiday mood. "The day-to-day filming was great, as I remember," she said. "We were given a proper wage rather than working just for the love of it, and Clive Parsons and Davina Belling were very gentle producers, keeping everything on an even keel while allowing us the freedom to do our own thing."

Clare would be picked up by David Brown and driven into Cumbernauld. Other cast members would be picked up in Glasgow around 7.30am in a minibus. Rab remembers one morning getting on the minibus and seeing Vanda, a friend from drama college days. He introduced her to the guys, Puff and Sanny. Yeah they'd been up late the night before, Rab explained to her, they'd been in the bushes watching a nurse strip naked. Well, they'd only been pretending to, they had to imagine the girl was there in the window. What was she doing today? Vanda, of course, was going to be playing the nurse.

The destination for the minibus might be Abronhill High or checking in at the film's HQ at 21 Pine Grove, a three-storied terraced house tucked away off Pine Road. Some of the new actors would wonder what kind of film they'd got themselves into when they turned up there. The mess inside, one room used for make-up, another for the wardrobe department, a few scruffy characters hanging around. There would be a bunch of kids there every day, ranging from 14 to 19 years old, from the GYT or other youth theatres who just wanted to make some money over the summer. They'd be hanging about in the school until they were needed, chatting; getting fed with baked potatoes, coleslaw and chips in Cumbernauld House; or just causing trouble behind the camera when their mates were trying to do a scene.

There were few actual rules imposed by the production team, but one was that no-one should flush the school toilets during filming because of the noise and the disruption to the sound recording equipment. Unaware of the rule, Caroline came upon the rows of rank and musky unflushed toilets, and was horrified. "Disgusting!" she announced to the world via the microphone she was still wearing, filling the headphones of the production team with the crash and roar of one flush after another.

Many of the GYT were thinking more about a big summer theatre tour still ahead of them, and it was *Gregory's Girl* that had to be squeezed in around these plans and learning other lines. "Fun but frantic," said Alan. "From what I remember of the filming days, they were a completely relaxed affair. You were never treated like a prop with a pulse around Bill. Like all interactions with him, and even though

in hindsight he was probably under some real stresses, he was only ever the twinkle-eyed guy. Our whole lives in those days were all about the pursuit of laughter and the need to

entertain. We knew nothing else and we cared for nothing else. The soundtrack of the time was [sunny Sixties classic] 'Happy Together' by The Turtles[27], and nothing could've been more apt." Sanny, though, was one of those disappointed at how different the experience of the new film was to the communal, mucking-in of *That Sinking Feeling*. "I was only in for a couple of days, so I felt like I missed out on things. But it was exciting, much more structured, with lots of PAs and make-up people and proper filming going on."[28]

When things got quiet, some of the cast would hang out at Cumbernauld's Village Theatre (where they might find John Baraldi). The older-looking ones would head for the Abronhill pub, and do the best they could to explain to the landlady why they were wearing school uniform. Sometimes there'd be an afternoon out. Bill, Eich and Puff once went for drinks and a screening of Woody Allen's *Everything You Wanted to Know about Sex (But were Afraid to Ask)* (1972) at the Village Theatre. "It was rare for Bill to consume any alcohol in daylight hours — something we could probably put down to the 'Eich' effect," said Puff. "Bill obviously knew the film inside out and prided himself on voicing the dialogue before the characters on screen had chance to do so. We were asked to vacate the theatre."[29]

There was trouble when Clare first turned up to meet the production team. Nothing to do with Altered Images. "I kept the two things separate, and few people on the film knew about the band. It's a Glasgow thing and a Scottish thing, nobody likes a show-off."[30] The problem was a scar across the left side of her face that wasn't in keeping with the schoolgirl look they needed. There'd been a fight in the union bar at the Tech college. One minute music and dancing, the next a scrimmage, punches, glasses and bottles being smashed and thrown. As she tried to run away a falling shard of glass had torn at her face. "It was a terrible incident, and I was kind of traumatised by it."[31] Twenty years' later, doctors had needed to re-open the wound and remove a largeish piece of glass that had been missed at the time and was still lodged in her flesh. There were some difficult conversations: Clive and Davina wanted Clare's part re-cast. But Bill wasn't having it, and wherever possible only the right side of Clare's face was filmed; when there were close-ups, the scar was filled with morticians' wax. "Bill protected me."

The young actors could sometimes struggle with the stop-start nature of filming. Gregory's sister, Allison, wasn't happy about being pulled out of a cinema mid-way through a showing — it was the only time they could film in the Cumbernauld shops — when she'd wanted an afternoon off with her friends. The make-up artist's legs had to be used as a stand in for Caroline (walking down the stairs to the clock in the Plaza) when she was stuck at work in her new job as a computer operator. The white nights of a Scottish summer meant the opening scene of the peeping boys couldn't be filmed until around midnight. Filming the football match took most of one day and was gruelling for the players. Contrivance is quick but naturalism takes time. "By the afternoon we had to stop," said Dee. "One of the boys had to be carried off with cramp — and it was at this point that Bill realised that if the boys were suffering, the players who were used to playing matches all the time, what was it doing to someone like me? I had to be taken for some emergency treatment with a doctor that evening because my muscles had seized up, I wasn't used to it. That kind of thing was just funny at the time though, something else to laugh about."[32]

Filming in the streets also meant there were unavoidable encounters with locals. When Gregory and his sister were trying to look at shirts in a shop window they were joined by a drunk Cumbernaulder who wanted to be part of things, pushing his false teeth in and out of his mouth with his tongue to make them laugh. A passerby was angry at the sight of Caroline/Carol coming out of the phone box in a mini-skirt and make-up, and confronted her in spite of the presence of the camera and crew, telling her she "looked like a prostitute"[33].

Actors were expected to supply their own clothes: Dorothy's white shorts and Susan's beret were borrowed from the wardrobes of their respective sisters. As the designer in charge of props, Adrienne remembers having to beg and borrow all kinds of stuff from the cast, Gordon Sinclair in particular. When the team needed more kids — pre-school-sized, the three and four year-olds to annoy Gregory with — they went round recruiting them from the streets of the Westfield estate, negotiating with payment of a 10p mixture of sweets. To keep one of them attached securely enough to a fledgling estate tree they had to resort to sticky tape.

Davina and Clive would wear headphones to listen in on every scene, picking up on any occasions when the Scots accents seemed hard to understand. "I could never say 'windows'," admitted Sanny. "It was always 'windaes'"[34]. A bigger problem turned out to be Allison's voice in general.

How did you tell a 12 year-old they weren't quite right for the film after all? In the final version, Madeline's lines were dubbed by Carol Macartney (who played Margo, Gregory's second date after Carol)[35].

Other little problems just worked out fortuitously — like the handmade sign that Andy and Charlie used to hitch-hike to Caracas with at the very end of the film. Adrienne, reasonably enough, had misspelt it as 'Caracus', and rather than making a new sign, there was the chance to include those deliciously ironic lines from Rab. A misspelling on his sign? *That* was why no-one had stopped to drive them to South America and the Promised Land of eight women to every man: "Could you not have told me that four hours' ago?"

Bill was living in Pine Grove during the filming, a walkable distance from many of the locations chosen for filming; the school itself but also the Abronhill shops, foot-paths and the country park. The house was the nerve centre for the production team dealing with logistics, finance and other admin, keeping the Cumbernauld Development Corporation on-side and negotiating permissions with its Chief Executive, Brigadier Colin Cowan[36] for use of the Abronhill house, access to Gregory's home, 29 Netherwood Place in Westfield, and to the town centre shops and Plaza. An officer during the Second World War, the Brigadier had been a defence adviser to the United Nations before taking on the challenge of establishing a new town in 1970. He wasn't a token figurehead for CDC, but an evangelist who believed in the new town ideal and lived himself with his family in Cumbernauld. He was keen to support anything that helped fix the town into the national consciousness as a place of youth and modernity (and if they could manage the odd shot of hi-tech manufacturing alongside the tidy new estates and play parks that would be nice). But there were some limits. The town centre could only be used for filming on one single day (8am to 8pm). CDC wasn't prepared to lay on catering facilities for them, or to provide any major funding (although £1,500 was donated as a gesture of support). Other permissions were needed from Mr Marchetti, proprietor of the Trio fish and chip shop in Abronhill Shopping Centre, as well as education authorities nervous about opening up their new school premises to film-making types. Not everything went well at Abronhill High either. At the end of July, Paddy received a letter from Strathclyde Regional Council complaining of damage. Fixed seating had been removed (to open up more space in one of the changing rooms); "heavy timbers" had been "welded into roof light openings" (for lighting rigs?); and tape used to support black-out material[37].

A list, written out in Bill's favourite green ink on A5 sheets of lined notepaper, set out the costs (estimated to come to a total of £6,245) along with the expected amount of time needed from actors. This included:

> Gregory £600 (six weeks)
> Andy £200 (two weeks)
> Phil Menzies £500 (six days)
> Dorothy £500 (two weeks) [Dee was given an
> extra £100 for the football training]
> Eric £200 (two weeks)
> Charlie £200 (two weeks)

> Alan £200 (two weeks)
> Steve £200
> Carol £200
> Miss Ford £150 (two days)
> Miss Welch £150 (three days)
> Kelvin ["Don't touch the ravioli, it's
> garbage"] £50[38]

Most of the actors with small parts received £50, except for the waitress in the Wimpy who, for some reason, was paid £75. Originally there was budget set aside for Dorothy's boyfriend, Ricky Swift (three days), and for a 'barman' who'd serve Gregory and Susan at the Mallard pub. The notes also included a rough idea of the volume of extra bodies needed (scaled down from the original script, which talked about having "500 girls" in the playground):

> 20 football players
> 10 schoolgirls
> 14 schoolboys
> 8 small children
> 2 grannies
> 10 hockey players

Pine Grove dealt with Equity Union cards for all the young actors with lines; tax and PAYE issues (especially to help people like Gordon, Caroline and Carol, who were in full-time employment); negotiating deals and discounts on film stock (10 reels, 10,000 foot from Fuji for £1,525) and lab processing fees (£37,151). Bill's 'Director's fee' amounted to

£7,500. The two producers were paid £13,000 between them.

Notes on props and costumes are a reminder of how every single detail had to be planned for, bought or borrowed: like the can of deodorant for Gregory, bundles of books, Gregory's wardrobe mirror, the Telstar 5 football[39], a hairdryer, Eric's camera, Mr Hall's car, what's described as a 'practical television', black lipstick, an afro comb, 'winkle picker stilettos', 'Carol's transformation gear', a 'nurse's uniform, bra and pants', even a sticking plaster. The costume and make-up team also had responsibility for keeping the big hairstyles trimmed for the sake of continuity, making them shorter, less wild than they would normally have been.

The production team worked from their mega-spreadsheet, a hand drawn and written table that cross-referenced each filming date against the planned location, particular props that would be needed, both the main actors and the numbers of extras (lumped together in categories of 12-14 year-olds, 15-18 year olds, and 'Wee kids'). The first day of filming — in the original draft schedule — was planned for Monday 9th June 1980: an easy starter of Gregory and Andy walking to school. Tuesday was going to be in Gregory's house in Westfield, followed by Phil Menzies "shovelling dung" in his garden with a 'tractor man' (a scene which didn't happen because of the lack of a crucial prop). Wednesday was Gregory almost getting run over by Mr Hall, the learner driver. Thursday, back to Gregory's house (filming there needed to be finished quickly in order for the property to be handed back to the CDC). 18th June was Chic Murray day. 20th was due to be the English lesson interrup-

ted by the window-cleaners. Filming was expected to be completed by 18th July — until the dreich weather and all the usual vagaries of production choreography made a mess of the spreadsheet. A second schedule moved the end date to 29th July.

A number of short scenes and diversions were cut or only partly filmed. An ensemble of motorway maintenance workers was led by the GYT's Gerry, who'd played the night watchman in *That Sinking Feeling*. They were filmed turning up in the background of a number of scenes, tidying flower-beds and verges, whistling the 'Heigh-Ho' song. "There was no dialogue, but the idea was of an almost fairy-tale element to them (*Snow White & the Seven Dwarves*), keeping the magical village of Cumbernauld tidy," Gerry explained[40]. Also, Gregory and Susan never got to make their detour to the Mallard, an actual pub on the Greenfaulds estate[41] (the barman was going to refuse to serve them anyway).

*

I'd read so much about Cumbernauld's town centre I was disappointed. Where was it? I could only see a retail park sliced in half by the main through road. Between gaps in the retail sheds there were views over to the opposite hills, a sense of meadows and swathes of woodland in the surrounding glens, of every blade of grass and leaf thickening, a wealth of thistles and dandelions. Treetops gleaming silver. Not like English meadows, so often damp and heavy and blue, the winds up there were too quick and restless. There was a vigorous kind of peace in those hills instead; a green abundance by comparison with what was meagre and utilitarian in the town centre.

There are standard types of human settlement: 'nucleated' (around a village green, church or manor house); 'linear' (along a main highway) and 'dispersed' (say, a loose scatter of farms). This was a new category, the 'ring-road' settlement. A town centre with no focal point and no streets, a kind of void. In our century, voids like these are filled eventually by big, anonymous sources of money that see markets and not places. And there they were: Asda, Tesco, McDonalds, Burger King. No sign of civic buildings. A single outsized office block, and the only pub was in the shopping centre, a Wetherspoons.

It was a Thursday afternoon, and the car parks and shops were mostly empty. Seagulls riding the winds. A thick feathering of cloud over the sky. A summer thwarted. I tried to find the original Copcutt mega-structure, but Cumbernauld's centre is a long funnel bordered by railed off roads, and the only way I found to go was into the shopping centre and its pipeline of stores. Poundland, Savers, Home Bargains. There seemed no option then but to walk up and over the road to the Antonine Centre (named after the remains of the Roman wall on the hillside). This is where the clock lives, the Victorian St Enoch Clock where Gregory waited for Dorothy. A sign points you up to an abandoned part of the new centre, empty steps, an empty corridor, more fire-doors and then warnings about the dead end that's coming. An information board explains the clock's story, how it had been saved from St Enoch Station in Glasgow after its closure and donated to Cumbernauld by a local entrepreneur. Unveiled by the Queen in 1977 in the original New Town Plaza (which no longer exists). But no mention of its part in film history. Heading back the same way down into the mall and another set of steps took me to Forth Walk, what had once been an open-ended arcade, including the shop where Gregory couldn't find any shirts with enough brown in. Forth Walk is now sealed up from the elements and modernised, the only trace of the original design being the awkwardness of some of the spaces, the number of slopes and ramps and steps that lead nowhere in particular.

Coming out of the Antonine, I found the alien's head by accident, trying to find a shortcut around another supermarket to the road. There it was, blocked in by the hulk of Tesco Extra, the remainder of Copcutt's vision and the only structure that hasn't been re-built or smothered with retro-fit. Hideous dockyard chic.

I'd seen enough. This wasn't Gregory's Cumbernauld anyway.

---

[1] An Englishman, Sir Hugh Wilson (1913-1985) had been the Chief Architect for Canterbury before being appointed to oversee the Cumbernauld Development Corporation's Master Plan between 1956 and 1962.

[2] By 1959 this ambition had grown to housing 70,000 people.

[3] Providing the set-up for the joke involving the learner driver almost running into Gregory: that's the good thing about a new town environment, "the absence of traffic lights — the absence of stray pedestrians."

[4] Geoffrey Copcutt (1928-1997) was a Yorkshireman who trained in architecture at the Edinburgh College of Art and found his first design posts in Edinburgh and Leicester. After Cumbernauld he became Chief Architect for what was intended to be a new town for Northern Ireland, Craigavon, but plans for the town had to be aborted when the Troubles escalated and money dried up. Copcutt went on to become Professor of Architecture at Carnegie-Mellon University in the US.

5 Another Englishman, Derek Lyddon (1925-2015) worked on the new town of Stevenage before being signed up for Cumbernauld. He went on to become Chief Planning Officer to the Secretary of State for Scotland, taking charge of sorting out planning rules for land development relating to the North Sea oil boom.

6 Rowan Moore, 'Rip it up and start again? The great Cumbernauld town centre debate', *The Guardian*, 3 April 2022.

7 Brian Miller (1934-2011) started out in the department as an engineering draughtsman but was given the role of 'Town Artist' for Cumbernauld, creating abstract expressionist concrete sculptures and painted elements to add interest to the look of public spaces, gables and underpasses. Some of his work around the town has now been listed by Historic Environment Scotland. He was a founder of the Cottage Theatre, and wrote and directed plays there as well as for the Cumbernauld Theatre.

8 Gair Dunlop, *Looking Back on Modern Living: Cumbernauld*, 2013.

9 Miles Glendinning, *Rebuilding Scotland: the Post-War Vision 1945-75*, Tuckwell Press, 1998.

10 Geoffrey Copcutt, 'Cumbernauld New Town Central Area', *Architectural Design*, 33 (1963).

11 Wolf von Eckardt, 'The Case for Building 350 New Towns', *Harper's Magazine*, December 1965.

12 Made by Robin Crichton's Edinburgh Film Productions rather than one of the more local Glasgow outfits. Crichton grew up in England but studied at the University of Edinburgh and settled in the city, going on to direct children's TV series such as *Moonacre* in the 90s.

13 A Cambridge University graduate in the 1930s, G.P. Youngman (1912-2005) abandoned his expected career route and paid a gardening firm £50 to take him on as an apprentice, ending up laying crazy paving in suburban homes. After bringing his landscaping talents to Cumbernauld, Youngman worked on Milton Keynes in the 1960s and is considered to have 'softened' the initial impact of the plan, bringing in more curves, undulations and woodland.

14 Owen Hatherley, *A New Kind of Bleak: Journeys through Urban Britain*, Verso Books, 2012.

[16] Geoffrey Copcutt, ibid.

[17] Professor Miles Glendinning, director of the Scottish Centre for Conservation Studies , Edinburgh University, quoted in *The Scotsman*, 16 May 2022.

[18] Jasper Rees, '10 Questions for Filmmaker Bill Forsyth', *The Arts Desk*, 28 April 2014.

[19] Jonathan Murray, 'Cornflakes versus Conflict: An Interview with Bill Forsyth', *Journal of British Cinema and Television*, Vol. 12, 2015.

[20] The film also featured the Penguin, Christopher Higson, with brother Michael, playing wolf cubs. Calum Malcolm worked on the film's closing theme song, a sound engineer who went on to work as a producer with Simple Minds, REM, Mark Knopfler, the Blue Nile, Aztec Camera, Orange Juice and Wet Wet Wet.

[21] Jonathan Murray, *Discomfort & Joy: The Cinema of Bill Forsyth*, Verlag Peter Lang, 2011.

[22] 'The Sitter's Tale: From the Scottish National Portrait Gallery: the film-maker has become a character in one of Steven Campbell's stories', *Independent on Sunday*, August 29, 1999.

[23] Bill Forsyth, 'Thermal underwear', *Sight and Sound*, Spring 1984.

[24] Since 2019, Scottish local authorities have been working to replace red ash with grass pitches.

[25] Jasper Rees, ibid.

[26] Dee Hepburn, Telephone interview, 16 January 2023.

[27] You know this: "I - can't - see - me - lovin' nobody but you/ For all my life/ When - you're - with - me, baby the skies'll be blue/ For all my life" (1967).

[28] Douglas Sannachan, Telephone interview, 9 August 2022.

[29] Alan Love, Email conversation, July 2022.

[30] Clare Grogan, Telephone interview, 27 February 2023.

[31] Ibid.

[32] Dee Hepburn, ibid.

[33] The Ross Owen Show, Interview with Caroline Guthrie, April 2016.

34 Douglas Sannachan, ibid.

35 Carol Macartney was working at the Royal Bank of Scotland in Cumbernauld at the time of the making of the film, but had previously been part of her school's theatre group in Greenfaulds.

36 Brigadier Colin Cowan (1920-2014) had taken command of his own regiment in the Second World War, aged just 20; he then achieved a triple first at Cambridge. He was awarded a CBE in 1984 (before leaving CDC after 15 years in 1985).

37 *Gregory's Girl* production notes, Moving Image Archive, National Library of Scotland.

38 Ibid. Kelvin was played by 12 year-old Patrick Harkins, who went on to become a film and TV director himself, directing many episodes of *Taggart, Waterloo Road, River City* and *Hollyoaks*.

39 The Telstar 5 was the 'official' football design used for major football tournaments at the time; made up of 32 black and white 'panels', 20 white hexagons and 12 black pentagons, it was meant to make the ball more visible on TV. The name comes from the design's resemblance to the dotted Telstar communications satellite from the 1960s.

40 Gerry Clark, Email conversation, July 2022.

41 The Mallard closed down in 2015, and in 2022 was still empty and boarded up. The new pubs in Cumbernauld were named after birds, the Jack Snipe, the Twa Corbies (ravens), and the Kestrel.

8. Looking

"I jus wanna stay here a wee bit longer and watch the traffic. I like lookin at the big trucks."

*G*regory's Girl is set in the Zone. Modern boys, modern girls, in a state-of-the-art setting on the frontiers of 20th century civilisation, filled with new freedoms, contingencies and emptiness. It's a location that Bill Forsyth found fraught with ambivalence.

On the one hand, the modernity of Cumbernauld meant a blank canvas, a simple way to be in tune with the everyday realities of a new decade — just as *That Sinking Feeling* had faced up to a new world of youth unemployment (and *Local Hero* would deal with the invasion of US business; *Comfort & Joy* with the rise of consumerism and the arrival of Scotland's own radio stations). It was also a chance to take an Existential approach (where the existence of individual responses and their integrity comes first, before labels are attached and made to explain things in a conventional way).

209

As the *New York Times*' reviewer, Vincent Canby, had realised, everything — every character, what they felt and saw, their gestures and ways of expressing themselves — was "miraculously seen anew", because "Mr. Forsyth accepts nothing at face value."[1]

We can't hear it now, but in 1981 the music of Colin Tully[2] was the soundtrack to a new Scotland. Scotland (and Glasgow in particular) looked to the US as its model of the future; as a source of new industry and jobs; for its blue-collar culture and music: Country & Western, blues, Frank Sinatra, soul and disco — all of which felt more relevant to the city's population than London's sour punk and New Wave. A Glaswegian from the south side of the river, Tully was 26 when he wrote and performed the film's transatlantic fusion soundtrack. He'd been a member of Cado Belle — a band named after a Mississippi steamboat — playing sunny New York street soul, music for rollerskating around Central Park, looking up at blue skies and the glittering faces of skyscrapers through the trees.

Cado Belle were regulars on the Glasgow pub and college scene and a fixture at the *avant garde* contemporary arts centre the Third Eye on Sauchiehall Street. They started out with Maggie Reilly on lead vocals (who went on to work with Mike Oldfield, most famously on 'Moonlight Shadow'), with Tully playing saxophone, flute and horns. A gentle, unworldly character, Colin was a virtuoso with every instrument he played. On stage with Cado Belle he'd be swaying off to one side, a lanky figure with long dark hair, thin sculpted features, flowery shirt and denim flares, waiting to come in to deliver another note-perfect, swooping line of sax.

Colin was one of Mick Coulter's flat-mates. Without a breakthrough record, Cado Belle had run out of momentum[3], and Colin was spending a lot of time in the flat with a borrowed Fender Rhodes electric piano writing bits of jazz. So when Colin met Bill at a party at the flat and heard about *That Sinking Feeling*, he was keen to get involved in producing the film score, even if it was more of a creative project than a money-making one. The soundtrack he came up with was inspired by the jaunty, street-wise spirit of American cop shows like *Kojak* and *Columbo*.

By the time work on *Gregory's Girl* began, Tully was in the limelight. He'd played sax on 'What's Another Year' — delivering a wistful intro that's instantly recognisable as coming from the man who wrote the *Gregory's Girl* music — and had performed with Johnny Logan to win the Eurovision Song Contest in front a TV audience of hundreds of millions of people. Bill travelled down with a videotape copy of the film rushes to Harberton in south Devon, the rural village where Colin was now living with his wife Anna, teaching the Alexander Technique (a way of improving posture and movement to reduce feelings of tension) at the local Dartington College[4]. Colin and Anna were living the Good Life in a cheap, out of the way place where they wouldn't have to rely on a big income or running a car. Anna took seasonal jobs picking strawberries; they made their own milk from oats and soya beans, sprouted mung beans in black bin bags in the bath, and experimented with eating only raw foods. To watch *Gregory's Girl*, Bill needed to give Colin a lift to the house of one his students who had a TV and a video player they could use.

It was interesting having Bill stay with us [re-
called Colin in his memoirs]. He was easy-
going and mild-mannered but capable of
delivering the occasional flash of wry humour you would expect from the creator of
such carefully observed films. After uncom-
plainingly chewing his way through his
breakfast of sugar-free muesli, Bill drove us
into Totnes where we spent the day at Tina's
house watching *Gregory's Girl* and plotting out
places where we felt music would enhance
the unfolding plot. In keeping with my current low-tech lifestyle, I used the second hand
of my watch to measure the approximate
length of each section and scribbled the timings down on a bit of paper along with a
brief description of what was happening in
the scene. If Bill was disappointed in my
lackadaisical, amateur approach he never let
me know.[5]

They returned to Colin's home for a dinner that would have
been a hardcore proposition in the parochial times of 1980:
"something along the lines of buckwheat topped with beans-
prouts in a miso and tahini sauce."[6] Bill retreated early in the
evening to the spare bedroom and Colin was left worrying
whether his friend had been put off by his encounter with
their alternative lifestyle. In a letter, Bill later referred to the
life of the Tullys in Harberton as "bucolic".

Colin got to work. He recruited former Cado Belle bandmates to play guitar and bass, a friend who'd often helped him out with a place to stay in London to play piano, and their girlfriend on cello. The Fender Rhodes had been re-claimed by its rightful owner, so Colin had only a "battered Hohner Clavinet", an amplified clavichord often used in the Seventies by artists like Stevie Wonder to produce a thick, funky sound, to work out the score. At the time, Colin was listening to *The Grand Wazoo* (1972), a big band album by Frank Zappa with a bittersweet citrus flavour, and jazz fusion in the form of Carlos Santana's *Welcome* (1973). Both, he felt, had ended up seeping into the film's sound-track (and you can certainly hear the easy, drifting shimmer of Zappa's 'Blessed Relief' and Santana's 'Samba de Saus-alito' in there). When it came to the recording — which had to be completed before the start of term at Dartington — Colin was taken aback when Bill booked AIR Studios, the facility set up in Oxford Circus in London by Beatles' produ-cer George Martin. His own side of things felt ramshackle and embarrassing when they first turned up in AIR's spa-cious, élite surroundings only recently used by Kate Bush, Paul McCartney, Queen and the Sex Pistols. Colin's usual saxophone was out of tune (an instrument he'd originally recovered from a "chicken slaughterhouse") and Bill had needed to hire another soprano sax for him just for the ses-sions. The cello player hadn't played or practised much for years and it showed. Watching the film projected onto a back wall — the kind of play-along method that had first been used by Miles Davis for the recording of his moody jazz soundtrack to Louis Malle's debut film *Ascenseur Pour L'Ècha-*

ufaud (1958) — helped hold them all together. The musicians not only had a clear idea of timings but also began to improvise in response to the film's look and feel.

> "The dancing in the park scene just came together so beautifully with the visuals – way better than I could ever have hoped for. Alan Darby's gorgeous sustained guitar work made that track almost luminous…On the scenes with Gregory and his various encounters leading up to the park scene…[Bill] wanted this section to be a bit of midsummer madness, evocative of the Shakespeare play. Musically I put together some dreamy chords without a particular tone centre, put a jazz groove under them and improvised some soprano sax on top. Again Alan did some very atmospheric guitar stuff."[7]

In the end Colin produced a whole suite, parts of which weren't able to be used, and the full original recordings have yet to be tracked down. Thinking the film would be another *That Sinking Feeling* in terms of commercial potential, Colin opted for a one-off fee of £750 rather than a percentage of the film's profits. It was a snap decision that, subsequently, he had the wisdom to know wasn't worth worrying about.

For anyone who loves *Gregory's Girl*, Colin's music is essential to the mood and lasting impression of the film. And in *Local Hero* the music takes on an even more central role, painting all those greyish coastal scenes with emotion and providing a cohesion to the piece. And that was exactly what Forsyth didn't like about it — to him, using music was like an admission of failure, it was basically telling an audience that a scene needed something else to make it work, it couldn't stand up without a prop. He loved music too much, he said, for it to be exploited in such a cynical way. Much of Tully's music, Forsyth has conceded, was really only there to "nudge" the film along, to move between scenes and provide some joins. Also, to fill in some of that extensive space and make sure the audience "wasn't getting bored"[8]. Unlike the typical film soundtrack though, the *Gregory's Girl* music isn't part of the narrative, there to signpost what audiences are meant to be feeling, not the sound of swelling emotions in young hearts. It's detached. More like the sound of the Cumbernauld landscape unable to do anything but be itself.

*

For Forsyth, there was another side to modernity that was junk. The pressure to conform exists in any society, but the intensity and form of that pressure had been super-charged by a modern consumer culture that kept telling the same stories about what 'success' was. Places like Cumbernauld were meant to be bright with a very middle-class modernity. Made from Colgate toothpaste, Daz washing powder, Flymo lawnmowers, Casio digital watches, Laura Ashley wallpaper, the smooth lines of a Ford Cortina estate and the crystal blue waters of a package holiday brochure — products from just the type of absurd, consumerist age that Ferdinand in *Pierrot le Fou* had needed to escape from, a place where people had started to speak and live in a language of adverts. Significantly, in the original script, Forsyth's name for Cumbernauld was 'Middleton'. The opening was intended to move from a soothing scene of old Cumbernauld village and its little rural cluster, so effortlessly settled and rooted, its church belfry, smallholdings and vegetable gardens, to a panorama of the new town and its football pitches and scurrying activity. "This town is football crazy. From every vantage point we are offered yet another football field with yet another game in progress."

As the 20th century's art form, cinema and its blockbuster movies have been a loudhailer for modern culture. But in an inherently fake and deceiving way: in the reassurance of black and white moral scenarios; the chance to identify with heroes and enjoy the journey to another happy resolution.

> "I don't know what people want happy endings for [said Forsyth]. I mean, life has very few happy endings. It seems to me a kind of infantile desire to go to the movies and want everything to be tied up in a bow in an hour and a half. What else resolves itself in that way? Nothing in life. My idea of entertainment would be something that engaged my mind and made me reflect and wonder about things. It wouldn't be switching my brain off, and that's what the cinema tends to do now."9

The modern world of stories had an insidious and prescriptive logic underneath the sheen of entertainment, one that undermined our ability to stay with reality, to keep on wondering and questioning. Forsyth said that: "once you've got a story you've got a happy ending. We take great comfort from that in our lives. To my mind it's polluted cinema."[10] Cinematic fantasies were damaging to the finer, more delicate machinery of everyday imagination.

> "I feel that movies have cheated on the audience by making magic into something artificial and putting it up in the sky or in space or, you know, ghosts. They are abstracting magic when I believe magic is a human resource that should be grounded. It is the strange way we try and understand things that we don't understand."[11]

An unpredictable, sometimes difficult and disappointing kind of reality had to be more rewarding in the end.

> "I'm not interested in telling stories, it's more about examining people in certain situations. Audience attention is made to follow stories when I'd rather spend time concentrating on the characters and how they respond, not chasing the story from A to Z....We use stories too much in our lives. We're taught that life is a story to an extent, hopefully with a happy ending. I want to subvert that view of

life…We're all removed from the real world
in certain ways. I'm trying to get a sense of
realness all the time."[12]

Which is why *Gregory's Girl* is populated by commonplace eccentrics. Even with the script in place there's a sense they're
following a less certain kind of pathway than in a typical
film, that they might, on a whim, decide not to bother with
football practice, drift out of shot to buy chips or go and
watch the traffic.

  With this in mind, what could work better as a window
onto everyday oddness than watching young men fall in love?
Seeing how they respond to the shock of new emotions —
strange, awful, ecstatic — so careful and nervous over every
shift of those feelings and their difficult progress, like swal-
lowing something they probably shouldn't have, wondering
what might happen to them next. The big King of
Everything one moment, as timorous as a baby goat the
next. Desperate. Ridiculous. But of course boys do their best
to let none of that show, and will even believe they're getting
away with it. These kinds of self-enclosed and self-determin-
ing characters are a reflection of Forsyth's philosophy. "I
think we're basically all odd," he suggested. "I think we all
have a tension between what we think we are and what other
people think we are. Everyone is like that and I just tend to
highlight it. I think I could make a detective story, or something conventional like that, and end up having odd characters in it too. Strangeness is in everyone, it's just a matter of
whether you choose to reveal it or not."[13] Forsyth said that
"the whole philosophy of *Gregory's Girl* was that especially in

adolescence you have a very precise image of yourself and you are completely unaware of the fact that the world sees you as something different."[14] We catch characters in the film, young and old, in their own little worlds: Gregory playing his drum kit in his bedroom, looking at himself in the mirror as he thumps away ("When he sees his reflection in the mirror on the wardrobe door he seems comforted," according to the screenplay); the headmaster toddling his head along to his piano playing; Andy and his universe of trivia; Eric and his elephants, Dorothy and her football. Forsyth was interested in individual responses to things and not what has been shrink-wrapped by convention: "Schools are little worlds — where all these young people are introduced to all these ideas and concepts, where things happen, where this creativity happens. That's what I was trying to embody."[15]

This world of non-conformists is an important part of the appeal of the film. We identify with the characters as real people, not fairy tale movie characters fulfilling a destiny, not story fodder. They don't seem to be 'living', in the sense of how they could be at the mercy of a plot and its manufactured twists and resolutions; not living at all, but 'being'. This lack of manipulation, Forsyth has hinted, might be the keystone to the singular quality of *Gregory's Girl*:

> "A film-maker with more nous would have
> been more manipulative. I hesitate to use the
> word 'innocence' about it, because the char-
> acters have attitude, have stories, have views,
> I don't think it was too innocent a film. But if
> there was a layer of purpose or intent miss-

ing, a layer of manipulation — here's where
we want the audience to feel this, or that, I've
always truly hated that — then, perhaps,
that's been its secret, if you like."[16]

There were few things that made going to the cinema
bearable for Forsyth, but one of them was when an audience
appeared to break up into individuals, when "one or two
people kind of giggle at something and no-one else will". In
making *Gregory's Girl*, Forsyth was giggling out of context,
taking a creatively illogical turn away from what might have
been expected from him and his career. Leaping into a
wormhole to try and make feature films. "If we hadn't made
a go of it, my plan was just to disappear."[17] It wasn't as if the
hole was ever intended to be the chance of turning up in a
classic Hollywood kind of story where the Scottish nobody
finds fame and fortune. Because *Gregory's Girl* was always
meant to be an artefact of anti-cinema. Nothing was going
to be smooth or slick. Forsyth didn't choose to write a script
about football just because of its mainstream popularity. He
wanted to stay "off-kilter"[18] throughout the whole process,
write about part of the modern world he knew nothing
about and had no sympathy with.

Perversely, there's no hero. Forsyth's original script
shows Gregory was meant to be unexceptional, self-obsessed
and silly. Mildly irritating. The film isn't meant to be about
Gregory's coming-of-age in itself: "GREGORY's story is
after all only one from a possible two thousand in the school,
and the film should keep a sense of this. A kind of rhythm
between the slightly distanced observation of lives in general

and the intense concentration on GREGORY. Anyway, GREGORY is the kind of guy you need a break from."[19] High School movies depend on their villains. There might be some switching of sides from bad to good or the other way round, but the friction has to be there or where's the interest? Still, Forsyth refused to get involved with portraying people as inherently right or wrong, it wasn't honest: "I suffer from it personally, because I know at home I'm always accused of seeing everyone's point of view. In my mind that's just the way things are…everyone has their own reasons….It's infantile to have baddies and goodies."[20] At the very least, Andy should have wanted to take revenge after losing his place in the football team; Steve's white jacket should have shrunk in the wash; the menacing figure of Ricky Swift, Dorothy's boyfriend, ought to have been the one waiting for Gregory under the clock in the Plaza.

Gregory's Girl includes no apparatus for creating drama at all, no design for ratcheting up the weight of tension or for the consequent snap and break, no certain movement to a resolution. And Forsyth makes a joke of it: at the very end of the film we discover the actual name of the place is 'Climackston'. Elements of confrontation and conflict aren't seen as being necessary. "If you're like me, or you're like Gregory, then you live without them," said Forsyth. "You can dance around these things."[21] So less of a plot than a jig or a reel. Like dancing, the impetus and direction of the film is based on a social memory, what people might actually do in their minor, unremarkable moments of intimacy.

"Talking about conflict, I remember Iain
Smith, who was line producer on *Local Hero*, I
was feeding him some script pages even before I sent them to [David] Puttnam when I
was starting to write it, because Iain was a
friend, and I sent him about twenty or thirty
pages and we were talking on the phone, and
he said: 'It's coming on fine, but there's no
cornflakes in it.' I said: 'Yeah well, I'm getting
away from cornflakes, you know, I had cornflakes in a couple of the other films: it's not
going to be a thing.' And he said: 'No: conflict. I'm talking about conflict.' That was
when I was suddenly informed that conflict
was good in movies and it was like a light
bulb coming on, I hadn't even thought of
that before. I'd managed to make two films
without conflict: cornflakes, but no
conflict."[22]

And, of course, there's no traditional happy ending to leave
an audience feeling fulfilled. There might or might not be a
Gregory's girl. No-one ends up being a local hero in Forsyth's next film; and — the final blow — there's no comfort,
let alone joy, to be found in the one after. In thinking about
life, or its representation in cinema, we should at least be
clear-headed and un-drugged.

"We're in the middle of something, but who's
to say that the end of it is going to be any

different or better than the start of it? To me,
it seems a kind of dishonesty, really, in film-
making. It's almost like a kind of propaganda, and I resent it a little bit . . . that's
what cinema, the kind of industrial cinema
we're all embedded in, that's the way it seems
to want to operate. It's almost as if it's telling
us this slight lie, almost as if it's trying to give
us some kind of pill, you know?"[23]

*

I went looking for the tunnel where Gregory and Andy had
traipsed into school. It was going to be somewhere on the
Seafar estate, I knew that much. But I'd already needed to
give up on finding the building where the nurse was caught
undressing. There were plenty of bushes around Seafar Road
to hide in, those young shrubs and trees of 1980 had each
grown into the size of a house — but the original building
they'd filmed had gone. It had belonged to the YMCA at the
time (who weren't that bothered about what was going on in
their windows), before it turned into a training centre for
Scottish Water and then premises for the Cumbernauld
Community Church.

As soon as I was past the town centre, Cumbernauld
turned into Middleton/Climackston. Blue pedestrian bridges
over cornflake-bearing roads. Metal-ribbed underpasses and
steps up and down through mossy belts of trees and greenery
with their own damp, sub-marine feel. Seafar itself was
spread with rows and blocks of little homes over a slope, a

Tetris maze with no regular streets or pavements but a flow
of pathways like water around rocks. Down they went
between the buildings, sometimes eddying around a feature
of cobbles, a mound of rocks, a tree or shrub. Gregory,
Andy, Steve and Billy could have turned up in any of these
places. Except this was a New Town that had relaxed into
middle age: what had been bright and modern was clotted
with weeds and moss, stickered with lichens. The original
planting, once laid out as formal gardens, had turned into fat
and scratchy jungles.

In a far-off echo of the film, these were strangely lonely places still. I met one mum and a toddler pointing to the cars passing under the bridge into Seafar. There was no noise or sense of movement in any of the houses, no-one else about on the pathways, not until I reached Our Lady's High School and a group of school kids (more tentative-looking boys and girls in black tights) climbing the slope during break-time. I quickly put my phone and its camera away. It might have looked a bit odd, what was there to take pictures of round there except weird anorak stuff? — but as a middle-aged man they didn't even see I was there.

When I did get lost, Cumbernaulders were genial and unsuspicious. Rather than a few directions to get rid of me, one lady carrying bags from the supermarket went out of her way to walk me round to where I should go, even when she wasn't so sure herself, the town centre being so oddly planned. A postman in Kildrum stopped and had a long think over the best way to get to the Abronhill estate. Abron-hill, from there? He wanted to puff his cheeks, but held back, not wanting to put a downer on things, not when it had started to rain. Gusty, unapologetic rain. I followed his advice and entered another web of alleys and pathways, suddenly slick and wet enough to be shining, reflecting the sky back to itself.

I found a way to the bridge over the railway line that separated Abronhill from the rest of town, and crossed over the steep banks of a wooded glen before heading up into an estate that was now doused in warm sunshine. There were blocks of low-rise apartments and rolling lawns. I was still expecting to find something of the *Gregory's Girl* mood in each place I came to. That feeling of being on the verge of something, an imminence. The sense that nothing was going to be mundane anymore. Anything was possible. A glad, uncomplicated happiness that wasn't won through money or privilege or even luck, but was somehow everywhere; communicated by the look of every simple thing. But in spite of my years of immersion in the film, the longing I'd felt for Cumbernauld places, I was still just a typical film tourist: taking snaps, caught up in a rigmarole of rucksack, mac and jumper.

I made my way to Moss Road in Abronhill, the place where Gregory was almost run down by the learner driver.

Around the corner there was a football pitch, not red ash but a perfect expanse of emerald astroturf. A shaggy, lustrous, white-shining surface, sensibly caged for convenience so that the kids didn't even have to run and fetch the ball. I took pictures of the pitch and felt kind of pleased that no-one had to play football on winter afternoons on the ash anymore, no more scabby knees and elbows.

It was only when I headed for Abronhill's shops that I saw my mistake — the old pitch was still there. It was like stumbling onto a landscape I'd only ever seen in a dream, that shouldn't be real, was never meant to be real. An old ash pitch with flaky goalposts. It couldn't have been played on for years and the dusty ash was now clotted over with summer beds of clover and islands of grass. A piece of wasteland scrub, dry and smoky, swallowed up by the open cloudscape and greater freedom of the hills; somehow light and fragile, like the whole lot could be blown away.

I was late to the party. The lights were all out, doors locked, no-one around. Not only a belated visitor, but so late that my presence around the town's pathways felt more fictional than the film itself.

*

The original drafts of Forsyth's screenplay were different. There were more characters (Gary, Pete, Lisa, Eddie, Mary, Anne, Margaret, Mr Wylie, the motorway gang; an entire spectrum of different couples, falling in love, falling out of love, arguing and pleading with each other), meaning there was a more desultory drift of attention away from the simple line of the plot, more tricksy experiments in the use of montage.

The biggest difference, though, was in tone. The language was harsher ("How can you stop a ball and trap it with big tits banging around?" asks Andy); the obscenities more casual ("Fuck, Andy grow up"). So when the filming began, the cast were given a script with a cold tangle of bitterness to it. Something less innocent and often more leery. Gregory keeps a copy of *Penthouse* under his mattress; takes the bus to school so he can exchange glances with the female bus driver. "I was up late doing some astronomy, checking out some heavenly bodies," explains Gregory to a neighbour, the morning after he'd been spying on the nurse undressing. Steve plans to be a "sex maniac" before he falls in love: "Get rid of my apron and let my hair down, put love potions in my biscuits. Anyway, I want to be rich first, so that I can love something really…expensive." Madeline is just used to her brother and his friends: "letting them get on with their silly
228

conversations, as always dominated by sex." Sex is the thing, even when they know it means trouble, one way or another.

> PETE: But its dangerous to wait too long. Its unhealthy. Its bad for you. I really love you.
> LISA: If you love me you can wait then.
> PETE: Shit, I knew you would say that, you got that in a book didn't you...

Gregory's friend Gary has got his girlfriend Fiona pregnant and is resigned to getting married: "It's a terrible thing, sex. I hope you're being good Gregory." The first stirrings of affection came wet with dribble. Susan tells Dorothy that Gregory is after her: "He was even drooling at your schoolbag." ("What a prick!" says Dorothy). The grown-ups are no different. When the girls walk into school, a "driver or two at the traffic lights gives them the eye." PE teacher Phil Menzies is a "born prowler" who's after Miss Welch. In the original script it's not just the "fifth-formers crying themselves to sleep" over Susan, according to Steve, but the music teacher as well.

The other sting to the screenplay was in the character of the girl power, the cool and well-adjusted females versus the weak and gawky boys. Gregory is seen playing with a model aeroplane in his bedroom; at break times the boys prefer to play chess while the girls — not just Dorothy — are winning at the game of modern life: they're the masters of football, vigorous and fluid and exact in all they do. "They are simply passing the ball backwards and forwards to each other about six of them, but they are doing so with skill and assurance and a few fancy foot movements." When a boy dares ask Dorothy about the ball they're using, her response has a note of condescension to it: "Nice ball? Its only a Telstar 5, its only the best professional ball in Europe." The girls' common room is a "lionesses den": "DOROTHY and four of her female friends are casually and slightly menacingly draped over chairs and desks." Their separation from the boys, a regal distance, is captured in one unused scene where Dorothy and her friends look down onto the boy's playground and speak to one another in cod-Italian. The translation is suggestive of something along the lines of this:

> "Look, 900 cocks."
> "Yes, with 900 kids attached to them, all on the hunt."
> "150 metres of cock…about 15 centimetres each."
> [They make a low whistle and repeat to each other]: "150 metres of cock."

The girls are made to be with a breed of man which is physically strong and athletic, like Dorothy's boyfriend 'Ricky Swift' (who's at a "Phys Ed College"). Then there's Renaldo. Gregory doesn't want to bother learning technical Italian for a good reason. "The whole things sounds grubby to GREGORY. He has an image of working in a filling station, filling up Renaldo's Maserati with petrol so that DOROTHY and Renaldo can zoom down the autostrada to the beach."

The script makes it obvious what 'love' actually means to Gregory: how it means being one of the chosen who have found a solution to their problems. Getting a date shows the world he's finally a player in the game, absorbed into the modern dream of success: "For lewd-thinking, self-satisfied, pampered, date-going GREGORY, the trials of life seem to be over or at least well under control." Inside his bubble of 'being in love', it doesn't matter that Steve's white jacket doesn't fit, "it makes him feel like Bryan Ferry going on a date with Olivia Newton-John." All he's thinking is: "How quickly should he try to put the evening onto a sexual footing? How do you get <u>that</u> underway?"

Dorothy is no more of a romantic hero. In the changing room scene where she and Gregory are comparing their old wounds, Forsyth adds a pointed running commentary on Dorothy's vanity and self-absorption. "I'm imperfect!" she exclaims about a scar on her knee ("The bit about being imperfect is her little joke," he adds in a note) "Its nice. I like it," says Gregory. "Really?" replies Dorothy ("Another concession she allows admirers is the illusion they can have original opinions about her.") When Phil Menzies gives Dorothy his idea for a fast trap and turn with the ball, she wants to call it the 'Dorothy Drop'.

The script was made from a cool-eyed kind of vision. Maybe a bachelor's take on the new 'kulture', hardened with a distaste for trivial obsessions (like football), along with a lonely man's sensitivity to what could seem less than romantic about modern relationships, with their machinations and ever-growing reliance on image and ego; perceptions over reality; an unattractive smartness in relationships, something self-satisfied and faithless.

This wasn't the film, of course, that he — and we — ended up with. There's still a sharp irony to the final movie, just as there was a strong element of romance and innocence, a tension with the smut, running through the first script. But why did the character and resonance of the film change so fundamentally? There will have been practical reasons for changes. Taking out the odd 'shit', 'fuck' and mentions of sex was an easy way to avoid an 'AA' (14+) rating. The producers would have needed Forsyth to ditch some scenes and characters because of limitations on time and cash. More than this, though, Forsyth and his script changed because of his day-to-day immersion in the process. Because he was no longer just a man with a typewriter. He was wooed along the way by working with the production team, with the GYT and his other young actors. As Forsyth has said, actors do their own thing, scenes are augmented and meanings come to change. The unaffected charm of Gordon and Rab; the shyness of Dee; the bounce of Clare and Caroline. Attitudes were softened, ideas fleshed out. He could see and feel something else happening to the script's logic — and this led to important changes, the bitterness was sweetened and *Gregory's Girl* was transmuted.

When Billy and his boss Mr Hall turn up to clean the windows, Gregory and Dorothy's English class was meant to be discussing VS Naipaul's *An Area of Darkness* (1964), a book banned in India because of its unsparing portrayal of poverty in the slums its links to government corruption. Naipaul had grown up in Trinidad and settled in Britain, but India was his cultural homeland, the beating heart to his sense of self. What he found during his travels, then, had left him angry and desolate. It's just the kind of politically-aware book that Greg would have used in his English classes in *Gregory's Two Girls*. But after his time in Cumbernauld looking at locations, Forsyth decided to go with *A Midsummer Night's Dream* instead. He'd seen and felt the ways in which those modern but still meadow-haunted spaces were right for the youthful, eccentric world of his script, in their atmosphere, a living silence; how they could even fill in for Shakespeare's balmy summer night in the woods, the moonlit madness and swell of romance. Poor mortal fools that we are. *A Midsummer Night's Dream* became an irresistible reference during the making of the film, not a calculated scheme: right from the opening scene with the band of rude mechanicals in the bushes; Susan reading Shakespeare's play in bed at night; Gregory's recurring romantic dreams. And no matter that it's Tudor poetry read by Andy in a schoolboy monotone, in a Cumbernauld classroom on a dull Tuesday afternoon ("What night-rule now about this haunted grove?… Titania wakes and straight away loved an ass"), or that no-one's taking much notice of him anyway. The spell is cast — a spell that's felt in everything that follows. In Gregory's adventure, his deception and confusion and rustic's wonder, the echo of mixed-up lovers overcome by the still magic of a moonlit wood. No-one understands what's come over Gregory ("So restless and I'm dizzy! It's wonderful. Bet I don't get any sleep tonight!"). "It's Dorothy," says a nonplussed Andy, "she's got funny ears." But she's already been transfigured in Gregory's eyes. Love means the reign of madness and stomach-churning mix-ups, an otherly dimension that even the film's rude mechanicals can sense: "there's definitely something in the air tonight," says Andy, walking past the country park bathed in the golden evening light. "I'm just a bit emotional tonight," admits Gregory, "Okay?" The camera tilts and turns, the world turns upside down. There's a lurch of disorientation. Vertigo.

Changes to the script also meant the convolutions of the evening's plot were simplified. Gregory was no longer overloaded by offers of advice, wit and wisdom from each of his dates. The handover scene where Margo and Susan do a hardboiled gumshoe routine is (thankfully) dropped — the plain flow of romance goes uninterrupted[24]. Gregory and Susan's gravity-dance together in the country park is given more time, and takes on more weight (in the draft screenplay there had been only a throwaway moment when Susan dances as they walk back home together and tries to get a reluctant Gregory to join in). According to Rab, the way the actor's voices and enunciation was monitored and managed for non-Scottish audiences, only added to the film's sound of innocence. No laconic drawling allowed.

Colin's music was allowed to seep over the entire piece with a single soundtrack and mood, rather than be interspersed by more comic interludes. When Gregory asks Dorothy out for a date, there was meant to be accompaniment from a band rehearsal near to the sports pitches, the surging chords of a cheesy rock ballad. In the bath, getting ready for his date, Gregory was to sing the Irving Berlin number from *Top Hat*, 'Cheek to Cheek" :'Heaven…I'm in heaven…" (no doubt one of the songs Charlie and Bill would have sung together in the Treemobile).

It's not as if Forsyth wasn't conscious of how actors can change the impression made by characters.

> "I don't like sentimentality and I spend most
> of my time self-consciously trying to take out
> any sentiment. Most actors, whether they
> would admit or not, are trying to make their
> characters as likeable and attractive as pos-
> sible. And while they're trying to do that, I'm
> trying to make them as unsentimental and as
> dark as I possibly can so we can meet in the
> middle and end up with something quite
> real…It's like the tension between who you
> think you are and how the world sees you."[25]

In *Gregory's Girl*, the balance is preserved. Romance without gooey sentiment. What we're left with is a curious sense of an ethereal presence. Love as something strangely imperson-al and insubstantial, everywhere and nowhere at all, only ever passing through. Sometimes all-consuming and yet leav-ing no impression, having no meaning in itself. A bit like gravity, it's just there.

*

Making anti-cinema wasn't about being subversive in a de-structive, punk kind of way. It was a method for creating bet-ter films. The defining quality of *Gregory's Girl* and its rebel-lion is that structure and tone of passivity. A slow pace, a simplicity of plot, an absence of tension and conflict that

235

takes away the noise of cinema. "It's a spacey story," explained Forsyth, "there's so much space you have to fill it out with things."[26] Not so much a film with an organised plan or architecture but a gathering of things to look at. And as a result there's an unclouding. A stillness and sense of flow that's so much closer to how we experience reality. Strangely light and drifting. A passivity that allows the universe to do what it does, to fill its cells with honey. In practice (taking a step back from my vague philosophising), that means a concentration on the seeing and nothing much else, the film-maker's gaze. Which is the way in which Forsyth made poetry. Because poems don't need to involve a narrative, they express moments of being.

Forsyth's approach came from his appreciation of the visual arts. Concentrating on what's seen, rather than said or told, makes for a simpler way of communicating. Like a sculpture in a garden. It doesn't mean something less sophisticated, only less hampered. Forsyth's ideal, he said, would be for cinema to be re-invented, for there to be "a direct engagement between the film-maker's mind and the audience's mind. That would dispense with the idea of having to appeal to another human being through narrative…narrative is nothing particular to film so it seemed to me to be a misuse of it. To be able to establish this direct link between the audience and their sensibilities was much more exciting."[27]

In the opening scene to *Pierrot le Fou*, that imaginative touchstone for Forsyth, Ferdinand is in the bath reading to his young daughter from the book *Histoire de L'Art* (1921) by Èlie Faure. The extract is a lyrical explanation of how the painter Velázquez broke the rules of his profession; and, in particular, how he managed to capture rarefied essences by no longer attending to outward appearances but only relationships with the aether:

"Past the age of 50, Velázquez stopped painting definite things. He glided round objects with the air, with the dusk. He elicited quivering colours from the shadowy transparency of the background and made them the invisible centre of his silent symphony. He gleaned from the world only those mysterious exchanges which allow shapes and sounds to intermingle in a secret and continuous progression that no collision, no involuntary movement can halt or betray. Space reigns. it is like an airy wave gliding over surfaces, absorbing their visible emanations to define and model them. It carries them along like a scent, like an echo, and scatters them everywhere like some imponderable dust... Velázquez is the painter of the night, of vast expanses and of silence, even when he paints by day, even when he paints inside a room, even when the sounds of war, or of the hunt, are all around him. As they didn't go out during the day, when the sun obliterates everything, Spanish painters communed with twilight."

Velázquez (1599-1660) was one of the first artists to paint landscapes realistically, directly from nature. A painting like 'View of the Garden of the Villa Medici' (1629-1651) was extraordinary for its time because Velázquez had attempted to convey faithfully the muted and sombre shades of twilight. Not only what the colours looked like, but what they felt like. It might seem too great a leap to connect Baroque art with a modest 20th century film-maker. But let's not underestimate the degree of Forsyth's interest in seeing and its relation to being. His attention to the 'gaze', to awareness, to thought and feeling, was intentional. This is how Forsyth chose to open his screenplay for *Being Human* (1994), his most ambitious and personal work: with a quotation from Nabokov (yes it's *Mary*), that he knew would draw impatient looks from studio bosses, but he included it anyway:

> "... and as he stared at the sky and listened to
> a cow mooing almost dreamily in a distant
> village, he tried to understand what it all
> meant — the sky, and the fields, and the
> humming telegraph pole; he felt that he was
> just at the point of understanding it when his
> head started to spin and the lucid languor of
> the moment became intolerable..."

We look at the world — in the most everyday places, at the most workaday times — and can see and sense that it means something bigger than itself. But what? In its arrogance (mostly benign but sometimes stupid), cinema thinks it knows already, thinks it has the answers in the stories it tells. But

Forsyth is happy to keep on looking, knowing it's the relationship with places and what we see and feel that makes for our most important emotions and memories — even what might end up defining our lives. Like what makes us fall in love.

It's an idea that's central to *Mary*. Nabokov describes how Ganin's love for Mary has been the product of a single place and an experience of passivity, his sickbed and the sunbright scene he was absorbed into: "In this room, where Ganin had recuperated at sixteen, was conceived that happiness, the image of that girl he was to meet in real life a month later…The burgeoning image gathered and absorbed all the sunny charm of that room, and without it, of course, it would never have grown."[28] His love for Mary is made up of epiphanies attached to landscapes, moments of seeing. His recollections of "the paths through the park"[29]. Being alone and reading Mary's letter in a desultory way, not conscious of her as an actual personality but only the heightened Romantic moment he was living through: the "delicate and amazingly distinct bare branches of an apple tree at the mellow pink of the sky, where the new moon glistened like a translucent nail clipping, and beside it, by the lower horn, trembled a drop of brightness — the first star"[30]. When Ganin can't contain himself any longer, excited at the prospect of Mary coming back into his life, he needs to talk to a friend "about many things". So many things, but none of them turn out to be about Mary herself, just "sunsets over a highroad in Russia, about birch groves"[31].

In the first drafts of the *Gregory's Girl* screenplay, the film opens with a moody oil painting of a village in the hills,

the pre-development Cumbernauld. It's a landscape by
Robert Russell MacNee (1880-1952), a graduate of Glasgow
Art School known for his mellow, impressionistic studies of
cottages and farmyards (he was known as 'Chicken MacNee'
because of how often hens appeared in his foreground
scenery). The very first film directed by Forsyth — his documentary of painter Sir William Gillies in 1970 — had begun
the same way, with a landscape in oils of twilight like an or-
ange-pink fire, a tiny figure walking across a blazing horizon.
The MacNee painting was a suitable beginning for a film
that's preoccupied with looking through windows: not only
the boys watching nurses undressing, but the perks of Billy's
window-cleaning job; Eric and his photography; looking
through cameras, seeing through different eyes. The plan
was not to begin with showing the place itself, but a painting
of a place seen and translated through the eyes of an artist,
then turned into a window for the audience to see how
places and our perspective on them had changed.

The 'ordinary' locations for the film were only
chosen after long days of scouting by Bill and Mick around
the backways of Cumbernauld, assessing the particular look
and feel of places and the pictures they would make. Nothing was background filler: "We didn't shoot from the hip...
we were precise about it."[32] In the resulting footage there is
still a sense of the documentary-maker who doesn't want
people to intrude and spoil a scene that has been found and
captured, not with everything else already happening in that
picture's landscape, when the gaze is steady, not if it means
breaking away from a lingering attachment to the potency of
places and everything that's mysteriously significant about

them. There's a visual love affair going on, a reciprocity. In its retrospective review, the BFI concluded that "Forsyth almost convinces us that the unglamorous, concrete new town of Cumbernauld is as romantic as Paris."[33] Film academic Jonathan Murray has even suggested that the scenery of Cumbernauld itself is Gregory's 'girl', the camera watches over it so intently and with such feeling[34].

Bill and Mick were equally precise about the light — another reason for them to have their eyes continually on the weather and its treacherous habits. *Gregory's Girl* is lit by a discriminate northern light, pearl-grey, white-clouded and unspectacular; enchantingly prosaic. Except of course when it comes to the quiet-coloured evening of Gregory's date and the coming of twilight. The existence of these scenes on celluloid is a rare and remarkable thing, because one of the first rules of cinematography had been to never film at twilight. Too fleeting and unreliable. Large-scale productions were slow and expensive to manoeuvre, so Hollywood had tended to either fake twilight or avoid it entirely. This is another reason why the scenes shot in the Cumbernauld House country park — cheaply and quickly, using just the one camera — look otherworldly. A summer's night in Scotland. A hazy sky tinged with the thinnest and palest of blues, almost transparent and yet still golden.

It's not just a matter of seeing places. The importance of the film-maker's gaze is equally obvious in Forsyth's feeling for things, prosaic things — what film writer Ben Lambert has called his "obsession with the thinginess of things", an "admiration for the inanimate"; going on to offer "a short illustrative list of objects that do work in his films:

portable electric toothbrush (in duet with can opener), string of Christmas lights, tape deck, telephone booth, attic trap door, scale model of the Scottish coast, chargeable suitcase, BMW 323i Baur convertible, pair of thigh-high leather boots, headlamp, cell phone, large rusty mildly phallic spring."[35]

Forsyth literally 'made' films — what have been, first and foremost, visual ensembles and artefacts: "The thing that interests me about anything I do is not the story but the use of film and the way that film manifests itself behind whatever surface there is."[36] He agreed with Godard about film scripts, they were just there to show the investors what the money was for, the script in itself was nothing to do with film-making. As film critic and festival curator Allan Hunter put it, Bill Forsyth was among the "modest ranks of film-making mavericks who dream in celluloid."[37] "It was absolutely pure film that I fell in love with," said Bill, "the stuff itself and the sheer business of being in the darkened room and have something engage your mind through your eyeballs."[38] The stillness of an art installation.

*

When audiences were leaving their seats back in 1981, titles rolling, each of them took their own *Gregory's Girl* with them. Out through the fire door and into the shock of the cold and the grey slush underfoot in the streets, wondering who Gregory's girl was meant to be in the end. Or where the hell Caracas was anyway.

We've seen some of where *Gregory's Girl* comes from, what Forsyth intended and the people who made it work.

Around a half or more of the mystery. The rest is about what happens next: what did we see in *Gregory's Girl?* Then, as a new cinema release; and since, as a classic we don't want to forget.

---

[1] Vincent Canby, *Gregory's Girl* review, *New York Times*, 26 May 1982.

[2] After Cado Belle, Colin Tully (1954-2021) played on singer/songwriter John Martyn's album releases in the 1980s and was part of the touring band. Rather than exploit his musical virtuosity more commercially, Tully moved to Wales with this family and devoted his time to teaching the Alexander Technique, playing with Celtic Jazz band Sensorium. One of his last compositions was an Edwardian-style musical about early aviator Charles Rolls (of Rolls-Royce) who was killed in 1910 in an aircraft crash at the age of 32.

[3] Cado Belle split in 1978 after recording just one LP.

4 Dartington College was set up in 1961, a famously Bohemian and alternative arts institution (with connections via the Dartington estate to Gandhi, Ravi Shankar and Rabindranath Tagore). One of last specialist arts colleges, Dartington was absorbed into Falmouth University in 2008 and the arts faculty was moved to Falmouth.

5 Colin Tully, *Earworm*, 2021, p154.

6 Ibid., p155.

7 Ibid.

8 *Gregory's Girl* DVD, audio commentary — Bill Forsyth and Mark Kermode, 2019.

9 Rita Kempley, 'Everyday of Bill Forsyth', *The Washington Post*, 15 October 1989.

10 Jonathan Murray, 'Cornflakes versus Conflict: An Interview with Bill Forsyth', *Journal of British Cinema and Television*, Vol. 12 (2), 2015, p245-264.

11 Rita Kempley, ibid.

12 Bill Forsyth interview, *Fresh Air with Terry Gross*, 6 October 1989.

13 Allan Hunter, 'Bill Forsyth: The Imperfect Anarchist', in *From Limelight to Satellite: A Scottish Film Book*, edited by Eddie Dick, BFI Publishing, 1990.

14 John Brown, 'A Suitable Job for a Scot', *Sight and Sound*, Spring 1984, p157.

15 *Fresh Air with Terry Gross*, ibid.

16 Euan Ferguson, 'I was quite naive. Probably still am', *The Observer*, 28 September 2021.

17 William Cook, Bill Forsyth interview, *The Spectator*, May 2014.

18 When Bill Paterson met Bill Forsyth, BBC Scotland, 2011.

19 Quoted in Jonathan Murray, ibid., p61.

20 Jim Healy interview, Dryden Theatre, April 2010

21 'An Afternoon with Bill Forsyth', FilmForum, 5 October 2019.

22 Jonathan Murray, ibid.

23 Ibid.

24 "Who's de guy?" asks Susan. "Sex maniac…picked him up at Capaldi's [the chip shop]" Margo tells her. What's the charge? demands Susan. "What about resistin a breast?".

25 Rita Kempley, ibid.

26 *Gregory's Girl* DVD, audio commentary, ibid.

27 Allan Hunter, ibid., p162.

28 Vladimir Nabokov, *Mary*, Penguin, 2007 edition, p39.

29 Ibid, p84.

30 Ibid, p106/7.

31 Ibid, p47.

32 Jim Healy, ibid.

33 Mark Duguid, *Gregory's Girl* review, BFI Screenonline.

34 Jonathan Murray, *Discomfort & Joy: The Cinema of Bill Forsyth*, Verlag Peter Lang, 2011.

35 Ben Lambert, Notebook: Bill Forsyth, MUBI, 29 July 2021.

36 James Park, *Learning to Dream: The New British Cinema*, Faber & Faber, 1984, p116.

37 Allan Hunter, 'The Imperfect Anarchist' in: *From Limelight to Satellite: A Scottish Film Book*, ed. Eddie Dick, Scottish Film Council, 1990.

38 Ibid.

9. Seventies

"I like to do something special on a Saturday night."

*G*regory's Girl belongs to a chapter of history that can't return. The hopeful naivety of the project, the simplicity to those wet summer days of filming in Cumbernauld, will never be recaptured. Obviously. Every year is unique, the stream of history is unstoppable. But some periods are more unique than others, and this was a revolutionary time in Britain. There wasn't only an acceleration of change along a groove, there was a painful buckling, holes and creases and a breaking apart, the slow making of new roots. A whole new course was being dug out for a society, its economy and way of life. That meant a mess of problems and opportunities that came and went before there was a new channel that settled and hardened again (around the rules of free markets and consumerism). *Gregory's Girl* was one of the happiest products of that upheaval. Less stability and fewer traditional jobs meant more time for the arts, and more energy — because people wanted a voice (either motivated politically or through some sense of personal philosophy). New kinds of enterprise became both necessary and possible. And it was only the arrival of cheaper technology — like the first sound-sync colour camera from Arriflex — that made filming outside of studio conditions possible. Would Forsyth have been interested in making films at all if there hadn't been an active 'Free Cinema' movement pushing for a realistic documentary style?

Very often, *Gregory's Girl* is pigeon-holed as an Eighties' classic. But like many other icons of the Eighties, it's Seventies born and bred. Like Thatcherism. *Dallas.* Out-of-town supermarkets. Sloane Rangers. *Smash Hits.* Ready meals. Computer games. All of them Seventies-made. Forsyth's film was written and workshopped between 1976 and 1979; its ethos and look belong to Seventies' Britain.

Forsyth has been a staunch realist: "I'm never going to be involved with a movie that has ghosts in it, that is about time travel or space travel or body-swapping or whether someone goes to Heaven or Hell."[1] And *Gregory's Girl* is a period piece, about a real time and place. It's also been made by someone who believed in the need for audiences to be part of the process by working out the relevance for themselves and not being spoon-fed. "The nicest thing anyone can say to me about *Local Hero* is, I saw your movie last week and I'm still thinking about it, and I might even go and see it again, because there were one or two things I was thinking about that I want to check out. That means the audience are really working hard and I think that's wonderful. They are the film in that sense."[2] Both real-life context and interpretation were meant to matter.

*

The most successful and technically-advanced film of the post-war period up to that point, *Star Wars* (1977), was made at Elstree, a studio that was cheap, discreet and came with easy proximity to pools of technical professionals and out-of-work actors. When George Lucas and his producers turned up in 1976 they realised the talk about the state of Britain was true. The studio was an unsightly husk of what might have been expected from a movie facility — not so different from what the National Film School had started out with at Beaconsfield — just some antiquated sheds, faulty electrics and mouldy toilets. In nearby London, the hotels they stayed in were expensive and dirty. Patched-up plasterwork, raddled furnishings, horrible food and staff with a superior attitude. Meat and cabbage smells in the corridors. There was also an unhealthy strain of mistrust in the air, especially when it came to 'foreigners'. When Mark Hamill (Luke Skywalker) got lost looking for the hotel he'd been booked into, he went into another hotel to ask for help. They demanded to know his passport number. When he couldn't give it to them, he was taken away by police as a suspected IRA terrorist[3].

Walking the streets, the Americans could see what a dismal nation Britain had become. So many fine old buildings left to rot. Flaky paintwork around the grand sash windows of Georgian homes; bags of rubbish left outside in gardens, dustbins tipped over. Empty factories like so many skeletons of industry left unburied. Victorian railway stations that were partly boarded-up and coated in dust and grime. A city with a drifting eco-system of fag packets, discarded newspapers, ring pulls and dog shit. And nothing was being done about it. Instead, the British seemed to be shiftless, stewing with resentment over their failures. According to *The Wall Street Journal*, Britain was the "sick man of Europe", and the reasons were pretty clear to commentators overseas. The post-war project of consensus politics, the middle way that tried to limit the excesses of capitalism, hadn't worked. It had only meant an insidious lack of competition: "labor indiscipline and overly ambitious welfare-statism", decided *Time* magazine[4]. Union pressure meant inflation and over-priced goods and services. British employees were slow, overworked and surly. At the sane time, there was a lack of political strength and will to do anything about the racial tensions simmering within communities or deal with issues like the Troubles in Northern Ireland.

For the inmates themselves though, life in the Seventies could look and feel very different to this. The visitors from *Star Wars* only looked around for confirmation of doubts expressed from a neoliberal perspective, and didn't consider whether the shabbiness might be superficial. Because the Seventies, for many people, were a Golden Age, full of communal human comforts and pleasures before the cold winds of the Eighties began to blow. The end of the Seventies saw relatively low unemployment, certainly lower than what would become normal in the next decade — and lower even than it would be in the late Nineties, the bullish era of New Labour and Britpop. Compared with that other fashionable era of popular history, the Swinging Sixties, households were more affluent: by the mid Seventies most homes had central heating, a car, a TV, fridge, telephone — about twice as many as 10 years previously, and average disposable income was no different than it had been in the Sixties. Society was a great deal more equal, and certainly more equal than it was going to become. Social mobility rates peaked and gaps between the incomes of rich and poor were at their lowest around 1977/78. Workers were getting twice the amount of paid holiday (up from an average of two weeks a year in 1960 to five weeks by 1980), and more people were having overseas holidays than ever before[5]. There was a boom in terms of funding for and interest in the arts. Sales of paperback books surged. Exhibitions of work by Turner and Constable at the Tate gallery in 1975 and 1976 were swamped with interest. More people wanted to sign up to art classes, take part in amateur dramatics or just pin an Athena poster to their wall[6]. It was only in the Seventies that the radical ideas of the previous decade led to any action or change in areas like environmentalism, feminism and gay rights. Even the introduction of the three-day working week, wasn't simply a 'bad thing'. Productivity levels went up; the Samaritans reported a fall-off in the number of calls "from would-be suicides"[7]. When the think-tank the New Economics Foundation looked at finding an alternative to straight Gross Domestic Product as a guide to the state of nations, it devised the 'Measure of Domestic Progress', using more of a balance of evidence from across sources of economic, social and environmental data. The 'best' year for Britain between 1950 and 2009 turned out to be 1976[8].

Still, we think of the Seventies as an embarrassment. A period as awful as the brown and orange decor, gypsy clothes and overgrown hairstyles made it look; its strikes and walkouts, inflation and oil crises; the need to stock up on candles for the next power cut; rubbish left out uncollected on the streets. No bunch of statistics or sample of events can capture the truth about a decade, so why is it there's been such an acceptance of the idea that the Seventies were 'bad' and the Eighties brought about a 'good' transformation? Because it's been convenient. Political rhetoric of the past 40 years has used popular perceptions of the Seventies as proof that socialism didn't work and collective action was our enemy. That a hive of hard work, enterprise and consumption by competing individuals would be the answer.

The Seventies made *Gregory's Girl* the film it is. An unappreciated decade: troubled and angry, brave and radical. Excitingly tasteless. Dreamily creative. Steeped in old-fashioned ways and pre-war memories, but with a thirst for the modern. Sometimes, even, a whole lot of fun.

*

Saturday night was about telly for most people. A living room jammed with family, fag smoke and trays of Mr Kipling cakes. Still a thick whiff of Crisp 'n Dry in the air. Everyone in the house sitting in a front of the box, burning with the coloured glare of studio lights, their feet up on the coffee table and the pouffe. The Ker-plunk and the Pong console are left under the sideboard, magazines stuffed in the rack, because no-one's doing anything else on a Saturday evening. Telly was like a Big Night Out in itself, with the kind of variety you'd find in the end-of-the-pier show in summer. An evening with the stars in studios caked with glitter and sequins, men in bow ties with music hall chutzpah; long-legged ladies in floaty dresses; sketches, dancing and songs. *Morecambe & Wise, Des O'Connor Tonight, The Andy Stewart Show, The Two Ronnies, The Generation Game, Mike Yarwood In Persons, Thingummyjig, The Dick Emery Show, Opportunity Knocks, The Val Doonican Music Show.* Undemanding, comforting razzmatazz.

TV reached its peak of popularity in the late Seventies. Audiences of more than 20 million were fairly common rather than being the signal of a special event. Beyond light entertainment there was a wealth of quality in comedy writing (*Dad's Army, Porridge, The Fall and Rise of Reginald Perrin, Rising Damp, Fawlty Towers*) as well as drama (*I, Claudius, Bouquet of Barbed Wire, Pennies from Heaven, The Naked Civil Servant, Tinker, Tailor, Soldier, Spy, Brideshead Revisited*). TV so dominated popular culture and consciousness that even current affairs was big: *Weekend World, Panorama, World in Action*, all heightened awareness of issues like police corruption, far right groups and declining standards in schools (while *John Craven's Newsround* made sure children had a knowledge of politicians and political strife like no other time before or since). Personalities from the telly had huge fame and influence, were accepted as occupying another, higher realm of existence, sometimes leading to an unquestioned power. (In 1973, Britain's favourite DJ, Jimmy Saville, was given his own TV programme, *Clunk-Click*, before the BBC moved him to a primetime Saturday evening slot with *Jim'll Fix It* in 1975). The pre-eminence of TV didn't mean it was imaginative in its programming, more the opposite. Even when there was only competition between three channels, bosses wanted to guarantee popularity first, because they knew video cassette recorders (VCRs) were becoming a threat, and that satellite channels and the opening up of the market to more production companies was coming (in 1980, with the Broadcasting Act). TV had to deliver what people wanted (or at least seemed to want): light, middlebrow entertainment, which meant more game shows and US soap operas.

But TV did change British film. By the end of the Seventies there were doubts about what would happen to Arts Council funding — as just another post-war consensus idea that was being questioned. Arts? State handouts for putting on dreary plays about social issues or some dancing around in tutus? At the same time, taking money from 'commerce' continued to be seen as a soiling of artistic integrity (in 1981, for example, the National Theatre would turn down a £750,000 sponsorship deal with Pearl Assurance). For film-makers, TV was "where the juice was," said Forsyth[9]. The opportunities in British TV programme-making, and TV advertising especially, had introduced new energy and talent into the moving pictures business. Like Ridley Scott (who made films for Hovis bread, Benson & Hedges cigarettes, Chanel No.5 perfume), and Alan Parker (Cockburn's Port, Pretty Polly suspenders, Birds Eye Fish Fingers). TV money had become essential, said Forsyth, before he could even contemplate taking on the financial risk of making a film. It was the TV industry that created the demand for less bulky 16 mm cameras, the game-changing tech for independent film-makers; and pushed through innovations such as high-speed film that allowed for shooting outside and in lower levels of light (in 1979, the *Brideshead Revisited* production was one of the first to take advantage, making use of the wan English light for its mood of autumnal sadness).

*

British cinemas were no longer the place for a romantic night out. The glamour had frayed and spoiled, become something louche. What had seemed a vault of dreaming starlight was now obviously just painted plasterboard and a job lot of light bulbs. The carpets were thin and sticky and the audiences were small (down from 193 million admissions in 1970 to 110 million in 1980)[10]. People were staying at home with the easy bonhomie of their telly, some even had a VCR for films (136,000 had been sold in Britain by 1978), and by the end of 1983 only 202 mainstream cinemas remained, around a quarter of the number open for business in 2023. This was a singularly British phenomenon. Cinema-going had stayed popular in the USA and the rest of Europe, but somehow, cinema wasn't for us. "Cinema and Britain have long seemed antithetical concepts," said Francois Truffaut. Even a British director, Alan Parker, was dismissive. The nation had had as much impact on world cinema as "a plate of cold haggis", he claimed. In 1984, film historian James Park concluded that the "history of British cinema has been one of unparalleled mediocrity." No new ideas, no daring. Somehow choked in its ambition. Was it because Britain, under the spell of its cultural heritage, had failed to understand the full potential of a 'new' medium? (There didn't seem any point in filming Shakespeare after all. Beatrix Potter and Edith Nesbit might be worth a go. Cinema, really, was for the great unwashed, the *Carry On* fans). Or was it a reluctance to take commercial risks, the belief that if a film was to be made at all, it needed to involve popularity, not an artistic martyrdom?[11]

The longest-running British film ever opened in 1977 and was still playing at the Moulin Cinema in Soho in 1981, the sex comedy *Come Play With Me*. A health farm can't pay its bills, so it turns itself into a brothel (with hilarious consequences). The most successful British films were part of franchise series, like *Confessions of a Window Cleaner* (1974), the *Carry on* films or Hammer House of Horror, and these were staggering on the last, weakening legs of public interest. Even TV sitcom spin-off movies could be better: like *Porridge* (1979), and *Monty Python's Life of Brian* (1979). There were exceptions, some eccentric personal visions that made it onto film, but at the time these were hardly noticed or seen by anyone outside of arthouse cinemas: Robin Hardy's *The Wicker Man* (1973), Nicholas Roeg's *The Man Who Fell to Earth* (1976), Derek Jarman's *Jubilee* (1978).

It was hard to be bold and creative about your film-making when the goblins of debt and bankruptcy were sitting on your shoulder. In continental Europe cinema was taken more seriously, there was a stronger resistance to Hollywood and its great sticky vats of investment money, and more support for independence. France had set up a film subsidy scheme in the 1950s, the *avance sur recettes*, which made the New Wave possible. The fascist regime in Italy built the biggest film studio complex in Europe, the 99 acre Cinecittà in Rome, giving access to funding for Fellini, Visconti and Bertolucci. Similarly, in Spain, there was the Escuela Oficial de Cine (and bingo, *Spirit of the Beehive* (1973)).

Sweden had a film policy linking up state funding with film and TV operations in order to help film-makers like Ingmar Bergman think about quality over bums on seats. Britain, instead, was a "country of significant film-makers in search of a significant film industry," historian Graham Stewart has said[12].

Taking funding from STV meant *Gregory's Girl* was a pioneer, and also a flagship for Thatcherite policy in the arts. Forsyth and his two early Scottish films made a difference, they led to the setting up of the Scottish Film Production Fund and to Channel 4 funding Charlie Gormley's *Living Apart Together*, Michael Radford's *Another Time, Another Place*, Murray Grigor's *Scotch Myths* (1982) and Bill Bryden's *Ill Fares the Land* (1983). But the change was relatively small, a local uprising that was always going to be crushed by crowd-pleasing competition. Buoyed by tax breaks for investors, more British films were being made, 32 in 1980 and 80 in 1985 — but that number had dropped back to 27 by 1989 (the tax breaks ended in 1986, and the investors' dollar was no longer as strong). So there was never any 'renaissance' in British film, James Park has argued: *Chariots of Fire* won the Best Picture Oscar in 1981 but was overpraised; the response to its success had an element of hysteria to it. The TV funding in itself, said some critics, had only led to 'made-for-TV' films, no blockbusters, and only a minor aesthetic. The national industry was still clinging to the US for financing and distribution, and its best directors kept on looking to Europe for its heroes. Like Michael Radford, who would head to his place in Paris to write. Because he knew he could wander into any café and be among people who would, and could, talk intelligently and seriously about the art of film.

*

Let's shut the front door on the scruffy British streets. The Seventies home was the place where the masses, not just the well-heeled, could have a better kind of life. The cork-lined wall in the living room and its wall clock with a ring of sun rays. Cream and avocado furnishings. A yellow carpet with a Cosmic-Onion pattern. And the royalty in the room: the TV, dusted and polished and topped with doilies, a china cat and a vase with dried pampas grass, wheat and honesty.

Popular TV comedies like *Whatever Happened to the Likely Lads?* (1973/74), *The Good Life* (1975-1978) and *Terry and June* (1979-1987), tapped into this domestication, a shrinking away from the rude world outside into some gentler middle-class occupations. Home decorating became a 'thing', along with gardening, home-brew kits and hobbies in general.

This might have been the age of teen rebellion, new fashions and bursts of punk and New Wave bands. But the punks and members of other sub-cultures stood out because they were still so unusual, like a tutti-frutti of exotic birds found perched on a street corner. Young people were mostly playing board games, doing craft kits, having a kickabout at the rec; going to the church hall for Scouts and Guides; trainspotting; doing their paper round. Even with all the free publicity in the press about how it was going to bring about the end of civilisation, punk music mostly sold badly. Only mainstream versions of soul and disco did any real business because the late Seventies was a world of easy listening and pop. ABBA, Leo Sayer, The Carpenters, ELO and the *Grease* soundtrack.

For teenagers, there seemed to be an endless amount of time for mooning about in bedrooms, thinking about love. A modern, Seventies kind of love: a combination of new freedoms and new anxieties. Everyone was doing it, said the TV and films. Song after song on the radio with the same message. Love was the best thing in the world, like hitting the jackpot on a fruit machine. Girls might flick through the photo features and get some advice from *Jackie* or *My Guy*, enjoy chatting with their friends from a phone box, ready with a hot fistful of 2ps. Boys, more probably, would be wondering what love had to do with sex; what love meant anyway, how they could avoid all that stuff about their 'feelings'. Old formalities and concerns over propriety had fallen away, which meant there were no excuses for not having a girlfriend or boyfriend. But whoever they were, they needed to be fanciable, trendy. Not a prat. Because love was sacrosanct and something to be fought for, not given away cheaply. Women, especially, were less likely to settle. The total number of petitions for divorce in the UK between 1961 and 1965 was 37,657. Between 1976 and 1980 there were 162,541 and rising[13].

Love was more vital and ever-present, but the mystery of how it could happen still remained. How were you going to cross the path of that special someone — and what could you do about it when you did? There was no social media platform to make the match and smooth the way for introductions. You had to be in the right place, at the right time, and that meant relying on luck or what might feel like the treacherous workings of fate. Who would you have met if you'd turned up at the cinema queue a bit earlier; or stayed on at the Social for another hour; or got that job at C&A? Life out in the streets was a labyrinth of possibilities, and most of them — maybe all of them — would end up being lost. Might-have-beens everywhere. Paradise mislaid.

It didn't help that the idea of girls and boys was more binary in the Seventies; identities were more strongly differentiated in ways that made simple friendships unlikely. Hobbies and interests didn't overlap; boys were still made from snips and snails and puppy dogs' tails — and with their beery breath, Brut and gobbing, knew how to show it. There was more sensitivity and insecurity around class, and the way clothes and speech and manner could give you away. All of this mattered because starting a romance was, at every step, a material, physical, bodily thing. Manual, analog and linear. A granular process of effort and risk: looking and willing the object of desire to look over and make that first connection with the eyes, the oldest form of communication and still the one capable of producing the sharpest bite; not being able to stop looking (because who were they with? where were they going?); getting close enough to make the eye contact obvious (proving you weren't just short-sighted or checking the clock to see if it was last orders). Some hovering might be needed, an inexplicable hovering that made every bone weak and stiff at the same time (which wasn't much good if dancing was needed). Then, the worst of it: chat-up lines for the brave, or getting a mate to have a word for the more constitutionally fragile, waiting for the final verdict to be returned.

Making Saturday nights special wasn't easy for teens. Pubs were for the regulars who'd settle into their usual places like it was their own front room, the drinkers who had an eagle-eye for any outsiders, the lame, the jokers. The kinds of places their parents would have headed out to as teenagers in the evenings, like the cafés and milk bars, were long gone. Cinema was old hat. So maybe a walk to the chip shop or just sitting around in the park wasn't such a bad option after all, because at least it meant being out of the house and in the streets, the places that parents didn't know about.

It was a quieter, emptier world. Not yet connected. And the reason why for so many teenagers that cars were so symbolic, not only as a symbol of having reached adulthood, but having achieved a different level of freedom — in other words, the possibility of sex. Which is why Gregory in the original script gets intensely irritated by the girls who keep on asking him whether he can drive, why he hasn't got a car like Ricky Swift: "Yes, yes, yes, I'm a mug and I can't drive and you're the tops…"

Gregory's Girl has a particular appeal to men, because it tells stone-hearted truths about the workings of romance, and relates to men's own, often lamentable and unreported experience. There's no Mills & Boon about it, no wish-fulfilment fantasy. The film's situations feel real — especially when it comes to a sense of intimidation and inadequacy, as well as the other side, the possibility of miracles. "For boys, it was just like that," said Caroline Guthrie, talking about the lasting popularity of the film. "It was how life was, and still is, and no-one had done it before."[14] And maybe it's that mixture of tense effort and occasional revelation that has made memories of first love from those times so forceful, and given *Gregory's Girl* its pinch.

*

When I met my first girlfriend in 1986, I was — somehow inevitably — wearing a white jacket. It was an after-play party, there were cans of cheap lager around and a disco on the stage where we'd just finished a three-night run.

The white jacket was a size too big and the sleeves hid my hands unless I rolled up the cuffs to my elbows, which I wasn't rock n' roll enough to do. So an oversized white jacket, shapeless white trousers and black shirt was the best I could manage. It wasn't enough to put off Tiffany, one of the girls who'd been working on the stage lighting. She was in the year above and I'd never spoken to her before. I'd not seen her during dress rehearsals, or even much noticed her other than as pretty and bob-haired and nothing to do with me. That is, until her friend turned up from nowhere, just when I was expecting a typical party of me and the other single males drinking beer, dancing to 'Blue Monday' and 'She Sells Sanctuary' and strictly nothing else — did I know Tiffany liked me? We had a slow dance in the choking mist of the dry-ice machine. Shy conversation took the place of any of the traditional smooching (which just seemed too earth-bound for such an unexpected and momentous occurrence).

Our first real date, just the two of us, was at the palatial Odeon cinema in Bedford. When we came out from the afternoon showing of Disney's re-released *Cinderella* it was a dark evening. The week before Christmas, snow in the air. Walking back to the bus station together I spotted my bus about to pull out and ran to make sure I made it. It was only when I looked back and gave a polite wave that I knew something had gone wrong. Had she expected me to wait with her? But my bus had come. There was Tiffany, in her pink woollen hat, standing alone in the bus station. And that was that. My first girlfriend, and my first failure to know what the hell I was supposed to be doing.

More failures were to come because I was making it up as I went along. Doing it badly. After I'd moved out of home and got that first job as a reporter in Milton Keynes, I invited an old girlfriend round. I was nervous. I'd not seen Pippa for a year or more, and was surprised she'd even said yes to meeting up. I wanted to impress her with how much I'd changed, with my independence and journo lifestyle. We'd go to the cinema (The Point, naturally), and yeah, course, we'd have dinner first. But dinner, for me, living on my own in a cheap flat with borrowed furniture, meant a cheese sandwich and a bag of Hula-Hoops. Ready salted. So that's what Pip got. Most depressingly of all, she looked completely unsurprised.

In the newspaper office I'd noticed Evelyn in telesales. Couldn't not have noticed her. A slinky, green-eyed red-head. I didn't really believe in my chances in someone older than me and a bombshell. Not me, the blushing trainee who'd already been nicknamed the 'Belisha Beacon' by the blokes in the production department. But as a hopeless romantic (irredeemably hopeless), I also believed in the Hollywood fiction that it was love and sincerity that led to happy endings, that they would happen against whatever odds. For a vision about the office like Evelyn it didn't matter if nothing came of it, I didn't care, I had to do something, make a gesture that could alter the mundane course of workaday things. So — anonymously — I sent a bunch of flowers. There was a lot of fluttering and excitement about the telesales department the day they arrived, and only I knew why; or so I thought. What I hadn't banked on was the unflinching tenacity of Evelyn and her telesales co-workers. They pressurised the florist into breaking its strict rules of confidentiality, having convinced them they were working with the police and I was a known sex pest. My name is probably still on a list somewhere.

*

The media saw *Gregory's Girl*, first of all, as a nice gimmick. Wow, a girl in the football team! Which says a lot about the times. The Sixties and Seventies were periods of radical campaigning for women's rights, and this had led to some of the most blatant inequalities being outlawed. It had taken until 1975 and the Sex Discrimination Act for unfair treatment on the basis of gender to become illegal (for things like job interviews, access to pensions, and segregation in pubs and clubs). In the same year, Angela Rippon started to read the *Nine O'Clock News* and Margaret Thatcher won the Conservative party leadership vote. Thatcher was the surprise winner, still best known as the 'Milk Snatcher' for abolishing free school milk in 1971, and the subject of mild disdain among her male colleagues. Who was this cold fish? A screechy voice and no sense of humour; a former tax barrister who'd helped the wealthy avoid/evade tax (well, they thought, at least that kind of thing could be useful). By 1980, Thatcher was PM — the first female leader of a European democracy — and women were being seen as role models in other places, like TV police dramas *Juliet Bravo* and *The Gentle Touch*.

Dorothy was no different to any of these examples: treated as an exception, a novelty. No-one was talking seriously about girls being inspired by *Gregory's Girl*; Dorothy United wasn't going to happen because it was only a 'what if' kind of thing. Much of the debate around feminism was still limited to universities and obscure publications, nowhere near the mainstream and its acceptance of the natural rule of gruff machismo. The number of female MPs had actually fallen throughout the Seventies to a low of 3% by 1979.

In an interview in 1984, Forsyth said he was hoping to make a film with just female characters as a way of counteracting film industry stereotypes[15]. *Gregory's Girl*, though, is not a feminist film as such. Or, it could be said, it adopts a common sense feminism rather than a political one. In his script notes, Forsyth was explicit about how he wanted his female characters to come across, with strength and maturity. Dorothy herself, as we know, is "very cool and self-contained"; at one point she is asked to give Gregory "a quick, almost motherly smile". Dorothy, said Forsyth, was not going to be a "love object", "she has her own journey to make."[16]

Carol is "business-like". With Madeline, he was even more careful. "Supersmart little girls have been done to death on the screen lately," he explained to his cast. "MADELINE is not a Jody O'Neal or a Tatum Foster. I want her to come across not as a child/Adult monster, but as a <u>woman</u>. It is based on the theory that a woman is a woman, no matter what age she is. In witness to the proof of this theory I think I could call on upward of 200 million males for testimony." Girls were on top in the script, whatever age they were. The following vignette (a difficult one to get local parents to agree to) was removed from the scene where Gregory leaves the house and is crowded by young children:

> A tiny girl is sitting astride a little boy, pinning him to the ground. She stops her throttling action on his throat long enough to say hello to GREGORY.

The boy/men were shown, at the same, to be obviously condescending. "What is it dear?" asks Phil Menzies of Dorothy when she arrives for her football trial.

Forsyth wasn't simply on the side of Women's Lib, as it was known in the Seventies. Dorothy could be tetchy: "full of concentration like one of those really wound-up lady tennis players at Wimbledon," he suggests. And he's not patient with PC language: "MARGO...is more outwardly 'emancipated' or 'liberated' or whatever the current word is." Gender tensions were what really mattered for a writer. "Football was for men and all that, so it had lots of nice anomalies in it," said Forsyth[17]. The girls were presented as self-assured and assertive simply because it was a reflection of little truths: "It's just the ways things were, and I suppose still are."[18] As the screenplay says, "the girls are being very much themselves". After all, isn't it patronising and wrong to suggest that only our liberated 21st century women have had the strength and sass to stand up for themselves? One way or another, it's always been happening[19].

*

Through the fog of net curtain there's a square of tidy lawn and a big spray of pampas grass, a single tulip between the lawn and the Ford Cortina — and at last the paperboy's come. He's late. NHS specs and a grimy old bag the size of a baby rhino. A rolled-up wedge of Sunday papers is lodged into the letterbox, then he's back on his Chopper, wobbling up the road and muttering as he goes. Nothing about the joys of spring.

There it was in black and white, the news from a planet of impending doom (plus, the big winner on the football pools! and why Isla St Clair — showing off her new frock — is simply buzzing about bees!). In 1979 the latest disaster being reported was the overthrow of the Shah of Iran, replaced by a radical extremist, the Ayatollah Homeini. That meant another oil crisis and prices going up again at the petrol pumps. By November that year, inflation had reached 18% and interest rates on mortgages were around 17%. Unemployment figures were followed by newspaper readers like the cricket scores, another big employer announcing redundancies was like the fall of another wicket. During 1980, the number of people in dole queues would balloon by 836,000, the biggest single increase in a year since 1930[20].

That was the landscape, the scenery. The starring role was taken by Mrs Thatcher and her campaign to re-make Britain. In May 1979, Thatcher was announced as the new Prime Minister on the back of a small majority and 43.9% of the vote. There had been a large swing away from Labour led by a new vanguard: women voters, skilled workers (the C2s in white vans carrying copies of *The Sun*) and 18-24 year olds. The old guard, the Establishment, the ABC1s, were still more likely to have voted Labour. Only someone like Mrs T, it was said, could make the tough decisions the country needed and be the hard, stiff brush that would get into lazy and complacent corners, address its outdated ways and fusty institutions.

In truth, different governments and political leaders since the beginning of the decade had all been talking in similar ways. Labour PM James Callaghan with his 'New Realism' manifesto for example, which questioned the effects of the post-war consensus and suggested more control of spending and inflation, more limits to trade union powers. What voters chose was an extreme version of that realism. Thatcher's policies were inspired by the work of academics (the Austrian School of economists from the 1930s who favoured the theoretical elegance of free markets left wholly untouched; and the 'monetarism' of Milton Friedman, American winner of the Nobel Prize for Economics in 1976, who argued that nothing should be controlled but the value of a currency, the rest of an economy could, and should, be allowed to collapse if necessary). These principles were cooked up and given credibility by the work of radical think-tanks.

In the new administration's first budget in June 1979, the top rate of income tax was cut from 80% to 60%. There was an immediate switch of focus to indirect taxation and increases in VAT, emphasising the importance of free consumer choice. The cost of NHS prescriptions went up 600%. Exchange controls were scrapped, allowing money to be invested wherever it could find the best returns internationally. This created a free market for investments that was heaven sent for London's financial services industry, delivering a new fluidity, speed and scale to how self-selected groups of élites could get rich. An American businessman was brought in to deal with the state-run British Steel operation. Ian Mc-Gregor stripped out 95,000 jobs between 1979 and 1983, and was then, fatefully, sent on to deal with the National Coal Board.

The whole nature of the battle with unions had changed by 1979 and the Winter of Discontent. This was the biggest wave of stoppages since the General Strike in 1926, and the strikes among civil servants and traffic wardens, dinner ladies and journalists, was for Tory followers another example of the insidious hand of socialism. But by this stage there was far less, if any, political dimension involved. Back in 1975, a poll of union members had found 86% believed in a free enterprise society, 66% were opposed to more nationalisation. A union card had become less about membership of a socialist brotherhood than the chance, at last, to afford a new car and a holiday in Marbella.

The early Seventies were the hinterland years of uncertainty. But by the time *Gregory's Girl* was being written
there was a sense of hope that change, at the very least, was
coming. The subsequent excesses of Thatcherism were less a
reaction against the mistakes of the Seventies than the result
of a hard gleam of confidence, encouraged by the growing
popular support for tough political radicalism. The Government knew vast revenues from North Sea oil were on their
way to buoy the economy, that council housing stock and
state-owned industries were a gold mine. They could afford
to be audacious, and turn away, unmoved, from the everyday
suffering being caused.

*

A special hatred for the Prime Minister was cherished in the
arts. Jonathan Miller, a gentleman of the theatre and opera
world, described her as "loathsome, repulsive in almost every
way". "Why hate her?" he pondered. "It's the same as why
the bulk of the human race hate typhoid."[21] Bill Forsyth, by
contrast, appeared on the surface to have pulled the covers
over his head. "Forsyth's Scotland," noted *The New Yorker* and
New York Times contributor Scott Malcomson, "is extremely
distant from the serious world of political conflict."[22] "I'm
very self-conscious about using politics in film," explained
Forsyth in 1986.

> "I don't want to make films that are about
> something, I don't want to make a film that is
> about a man in a post-industrial urban soci-

ety who is trying to find out who he is and
what he is doing. I want to make films about
what it is like to be him. I don't want to make
films about situations but what it's like to be
in situations and that's why I always avoid
issues. I want to make films about what IT is
like, rather than about IT."[23]

Showing not telling. Life as it as actually lived, not told
through man-handled concepts. And the film vocabulary he
used, again, was humour and irony. Like Ronnie in *That
Sinking Feeling* trying to end his miserably dull life by drowning himself in a bowl of cornflakes. "I wanted to capture the
sense of the kids' isolation and emptiness."[24] The toy town
of Middleton is the anti-Glasgow, "overindulged":
"Gregory's life is all organised for him, he doesn't have to
worry if somebody's going to feed him, and he's got his best
friend and his sister to turn to, to sustain him emotionally. All
he's got to do is worry about who he's in love with. And the
environment, the layout of the New Town, is antiseptic and
almost luxurious, so I was seeing all that not just in relation
to *That Sinking Feeling* but also in contrast to the real lives of
some of the kids who were acting in *Gregory's Girl*."[25] Privileged but no less banal and lacking in real chances of a
meaningful life. In the draft script, teacher Alistair observes
that the Middletown kids' "chances of getting into university
are ten times less than those of ending up in the 'loony bin'".

*

The English newspapers had plenty of other frightening things to write about, like the invasion of the Scots. Every two years, Scottish football fans would arrive at Wembley for the Home International series in May. For a big Tennents-flavoured embrace. The last clash at Wembley in 1977 had ended in an historic victory for Ally MacLeod's Scotland, 2-1, in front of 100,000 fans — most of them Scottish, Rod Stewart and Gordon Strachan among them — who'd ended up pouring onto the pitch to celebrate. The Scots players were lifted onto the shoulders of the crowd as heroes, decked out with Tartan scarves and flags; fans flocked to swing on the goalposts until the bar snapped, and there was a final swell of emotion as they came together and sang Stewart's mega-hit from 1975, 'Sailing'. The next day, the poor fretful souls at the *Daily Mirror* wrote about "Scottish hordes" having "mutilated" Wembley's "hallowed turf". Reports suggested "riots" in the streets of London. Scottish fans had been seen getting onto trains home with armfuls of muddy football pitch, and at least one group had been carrying a section of crossbar.

Scotland weren't brave no-hopers anymore. The spine of the two most successful football clubs of the late Seventies, Liverpool and Nottingham Forest, was made of Scottish players: Kenny Dalglish, Alan Hansen, John Robertson, John O'Hare, John McGovern, Graeme Souness, Archie Gemmill. It was Scotland, not England, that represented Britain at the 1978 World Cup and Ladbrokes made them 8-1 to become world champions. Merchandisers went into overdrive, selling greetings cards with pictures of the Scottish team, celebratory aftershave, blokes' soap-on-a-rope, a collectable range of beer tankards at Esso petrol stations. The tournament itself, though, turned out to be a nightmare for the team and the fans who'd travelled to Argentina for their once-in-a-lifetime football carnival. Scotland were beaten 3-1 by an unfancied team from Peru, followed by a draw with Iran. "All this way for SFA" said one press head-line; angry fans got themselves into punch-ups in the Argen-tine streets; one record shop in Dundee ended up selling off its unwanted stock of 'Ally's Tartan Army' vinyl singles for 1p, encouraging customers to smash them with a hammer on the counter. The lasting memory for fans though would be Archie Gemmill's belated goal — a beautifully fluent football doodle — that meant Scotland ended their World Cup with a win against the mighty Holland. Who needed Johan Cruy-ff?[26]

Then there was the Bay City Rollers, the first boy band and Britain's most popular musical export since the Beatles. Rollermania had spread to the USA and Australia, and just the filming of the Edinburgh lads' weekly show for ITV, *Shang-a-Lang*, was a hazard to public health. One distant sighting of Les, Woody, Eric, Alan and Derek in their clingy v-neck tops and Royal Stewart tartan trousers, would fill young hearts with madness, there'd be a swarm and crush of fan girls in their home-made tartan-trimmed outfits, tartan caps, rosettes and pin badges, a blind surge through the po-lice cordons. While the Rollers went out of fashion (tartan scarves tossed to the back of wardrobes), *Gregory's Girl* came into a world of Cool-ish Caledonia. It was no surprise to anyone that Scotland had produced such a refreshing piece of cinema, an artefact of what we might now describe as nerdy outsider hip. Scotland was less stuffy, less tainted by the Seventies malaise, more easily able to shake off seedy old habits and say something different.

There was more to perceptions of Scotland than pop culture. For hundreds of years, Scotland had been trying to assert its own distinctive identity separate from the English, driven for the most part by the romanticism of Sir Walter Scott and his novels and poetry, a need to preserve the particular rural tang of Scottish life and culture from urbanisation and the commercial energy of England, with its rationalising and standardising tendencies. The bullying nature of the relationship over history — the bloody wars of independence, English violence against the clans — couldn't be forgotten. This led to an emphasis on the folk roots of old Scotland, what became known as 'tartanry' (using the kind of romantic Highland symbols, settings and costumes that would feature on millions of shortbread biscuit tins and boxes of porridge, and be the template for films like *Rob Roy* (1953) and *Kidnapped* (1960)). There was also the 'kailyard' tradition (taken from a Robert Burns poem, meaning cabbage or vegetable patch, the main form of sustenance for the simple souls of villages, full of rustic nous and wit). Both involved a soft, twilit nostalgia rather than specific relevance to the changing times and lives of Scots themselves. A stunting of imaginative possibilities, and as a consequence, there was never thought to be a separate Scottish intelligentsia.

At the same time, it should be said that cultural influence was far from being one way. Victorian Britain was notably Scottish and Presbyterian in character, with its popular enthusiasm for thrift and self-help. Empire-building and colonial rule was very much a joint venture that the Scottish population both influenced and benefited from at least as much, if not sometimes more than, the rest of Britain[27].

By the Seventies there were new reasons for tension in the union. In 1975 the Queen had pushed a gold-plated button in the headquarters of BP in Aberdeen to mark the opening of the first oil pipeline from the North Sea. Oil was going to make Britain (yes, *Britain*) rich. Police were everywhere, locking down the area to keep out members of the Tartan Army, a nationalist group that had previously planted bombs around the pipeline works in protest. "By 1985, the Labour Secretary of State for Energy will be chairman of OPEC," predicted Harold Wilson, in jaunty mood[28]. The Scottish Nationalist Party, meanwhile, had adopted a straightforward slogan: "It's Scotland's Oil". The SNP argued Scotland alone should be on the road to becoming the wealthiest country in Europe, and started warming up its contacts in OPEC, the US, and the other main oil producer in the region, Norway. The referendum vote on Scottish devolution, when it came in 1979, became mixed up with more immediate issues. The oil revenues were still only an unconvincing trickle and Scots were worried about unemployment and a weak economy, which meant the turnout wasn't big enough to make the majority vote for independence legally binding. If the vote had happened two years later, once the effects of Thatcherite policies had been seen and felt, the turnout would have been different. Things got worse, far worse, than the bitter days recorded in *That Sinking Feeling*. Between 1981 and 1983, the number of jobless in Scotland doubled.

Forsyth always felt at home in Scotland. His early inspiration had been to make films for Scottish people. "I live in Glasgow at the moment," he said, in 1986, "because it's comfortable for me to be here and there's nowhere I've worked that I'd prefer to be. Also in a certain sense I have a backlog of living and ideas that rest within this city. I did not start making feature films until I was 30 years old, so that means that there is 30 years worth of material waiting to be used in this city."[29] He didn't think there was anything wrong with films that were provincial, they were stamped with character from a cultural identity: "If a film isn't provincial then it's from nowhere."[30] Later, working on Dylan Thomas's piece of Welsh history, *Rebecca's Daughter*, Forsyth planned for the setting to be transplanted to Scotland. By 2008 he was talking about himself as a Burns-like figure (celebrated and then ditched by the English establishment): "the retiring ploughman poet of Scottish cinema (living up a hill with some trout as neighbours)."[31]

Even so, Forsyth's films have sometimes had a lukewarm response from Scottish film academics and commentators. The influential *Scotch Reels* essays[32] in 1982 placed Forsyth more in the tradition of *Whisky Galore!* and *The Maggie*, and uninvolved with the job of creating a genuinely modern Scottish cinema. When it arrived, *Local Hero* was written off in Scotch Reels quarters as just another unhelpful *Brigadoon*. Like a Scots hero of his, the Orkney poet George Mackay Brown, Forsyth's attachment to Scotland was through people and places, not politics. He never wanted to be part of the loaded debate on Scottish film, what was 'right' and 'wrong'. Cumbernauld had been such a useful setting because there was nothing very obviously Scottish about it. "I wasn't trying to say something culturally about Scotland," admitted Forsyth, perhaps tired of being expected to speak for Scotland rather than himself.

> "I don't know what Scotland means to the guy next to me on the bus. It's too dumb an idea to want to nail. A culture comes from making stuff, and the accumulation of that stuff finally reflects a culture. Scotland's always been one of these little countries that had an identity problem. It's either had an inferiority complex, or the opposite. It's just a little schizophrenic nation like most little nations seeking an identity. There's nothing awfully special about it. There's history, but every place on earth has its history."[33]

*

Yawning, still on the sofa with the papers, the nest of tables littered with teacups and the Rover biscuit tin. Nothing on the telly until *Worzel Gummidge* and then later there's a showing of *Jesus Christ Superstar*. Back to the ads in the *Mail on Sunday*, the chipper voice of Noel Edmonds on the radio in the background. Must be time for a new car — even Keith and Joan had got another one. The Fiesta looks nippy, kind of sleek. If a bit pricey at £2,260. The kids want a fizzy. And everyone wants one of these: a Ferguson VHS Video Cassette Recorder. Christ alive though — six hundred quid. I mean, how many times over would they watch want to watch

Goldfinger or *The Sound of Music* again anyway? A two-bed house for £18,000 and it's only terraced. Fitted kitchen units though — and trees and space. Looks like it could be a country cottage from the picture, a brand new one. New houses being built everywhere on the outskirts of places nowadays. You need a car to do anything.

New towns and the growth of suburbs were a familiar post-war phenomenon across the world. Within the US psyche the suburban home was a centrepiece, the neat green lawn and white picket fence, the giant tub of car in the drive. Before 1939 just 13% of Americans lived in suburbs; in the 21st century the proportion has become closer to half the entire population. The popular image was powerful enough to obscure the truth about what living in such well-organised and managed domains was actually like. In the US, the suburbs meant stratification by class and race, whether through legal covenants preventing the sale of property to 'less desirable' occupants or through social pressures and pricing. Unlike traditional towns and their hubbub of homes and shops and factories, suburbs felt mass-produced, antiseptic and isolating. The same was happening in the UK. "Used to the grubby intimacy of city life, transplanted urbanites missed the profusion of corner pubs, neighborhood dance halls, local cinemas, and the ready help of neighbors and friends," reported *Time* magazine in 1961. "Psychiatric cases are significantly higher than in the rest of Britain."[34] But people want shiny new things, wrapped in cellophane, factory fresh. The British in the Seventies were becoming far more self-conscious, comparing themselves with lifestyles they saw in the magazine ads and on TV. There now seemed nothing wrong with aspiring to more gracious and affluent ways, even if that meant becoming detached from the old (and, frankly, 'common') habits they'd been brought up with. The insular little worlds made up of the factory, corner shop, family and pub — involving membership of a community of gossip, rough jokes and nosy familiarity — was being superseded by individual lives and the space and air that came with them. Marks & Spencer-style. The ease of wheeling a trolley through the supermarket; the soothing soft lighting of shopping centres, cool and natureless; dinner parties and drinks at home; package holidays abroad to places where the rest of the estate wouldn't follow. People were becoming more like customers — not members of anything that would oblige them to give up their time and attention to people wanting protracted conversation, company, favours, or sympathy for their ailments.

A boom in the development of out-of-town supermarkets took place in the late Seventies, led by Asda, Co-Op, Fine Fare, Tesco and Morrisons. In 1973 the average adult was drinking nine pints of wine a year (pints? only the British would have measured wine consumption that way); by 1980 the figure had climbed to 20 pints a year. Shoppers were starting to buy more olive oil, and for cooking with rather than cleaning out their ear wax. The most watched TV programme of the decade (with more than 23 million viewers in October 1979) was the last episode of the first series of *To the Manor Born*: another signal of how sympathies and aspirations had been changing in the mass of British homes. Penelope Keith was no longer the awful snob Margo Leadbetter, but the upholder of a very British heritage and civil-ised values that were admired and needed protection.

In the late Seventies there was still friction between working-class and middle-class identities, with one not yet dominant over the other. The standard of what made people 'normal', in their fashions and attitudes and beliefs, was far more weakly imposed, and so people and personalities were more various, less smoothed over by media and marketing (the kind of mass messaging and reinforcement that makes us cool and smiley consumers, love our me-time, expensive trainers, iPhones and streaming services). Seventies life, in the shopping streets, the estates, around the pubs and foot-ball grounds, in the cinema queues, was more roughly tex-tured, more smelly; harder and slower, without the support of digital aids and navigation, more exposed and susceptible to the seasons, the smoke and chill of winter in particular; a life that was seen and felt in less mediated ways. There were fewer expectations and lower expectations — and when happiness came, because of love or children or a windfall of money, or maybe just out of nowhere while crossing the street, it was more in the form of momentary sparks and glow of embers to be grateful for, not a comfortable asset that could be kept in the bank as a prop to health, wellbeing or identity.

*

Abronhill High School was demolished in 2013, just 35 years after it had been opened. Cumbernauld's population had stopped growing and the school had been half full for years.

There's nothing left now of the school or its red ash playground (the one physical object from the school that still exists is the piano played by Chic Murray, now installed in Cumbernauld High down the road). Ten years on, the school site is still unused but earmarked for another phase of 're-generation' from 2028 at the earliest, two new primary schools, smarter shops and housing, a central hub to bring the community together — as if none of the past decline and slide into dis-use had ever happened.

I went to the old Abronhill Shopping Centre instead. It was lunchtime by now and some school kids were buying pies from the Spar and standing around with their smart-phones. Metal shutters were pulled down on the Trio fish and chip shop where Gregory took his dates (called Capaldi's in the film). There's not much else to the place. Some benches for sitting and eating your chips, and a dingy plastic-roofed arcade. The planting and greenery that can be seen in the film has gone. I bought a Spar sandwich and wandered over to the bus timetable to see if I could save myself the long walk back into town.

"You don' wannae be takin notice of that. It's BC," said a voice behind me.

"Sorry?"

"Before Covid pal."

A feller in a shell suit. We exchanged knowing shrugs and smiles about the state of the world and its mess. He sat back down with his mate on the bench by the bus stop, and I went on looking for the phone box where Carol changed outfits for her night out (transformed into a 'punk witch' according to the script), a petite 17 year-old who'd needed to stand on a

box so the camera could see her. Many of the pathways close to the film's Pine Grove HQ were used to film scenes of the lads going home from school, bragging about the importance of "doing it", as well as Gregory's evening out; but they're snippets of places, separate locations from around Abronhill that were cut and gummed together. For the *Gregory's Girl* tourist it's a spiral of grey blocks of flats, bridges and tunnels, with no sign of a phone box or where it might have been, and no-one around to ask or who'd even know what I was talking about. Driving the bus for the 'Forsyth Safari' movie location tour would be a shit job in Cumbernauld. Always backing in and out of dead-ends, gears crunching, back on the ring road again to find the site of another brief clip.

I ended up back at Abronhill's Shopping Centre. A place that on a return visit looked even more like it was waiting for demolition. The shell suit man was still there. A bus finally arrived, but he wasn't interested in getting on anyway. Just sitting on the bench, calling out to anyone passing by to see if he could start up a conversation.

*

In Scotland, *Gregory's Girl* premiered at the Odeon in Renfield Street, a monumental piece of Art Deco design with a mighty set of lines and curves reminiscent of 1930s New York. By 1981 the epic grandeur of the original's internal arrangement had been modernised to suit changing business models, and the auditorium which had once seated a giant crowd of 2,800 people had been broken into three screens[35]. It was still a big cinema in Glasgow and a big night. Everyone was there, the cast and crew had got dressed up and brought their friends along; even some Scottish showbiz celebrities had turned up. This was suddenly more exciting than they'd expected, a real buzz. "I was standing around with my friend Grace Glover," remembered Rab.

> "We were next to this group of women who kept looking over at us, and I thought, okay, they've recognised me. They kept looking over whispering to each other, looking over again, giggling. I thought, y'know I'm going to have to get used to this now. So I said to Grace, quick! they're coming over for an autograph and I've not got a pen or anything! She finds me a pen and a bit of paper and these women start coming over. They walk straight past me, they've seen Johnny Beattie

World Charity Premiere

Gregory's Girl A

Written and Directed by Bill Forsyth

Released by ITC Film Distributors Ltd

All proceeds to The Variety Club of Great Britain (Scottish Committee)
(Tent 36: the greatest children's charity in the world)

Sunday May 3. ODEON 1– ODEON FILM CENTRE – GLASGOW

DOORS OPEN 7.15 p.m.
PROGRAMME COMMENCES 8.00 p.m.

DRESS INFORMAL

ROW/SEAT

X   9

Courtesy of Douglas Sannachan

[a stand-up comedian and actor famous for the *Scotch & Wry* sketch show on BBC Scotland, as well as *Johnny Beattie's Saturday Night Show*]."[36]

Chic Murray, was asked to say a few words to introduce the film to the audience. "He gets up and starts telling everyone what was going to happen in the film," said Sanny, "he's ex plaining the whole lot of the story, everything. Someone had to basically go and rugby-tackle him to get him off the stage. It was brilliant." The evening got even better with the reception held at the City Chambers in George Square. Party guests climbed the marble staircases to its illuminated galleries, lit up like a set of golden jewellery boxes. An ornate heaven, blessed by bottles of drink everywhere. "I found a plastic bag and was clinking on the way out," confessed Sanny[37].

For some of the cast, the first time they saw the film was at the National Film Theatre on the South Bank in London. Another big party. Clare remembers the fun of a group of them taking the sleeper train down, arriving in the city and going to Michael Radford's flat to change and get ready. "We didn't know anything about the significance of the film then, so no pressure. Those days I just couldn't get over the amount of free drink on offer." Watching the film itself proved the hard part. The first time Clare saw the film in its entirety was at a BFI event in 2018. "But it was the most amazing calling card for me. I've been so many places and had a lovely welcome, because of *Gregory's Girl*."[38]

"I was very excited to show my girlfriend some proof of my showbiz career, so we both went along," said Gerry.

> "On the night I introduced her to Bill and to John Gow, the editor. From the beginning I was nudging her and whispering, 'Right, this is one of my scenes coming up now'. This went on far too long, and I realised all my scenes [with the motorway gang] had been cut. Later I asked John why Bill hadn't thought to mention the small matter of my being dumped on the cutting-room floor. John reckoned that Bill was just too scared to tell me in case I freaked out."[39]

Gordon hadn't seen the film as a whole before, the filming was just bits and pieces, and also hadn't really thought about how he might come across on the big screen. But he was the hero though, right? All Gordon saw was awkwardness. An un-faked awkwardness that, he thought, made Gregory look like a fool and ruined the film. He "stormed out" of the screening early.[40]

While Sinclair has long been reconciled to his youthful contribution to the film, turning up for BFI anniversary events and interviews, he's become tired of being asked about it. Since 2012 he has been JG Sinclair, the writer of a series of unsparingly dark crime thrillers. (Soft like Gregory? Nah, put some Mafia brutality and slasher killings in your pipe and smoke it). At book signings, people still want to talk about Gregory. He's polite, of course, but tends to change the subject.

Arriving at the special screening at the Odeon in Leicester Square, Dee Hepburn remembers a growing sense of wonder at what was happening.

> "When they said it had a guaranteed general release, I just thought it meant it wasn't going to be ditched at least, it was going to get shown somewhere, not that it would go everywhere. There was a Q&A on stage before the film was shown and Gordon was holding my hand grimly as we walked back to our seats, like we'd been fed to the lions. When the film started it was amazing to see and hear everyone around us laughing. Gordon pointed out a large man behind us who'd taken out his hankie, he was howling. For Bill it must have been incredible to see that — to

know he'd accomplished what he set out to
do, make people laugh."[41]

None of this means it's made watching the film any easier for
her either. Since that night at the Odeon, Dee has only seen
Gregory's Girl three times. In the aftermath of the film's release, Dee also had to fend off an industry that saw commercial potential in Dorothy, or, at least, in the end of Dorothy's
tantalising innocence. The film offers came rolling in, like
the female lead in *Bolero* (1984) (about a young woman's
search to find the 'right man' to take her virginity); and *Cast-
away* (1986) (getting naked on a beach with Oliver Reed).
Even back at home in East Kilbride there were problems. "I
started getting calls from this weird guy threatening to attack
me. He'd say that he'd seen me and he would recount exactly where I had been. It was horrible. One day, he said:
'I'm just going to have to kill you.' We phoned the police.
They never found out who he was, but things like that don't
go away, do they?"[42]

For most of the cast there was an all-too sudden return
to reality. A few months before the film's release, Rab had
found a backstage job working at the Cumbernauld Theatre.
So when *Gregory's Girl* was first shown in the town, Rab was
both one of the stars on the screen and the film's projectionist. "Reality kicked in when I headed back to Glasgow after
the shoot days," said Sanny. "It all felt like a bit of a dream
really, the portrayal of that working boy in an awesome new
town with a bright future ahead. Then you wake up unemployed in the east end of Glasgow."[43]

The film's legacy has been soured in other ways. It's now out-of-step with 'woke' critics and viewers who can be ever-alert to the pleasures of being outraged. The night nurse scene — with the boys who consider seeing a naked woman through a window as one of the wonders of being alive — has been singled out as inappropriate. Amoral[44]. Misogynist. Academics have argued that while women might seem to have the power in the film, they are only powerful for the sake of Gregory's experience. And it's *Gregory's* girl isn't it — so he *possesses* her. Should Billy really be offering cigarettes to a young girl? The list goes on. "Intolerant (and ignorant) film commentators are watching older films through a Millennial retrospective lens and making value judgements based on fashionable, modern interpretations of ethics," Gerry has said, reflecting on the survival of the film's reputation. "For example, I recently heard a podcast 'review' of *GG* in which the commentators wondered why Gregory and Madeleine are apparently parentless. Where are the adults in charge of all the kids outside his house? Why does his dad (when he does make an appearance) casually allow his driving pupil to continue to steer towards Gregory? Why is the coach allowed alone with a female pupil in the female dressing rooms? And so they go on and on, utterly failing to understand the concepts of fiction and humour, let alone make allowances for alternative perspectives from previous generations."[45]

[1] Allan Hunter, 'Being Human', *Sight and Sound*, August 1994, pp. 24–28.

[2] John Brown, 'A Suitable Job for a Scot', *Sight and Sound*, Spring 1984, p157.

[3] JW Rinzler, *The Making of Star Wars*, Aurum Press, 2013.

[4] Dominic Sandbrook, *Seasons in the Sun*, Allen Lane, 2012.

[5] Andy Beckett, *When the Lights Went Out: What Really Happened to Britain in the Seventies*, Faber and Faber, 2009.

[6] Dominic Sandbrook, ibid.

[7] Andy Beckett, ibid.

[8] Ibid.

[9] Bill Forsyth, contributing to a panel discussion on the 80s 'renaissance' in British film-making, Torino Film Festival, 25 November 2008.

[10] British Film Institute figures.

[11] James Park, *Learning to Dream: The New British Cinema*, Faber & Faber, 1984, p13.

[12] Graham Stewart, *Bang! A History of Britain in the 1980s*, Atlantic Books, 2013, p261.

[13] Ibid.

[14] Caroline Guthrie, Telephone interview, 27 June 2022.

[15] John Brown, ibid.

[16] *Gregory's Girl* DVD, audio commentary — Bill Forsyth and Mark Kermode, 2019.

[17] Bill Forsyth interview, BBC Scotland Afternoon Show, 19 April 2021.

[18] Radio interview with Bill Forsyth, The Leonard Leopate Show, 2010.

[19] Dee Hepburn got involved with supporting fundraising and awareness-raising campaigns for women's football after 1981, laying the foundations for the sudden rise in popularity of women's football in the 21st century.

[20] Andy McSmith, *No Such Thing as Society: A History of Britain in the 1980s*, Constable, 2010, p27.

[21] Graham Stewart, ibid., p227.

22 Scott L Malcomson, 'Modernism Comes to the Cabbage Patch: Bill Forsyth and the "Scottish Cinema"', University of California Press Film Quarterly, 1985.

23 Dominique Toyeux, 'Tidings of Comfort and Joy, an interview with Bill Forsyth', *Cinema Cessenta*, March/April 1986.

24 Gerald Peary, 'Bill Forsyth', www.geraldpeary.com, September 1985.

25 John Brown, ibid.

26 The world's most famous footballer at the time and the star of the Holland team. Cruyff had decided not to travel to Argentina for the World Cup because of fears over security. There had been a recent attempt to kidnap him and his family at gunpoint in Barcelona.

27 TM Devine, *The Scottish Nation 1700-2000*, Penguin, 1999, p291.

28 Andy Beckett, p189.

29 Dominique Toyeux, 'Tidings of *Comfort and Joy*, an interview with Bill Forsyth', *Cinema Cessenta*, March/April 1986.

30 Bill Forsyth, *Sight and Sound*, Vol. 50, 1981.

31 Tim Teeman, 'Bill Forsyth: the reluctant father of Gregory's Girl', *The Times*, 6 February 2008.

32 Colin McArthur ed, *Scotch Reels: Scotland in Cinema and Television*, BFI Publishing, 1982.

33 'Director Bill Forsyth: Nothing special about Scotland', *The Scotsman*, 22 February 2016.

34 'The City: New Town Blues', *Time*, 18 August 1961.

35 The Renfield Street Odeon was closed in 2006 and the building was left empty and boarded up for many years. It's now a German Doner Kebab restaurant.

36 Rab Buchanan, Telephone conversation, 10 August 2022.

37 Douglas Sannachan, Telephone conversation, 9 August 2022.

38 Clare Grogan, Telephone conversation, 23 February 2023.

39 Gerry Clark, Email conversation, 15 July 2022.

40 BFI *Gregory's Girl* Q&A session, 5 December 2015.

41 Dee Hepburn, Telephone interview, 16 January 2023.

[42] Mary Hannigan, 'For a young one obsessed with football, *Gregory's Girl* was heaven', *Irish Times*, 3 March 2021.

[43] Douglas Sannachan, Email, 24 March 2023.

[44] Ben Lambert, Notebook Primer: Bill Forsyth, MUBI, 29 July 2021.

[45] Gerry Clark, ibid.

10. Alone

"In another million years...there'll be no men, no women...there'll just be people...
Just a whole world full of wankers."

A *ndrina* was like a ghost. A gentle apparition made from rain and mist and shadows on stone, a visitor for St Andrew's Day in 1981. A short TV drama set on the lonely shores of Orkney, where the fire in the grate and sounds of curlew calls from the marshes are like company. A piece that has since disappeared into the aether.

Andrina was shown on Monday 30 November, BBC 1, 9.25pm until 10pm (followed by highlights of the snooker quarter-finals from Preston)[1]. Bill Forsyth adapted the script from a story by George Mackay Brown, and directed the filming with actor Cyril Cusack in the lead role. Gregory's Dad, Dave Anderson, turns up as the pub landlord. There have been no repeats and the master negatives and soundtrack have stayed in their original, unrestored state in the BBC Scotland archive. Mackay Brown's biographer doesn't mention it — even though it's the only filmed adaptation of his work in existence. So *Andrina* is a dim memory shared by the few who took notice of its fleeting visit. A face at the window.

The author, the bard of Orkney, would have been one of those watching TV that night, a reclusive figure holed up in his ex-council flat in Stromness. For many years he'd railed against the intrusion of modern technologies and attitudes into the life of the island — wrecking age-old harmonies, such as our susceptibility to the moods of natural landscapes — but he'd changed his mind about TV. *Horizon* documentaries and *Countdown* were among his favourites. As a Catholic, George loved Evelyn Waugh's novel *Brideshead Revisited* and would have been glued to the TV adaptation, airing weekly during the same period that *Andrina* was broadcast.

In his short stories and poetry, Mackay Brown managed to generate a vivid sense of life from a spartan stock of materials. A single, sea-bound location. An intimate, hand-to-mouth reality of living, but one that's suspended in great gulfs of space and time, suggesting how thousands of years of history always remain with us. Time collapses — because time is just an idea after all, it has no physical reality. Orkney, by contrast, is the ever-present, material proof of his thinking. Its rocks and boiling seas are a constantly pressing argument for not taking the modern world too seriously, for never believing that contemporary life — with all its silly obsessions with careers and status, fitted kitchens and dances and make-up — is more than a paltry distraction, a moment's gloss. That kind of perspective didn't mean people's lives couldn't be painful. Mackay Brown was always aware of an immanent sadness to human relationships and how small acts of carelessness and pettiness could lead to broken lives, never mended.

Andrina is one example of that. An old seaman, Captain Torvald, lives alone in an Orkney village. A young woman starts to come to visit his cottage every winter afternoon before it gets dark. "She lights my lamp, sets the peat fire in a blaze, sees that there is enough water in my bucket that stands on the wall niche."[2] The Captain tells Andrina stories of his life, including some fragments about his first love, Sigrid. "It was a tale soaked in the light of a single brief summer. The boy and girl, it seemed, lived on each other's heartbeats...They walked day after day beside shining beckoning waters."[3] She'd become pregnant, but, as he explains (and more to himself than to Andrina), he was just too young to be a father then. So he'd booked his passage to the other side of the world, left Sigrid behind and only returned to the island after 50 years of being a working sailor. The day after telling his story the Captain falls ill, but Andrina doesn't arrive at her normal time that evening — and doesn't come again. He asks around in the village about her, but no-one knows who she is, or has ever heard her name.

Forsyth turned this 10 page short story into a 35 minute TV drama — so it's more than an adaptation, it's a Forsyth script built around Mackay Brown's theme. The bond between the Captain and Andrina is given more time to grow. We see the beginnings of affection start to kindle

and flicker up into the jokes and banter they share, how it
becomes a saving infusion of comfort and peace into the
cold bones of the cottage. We get to know Andrina as a confident girl, full of both grace and fun. The first time she
meets him he's had too much whisky: "C'mon you old fool,"
she says, "unless you want to spend the night in a ditch."[4]
Forsyth stokes up the warmth of their relationship through
desultory conversations and teasing. The Captain enjoys
telling his tall stories, like the one about a shipwreck where
the crew ate everything they could find, the wood of the ship
and the oil, before they eventually turned to cannibalism and
ate each other. "What did the first mate taste like? That's the
question." There was only one survivor, one cannibal left,
the Captain tells her. Had he ever met him? Andrina asks.
No, but he'd been pointed out to him once when he was in a
bar in Hong Kong. "He was looking peckish when he came
in —" and then he lunges to try and bite Andrina.

The Captain knows she's fishing for his secrets, she's
curious and coaxing: "I've laughed at your silly jokes, tell
me." She reads Joseph Conrad to him and an old Scots
poem. "Not all sad things are beautiful," concludes the Captain.

The underlying lyricism of the piece is brought to the
surface in the TV version. By emphasising the silences of an
old man's life on a remote island, the sounds of sea birds
crossing open skies; sweet low calls and twittering from
somewhere in the wet sands, the curlew and the eider duck.
Forsyth contrasts timeless Orkney with snatches of pop culture from 1981 — the past and present rub against each other so we feel the passing of time, how distant and unrecover-

able the Captain's past has become to him. A folksy DJ (a forerunner of Dickie Bird) reads out announcements about the lifeboat guild annual sale and the local ladies group, and plays a mix of different memories: Jona Lewie's 'Stop the Cavalry', a recent Christmas hit; Merle Haggard's 'Okie from Muskogee' ("We don't smoke marijuana in Muskogee/ We don't take our trips on LSD."); Shirley Lewis's 'The Clapping Song'; Ella Fitzgerald and 'Sentimental Journey'.

The pair sit together in the evening and look at the stars. Andrina fusses over him, how he really needs to be wearing an overcoat. The Captain knows he doesn't deserve the attention he's getting, the gift of her presence, knows he owes her the story she's been waiting for about his first love for Sigrid — so he tells her the story, in a breezy, raffish way, as if she should be sorry for him: "All the love I've given or had was in that one summer. It's had to last me a lifetime." This is where the mood changes, with Andrina's soft, quiet, emotional whisper: "What a sad, bad man you are. What a sad, silly boy. That's more horrible than your cannibals."

The Captain's ill-health and Andrina's troubling disappearance is balanced by jokes. In the village pub, the landlord is complaining about the arrival of new gadgets: "Aye, you get batteries for everything now, even for hens." The Captain tells him about Andrina and his feverish illness. Maybe she was just a figment of his imagination suggests the landlord. "You're lucky," he adds. "I keep seein the wife when I'm in fever — whas your secret?"[5] In the post office, they're more interested in another local character. "Ahh, another plain brown package for Alec." "Hmm," says the dubious postmistress. They've also received a letter for the Captain that has taken months to arrive from Australia. It's a letter from Sigrid. She's been trying to find him for the past 50 years and wonders if he has finally returned home from the sea. Sigrid tells him about his daughter, and that she now has a granddaughter, Andrina, who has often wondered about the Captain and if he might be lonely: "I wish I knew that grandfather of mine," Andrina had often said to her. "I think he would be glad of somebody to make him a pot of tea and to see to his fire. Some day I'm going to Scotland and I'm going to knock on his door, wherever he lives". But this was not going to happen, Sigrid had written, so many months ago, because Andrina had died "suddenly, in the first stirrings of spring".[6]

The film ends with the Captain sitting alone with his radio. The presenter reads out a notice about a lost cat, a Django Rheinhardt number plays that's reminiscent of old times and that long-ago summer.

Andrina was included in both the *Penguin Book of Ghost Stories* (1985) and a collection of *Scottish Love Stories* (1995). The piece, though, is too delicate a construction, evanescent with different strands of feeling, for genre categories. The mystery for us is how Bill Forsyth came across the story in the first place. It wasn't published until 1983 (in a collection which is regarded overall as Mackay Brown's weakest, from a period when he'd grown tired of the hamster's wheel of writing). The most likely explanation would be a recommendation from Steven Campbell via Gunnie Moberg, the Swedish photographer who'd moved to Orkney with her family in 1976, becoming close friends with Mackay Brown. They worked together on a number of books, her pictures, his poems. We know Gunnie was also friends with Steven and Bill from the photographs she took of them together (and of Bill during a film shoot, asleep under his hat)[7]. Mackay Brown involved Steven in providing illustrations to his *Scottish Bestiary* project in 1986, so may well have had connections for years before then.

Andrina and Forsyth were made for each other. Scotland's cool summer twilight, the one that the Captain and Sigrid (and Gregory and Susan) once met in, is part of Forsyth's psychological landscape. *Andrina* is about another nuanced, non-traditional love story (like that of Gregory and his sister), and how feelings of 'love' shouldn't be confined by stereotypes. The most rewarding relations between people — like the temporary light and warmth brought into the life of an old man — don't need to be signposted and self-conscious, or even have to make sense in ordinary terms, they have their own value and meaning.

There might have been another kind of sympathy between Forsyth and what he'd read in Mackay Brown's work. In the short stories, love recurs as something that appears briefly but never matures or evolves. It's not allowed to stay, it can't stay. The pattern is a mirror to Mackay Brown's own life. Catholicism, along with a shyness caused by years of illness and self-consciousness about the physical effects of tuberculosis, meant he backed away from love-making and ended relationships early. He was very used to younger women, often fans of his work, coming into his life with their sunny presence, as well as their eventual leaving for one reason or another; it happened many times. What this means is that Mackay Brown worked with loneliness, used it as a resource, made it a part of his modus operandi. He spent months at a time in hospitals convalescing from TB and bronchitis throughout his life. Himself, a bed and a heap of books.

As author and Forsyth fan Jonathan Coe has pointed out: "it's kind of the missing piece in the Bill Forsyth jig-saw…There seems to be a big shift in tone and ambition between *Gregory's Girl* and *Local Hero*, and that makes sense if you've seen *Andrina*, because that's the film that kind of links the two."[8] *Andrina* has been ignored — not only because of its transience — but because it doesn't fit the expected arc of a career: how Forsyth went from the success of one film to a bigger budget, working with bigger name actors and in the US. In-between was this telling clue to the man, because it was something personal that he had chosen consciously to do.

"I'm a writer at heart," said Forsyth in 2011[9]. Writing made it possible for him to be in charge of the ideas and for the emotional language to stay intact. "I wouldn't know how to make *Robocop 3*, wouldn't know how or why. I'm not a film-maker, I'm just someone who has put certain ideas on film."[10] Writing came with "a feeling of freedom…because you can write whatever you want."[11] Filming things didn't give the words life, but was a kind of death: "The camera limits everything. When you shoot the scene that you have written, you are killing it. Up until that point it could have been anything, but everything that an actor does is there and it can not be anything else."[12] Forsyth was always worried about what happened to the writing, the fragile integrity of the ideas within, the cyclical pain of miscommunication and misunderstanding (even before the critics and audiences had been given the chance to sink their teeth into it).

> "Everything about making a film — and I hate to be negative — but it's a process of failure. You spend a year writing a script. You go in the first day and film a scene, you've finally filmed it, it's in the can. Nothing can change. The director fails the writer. The writer fails the director. The process goes on and on."[13] [14]

The ideas aren't about having a message, nothing didactic. As we've seen all along, *Gregory's Girl* doesn't *say* anything. But what is happening under the surface of Forsyth's films is something much more simple and personal — and, in the end, more engaging and resonant: a working out of human problems we all feel and know intimately, but whose machinations aren't recognised (or much wanted) in a mainstream screenplay.

Most of all, the loneliness. "The ultimate bravery is getting out of bed each morning," Forsyth once said about the angst of the individual in our modern world[15]. But loneliness in itself isn't a curse.

> "We are alone. No other individual has any idea how you see the world. You have no idea how I see this room or the street outside or what Sunday means to me. We are alone, but that's not a negative thing. It's something to

be celebrated. A lot of Hollywood movies try to comfort people with the idea of something beyond them — a god, or a ghost of someone they love. I think that's a cheat. Movies about time travel or space are entertainment, but in a more subtle and sinister way are also telling people 'don't worry, don't think, whatever fears you have you're not alone...every human being that has ever lived and breathed has been just as alone as you, but that's great...You're going to live and die and you're going to cease, you're going to be an absolute nothingness. Instead of that being a problem, celebrate it and celebrate that you are connected to every living being in the sheer fact that you've shared these experiences and that never stops."[16]

Gregory's Girl is a lonely film, made from a lonely method: the writer and his windows, the film-maker and his gaze, always one stage removed from the action. Forsyth's films have nothing to do with the noisy burble of their times, they come from a place of stillness; the kind of space where we work things out for ourselves. "That's what I used to enjoy about cinema," Forsyth said, "it was the bus ride home. It wasn't, you know, standing there watching the credits, it was what was going to happen to me afterwards, having watched the movie. So I think I was always trying to stay loyal to that [in the films]."[17] In other words, "emotion recollected in tranquility": Wordsworth's definition of poetry.

Being a teenager means waking up to a basic state of loneliness. The problems of connection and communication; the difficult making of an identity for yourself; the confusion that comes with freedom. The loneliness is there, in Andy standing watching the trucks. With Dorothy out on her solo runs. Steve making his buns. Eric in his dark room. Gregory relying on jokey chats with his little sister (because the family home is empty and made up of disconnections: "Do you remember your mother?" asks Gregory's Dad — or 'Mike' as Gregory calls him). Even when scenes are made up of groups of people, a reserve and awkwardness makes them feel even more alone than when they were separate. Forsyth once described his characters — all of them — as "marooned"[18].

This may well be the source of the problem with "whimsy". What might look whimsical is actually a reflection of Forsyth's awareness of the absurdity of the human predicament, how we are each of us alone on a planet of love and death. Rather than chilly existential despair, Forsyth's response has kept on being one of humour, accompanied by a sense of how, in spite of our solitary state, there keeps on being a deeper human connection between all of us. We are together alone. We share ideas and experiences while we keep on looking and thinking. And this is where some of the sheer loveliness of *Gregory's Girl* comes from: the heightened feelings that come from a lack of certainty, of there being no fairy tale endings, no truths or resolutions. Just everything in motion, a flow of occasional poetry. Arrivals, but also loss and leaving, the transience which gives the film its background note of melancholy.

*

I only had a day in Cumbernauld. Duty called. I needed to
catch a bus back into Glasgow and be there in time for the
sleeper train, and I still hadn't seen the country park. Had to
tick it off the list. Because by that stage, trudging along the
grassy verges of another of Cumbernauld's arterial roads,
not able to find any footpaths, that was what it had become.

Park Way. The pebbledash bollards where Susan was
waiting for Gregory. Mysteriously, it's one of the most affecting scenes in the film. Just in itself and how it looks. A suburban lane where mum is out mowing the lawn with help
from her little son; the summer light starting to soften and
grow wan; you can almost see the scents of cut grass moving
through the thin evening air. A scene that somehow suggests
how even routine domesticity can be an escape and a consolation, at least sometimes.

Nothing much has changed in Park Way, it's still an area of well-kept bungalows on the brink of rolling parklands. Clipped hedges, wind chimes and garden gnomes. A look of wood-framed Skandi cool and hygge about them. There are a lot more cars lined along the road than there had been; the area around the bollards is tufted and padded with grasses, moss and lichen.

Nearby, the park of Cumbernauld House feels like a baronial estate that's been gatecrashed, a modest neo-classical monument now subject to public trespass. The House itself is an unremarkable part of landscaped gardens with their own dovecote and summerhouse and skein of footpaths; what would once have been an idyll away from the clamour of 18th century Glasgow and its crowds and messy affairs of commerce and politics. No longer a family home, the House has been stripped of Georgian bling, the stag heads, brownish oils of naval battles and cows, Chinese porcelain and mildewed Persian carpets. The parklands themselves would have been a must-have feature for the gentry. A playground for weekend guests who could follow the winding footpaths as part of their after-dinner constitutional and take in the agreeable country air. The glen and the distant hills were there to be sighed over; a summerhouse that would be the place for conversation on warm afternoons. In his script notes, Bill talked about it as a "one-time country estate which has mated itself with the New Town so now it has nature trails and picnic areas...for most people around these parts it does an excellent job as 'the countryside'. And what's wrong with a fancy estate having 70,000 lairds instead of one?".

There were only a few of us commoners on the estate that afternoon, a grassy sea combed into wavy lines by a ride-on lawnmower. Walkers were throwing balls for their dogs, probably wondering where my dog was. I stopped at an information board which confirmed the tree was there, behind me up the slope. In the rain-light it looked like an eldritch stump meant solely as a home for owls and beetles. I sat on a bench and put my mac on, the rain spotting. Clouds slid past like scenery seen from a train window, an unsettlingly dark and mountainous landscape shaded in pewter and blue. The park had that inimitable British summer look, dolefully green. Nothing close to what summer was supposed to look like. Disappointing because it's all we have from one year to the next, just another summer that was no different from any other time of year, a lost opportunity; balmy enough but only in a dampish and dimly-lit kind of way. An elegy for summer.

Maybe though, the British summer works better without being what the ideal says it should be, without the endless days of golden heavens, remorseless sun and heat, because our blue-misted, rain-filled places have a living, breathing softness to them. The dry plains of San Gimignano and their beating sun would be like a war for anything that tried to grow there, the dust and the ants, I thought, while summer in Cumbernauld worked out fine. Delicate moods, reflected back to us in puddles. The occasional sunshine, when it came, was like a blessing, a true spectacle, a warmth that filled our green hedgerows, the ditches and meadows with masses of unshowy flowers, hard little seeds and fruits.

Other than a few snapshots of familiar sights, there had been nothing much in Cumbernauld, no easy revelations. And maybe that was the point. If Cumbernauld had been a *Gregory's Girl* theme park, with interpretation boards spelling out the arc of meaning and significance to the film, it would have been a disaster. Any sense of proper purpose or achievement would have broken the spell. Clogged the little flow of tenuous beauty.

In the final chapter of Flaubert's *Sentimental Education* (1869), the hero realises that after all his woes and striving to be with his first love again, an entire career of hard-won romance, the best and happiest moment of his life had actually come much earlier, when he was a schoolboy. He'd been about Gregory's age when he and a friend had gone to the door of a well-known place of ill-repute, "the secret obsession of every adolescent", where there were girls "in white dressing-gowns, with rouge on their cheeks and long earrings"[19]. The boys turned up with their hair curled fussily and a bunch of flowers taken from their neighbour's garden. But they could only stand there, frozen and silent, until the girls burst out laughing at them and the boys had to run away. That was the happiest he'd ever been. And the same idea is there in *Mary*. The moment that Ganin "now rightly regarded as the highest and most important point in his whole life" had been when he was sitting on the loo, resigned completely to the knowledge that he was never actually going to meet Mary, the girl with the black bow in her hair, not ever[20].

That was *Gregory's Girl* for me. That was it. Not the having and getting, but that sense of being on the brink of discovery, knowing the world had secrets. Lonely, thoughtful views along the way. Sometimes being able to catch at something magical in the air.

---

[1] There was one previous showing, at the London Film Festival on 22 November 1981.

[2] George Mackay Brown, *Andrina and Other Stories*, Polygon, 2010, p69.

[3] Ibid, p73/74.

[4] *Andrina* (1981), BBC Scotland, British Library audio archive.

[5] Compare this with the Mackay Brown original: "The only women I saw when I had the flu were hags and witches. You're lucky, skipper — a honey like Andrina!"

[6] George Mackay Brown, ibid., p77/78.

[7] Photographs by Gunnie Moberg, held by National Galleries Scotland.

[8] Jonathan Coe, interviewed by Anna Cale for the *Ten Thousand Grains of Sand* podcast.

[9] *When Bill Paterson met Bill Forsyth*, BBC Scotland, 2011.

[10] Bill Forsyth interview, Ibiza Film Festival, 2009.

[11] John Brown, 'A Suitable Job for a Scot', *Sight and Sound*, spring 1984, p157.

[12] 'Morning Discussion with Bill Forsyth', Midnight Sun Film Festival, 2016.

[13] Bill Forsyth interview with Jim Healy, Dryden Theatre, New York, April 2010.

[14] Forsyth's attitude is the polar opposite to that of Mark Kermode, who once said to Bill (at a screening of *Local Hero*) that what he loved about film was its immutability, it wasn't ever going to change — it was perfect just as it was — and wouldn't suddenly be different the next time he saw it. A difference in experience or temperament?

[15] Kevin Courrier, Interview with Bill Forsyth, *Critics at Large*, 1985.

[16] Allan Hunter, 'Being Human', *Sight and Sound*, August 1994.

[17] Jonathan Murray, 'Cornflakes versus Conflict: an Interview with Bill Forsyth', *Journal of British Cinema and Television*, 2015.

[18] Jonathan Murray interview with Bill Forsyth, Edinburgh International Film Festival, 2009.

[19] Gustave Flaubert, *Sentimental Education* (1869), Penguin, 1964 edition, p418/9.

[20] Vladimir Nabokov, *Mary*, Penguin, 2007 edition, p56.

11. Movies

"Just keep the doughnuts coming Steve, we're on the gravy train, but what the public says is ease off on the marzipans."

What was supposed to happen next was Big Time Forsyth in Hollywood. *Gregory's Girl* had given him his chance, but all those dreams would be broken on the rocks of American studio demands and commercialism. We love a tale like that, even when it didn't really happen.

Bill was hardly ever in Hollywood and had kept his distance as a separate "one-man business". He went on occasional trips to the US, became pals with Bill Murray ("We were always planning to do something together and it was at the time of *Ghostbusters* [1984]. I would hang out with all those guys from that film at a house in Malibu"[1]); but he didn't move away from Scotland, or take up a seat on the Hollywood Big Wheel. Even the scenes in *Local Hero* of Burt

Lancaster in his Texan boardroom were filmed in Fort Williamam, inside an old distillery warehouse. So there was no concerted effort to get noticed or 'get on'. "I never had this idea of a career, like when you climb a mountain and reach the top. Filmmaking has always been something that I do, rather than something that I strive to do."[2] He was drawn into the Hollywood vortex simply by the power of its reach, an unavoidable sucking magnetism that pulled Forsyth ever closer to its centre, not either pushing forward or resisting.

His early success had provided the momentum, and was perhaps too much, too soon, because it meant he was speeding into the mainstream before he had chance to make more conscious decisions about the film-maker he wanted to be, with no way back to arthouse cinema. He stayed an awkward fit for the business — an auteur, so harder to control and more capable of making an expensive mess (by this stage, Cimino's *Heaven's Gate* and its $40 million loss had changed the movie business forever). If anything, he wasn't asking for enough money from investors. "It's easier to fund a $10 million film than a $3 million one," said Forsyth. "Investors understand $10 million but not $3 million. They're suspicious — they're terrified it might be art or something."[3]

> "If you ask for relatively little money, they worry that you are going to get involved in something that is unwatchable or, worse, unmarketable. Unmarketable is a much more worrying term for them because if they can find an angle to make something unwatchable marketable, they'll do it every week. The

> studio system reminds me of the stock market. People think the stock market is a place of levelheadedness but it actually works in a totally emotional way: the President gets a pimple on his nose, and the thing plummets. The movie business is very much like that: people in authority making purely emotional decisions instead of interesting rational ones."[4]

There was always something not quite right for the industry about Forsyth's films, his talent didn't come out on the screen the way studios were expecting. Too small-time. Comedies that weren't entirely heartwarming, without much in the way of laugh-out-loud gags. Then a literary adaptation without the (Oscar-friendly) emotional gush. Then, when there was money available, he wasn't that bothered about recruiting star names — why cast Burt Lancaster when there'd be more menace in a TV tough guy like Brian Keith[5]? Why cast Robin Williams when you could have the ambiguous presence of another movie-hater like John Malkovich? Altogether too much marzipan. "There's a huge discrepancy between what a studio expects of a movie and what an eccentric filmmaker like me expects," said Bill. "The notion that we could inhabit an idea together, let alone finish a film, is a miracle."[6]

While the differences in outlook and ambitions were clear between Forsyth and the studios he worked for, there was no war. Bitching was saved for conversations among his indie director peers. Forsyth didn't make compromises when it came to his principles (you can afford to be stubborn when a 'career' isn't your main priority), only over details that wouldn't matter too much, or in situations where there seemed to be no choice.

> "I know there's a myth about this thing: go-
> ing to Hollywood and being taken to pieces
> and all of that. But it's not really true, be-
> cause any film-maker who works inside the
> system has these pressures daily. I don't care
> who you are, 80 per cent of film-makers are
> probably quite happy to work in there at least
> some of the time, a lot of them most of the
> time. Some filmmakers are quite happy to go
> out and shoot four endings on the main shoot
> and then they'll pick the best one according
> to what the audience wants, and that all goes
> on. So it's only for a slight outsider like me
> that these things become at all controversial,
> or whatever. But to my mind, it was quite a
> normal process because I knew all of these
> things would happen, I knew they would go
> on."[7]

The first experience of a push-back came over *Local Hero*. The ending was too downbeat — couldn't Mac change his mind and stay in Scotland?

> "I was sat down in Los Angeles with a couple
> of Warners' executives and asked if I'd like to
> reshoot the ending. I don't precisely know

what ideas they had, but I said, 'No, I'm not interested.' The movie had been finished seven months before, and the last thing on my mind was to retire to one of those beaches and try to think up a new ending. That experience was quite a surprise. That was very benign pressure because Warners was very happy with the movie and happy to distribute it. 'Well, I thought, 'if this is the best, God help me if they ever get serious.'"[8]

In the end the editors just added on an unused section of film showing Mac and Danny arriving for the first time in the village, overlaying the sound of the phone ringing. Any more than two rings at the phone box and audiences would have seen the Cortina pulling up to start the visit all over again.

Forsyth, though, wasn't immune to the effects of studio disease:

"I have to work in London for practical reasons like the editing of my films. I probably spend a third of the working year in London but I always feel the need to get away from there after two or three weeks. I don't like being that close to the film industry. If I'm in London too long I become bitchy and competitive when there's no real need to because I'm not competing with anyone in the British film industry at the moment. It came home to

me recently when I found myself in a London bar quite heartily moaning about a film
director that I hadn't met and whose work I
had never seen. It was then that I realised
that London was quite unhealthy for me."9

*

There were five Forsyth films in 18 years after 1981. Each of
them helps put *Gregory's Girl* into perspective and confirms
the attitudes and themes exhibited there as essential rather
than early, have-a-go Forsyth.

The original idea for *Local Hero* came from David
Puttnam. He knew he could get Bill money for a culture
clash film about American oilmen in Scotland. *Dallas* meets
Brigadoon. When he worked on the pitch, Forsyth made it
simple for studio executives by making comparisons with *The
Beverley Hillbillies*, the hit Sixties TV show: think backwoods
yokels and their big chance to get rich. We know another
likely influence was the John Byrne play, *The Cheviot, the Stag
and the Black, Black Oil* (1973), an angry collation of songs,
sketches and interviews explaining how the Scottish Highlands had been exploited since the 18th century. Bill Paterson and Alex Norton were stars of the piece (and Forsyth
remembered them afterwards as actors he wanted for his
films). The story of the eviction of crofters to make way for
the Cheviot breed of sheep, is compared with the arrival of
oil prospectors, more coldly efficient and brutal than ever
before in their destruction of the shoreline, their pollution,
and the way the property boom in Aberdeen pushed out loc-

al families. With the involvement of Puttnam and Burt Lancaster, Forsyth knew the money was safe and the film would get a distribution deal. At the same time he was suddenly under more pressure. Bill "knew in his heart of hearts", argued Puttnam, "that *Gregory's Girl* was an over-praised film" and that he had a point to prove[10].

The fishing village setting was the flip-side to modern Middleton, an appealing return to simplicity. Forsyth was again making a point, this time from the other direction, about the consumer culture: "It was the 80s, I think people were losing it slightly. It was a decade of excessive acquisition, all of that stuff."[11] The US money man, Felix Happer — a name that essentially translates as 'Mr Happy Happy' — has everything but happiness. "Happer is a madman," clarified Forsyth, making sure no-one would think the oil boss was in any way an eventual saviour of the village or its coastline. "He's insane."[12] It was a basic truth to Burt Lancaster's character that the director decided to keep from his star, knowing that Lancaster had begun to identify with Happer and would have struggled with such a negative back story. Peter Riegert's character MacIntyre doesn't have a first name because he's just 'Mr Business' ("call me Mac") and nothing else. The modern world has stripped him of a personal life and any purpose other than a career.

The determined realism of *Gregory's Girl* is just as persistent in *Local Hero*, in spite of the wistful sorcery of northern skies and stars, the florescence of the aurora borealis — and the suggestion that Marina might be a mermaid. "People in Scotland have less difficulty believing in mermaids," explained Forsyth. "It's still possible to meet the cousin of someone who married a mermaid in certain parts of the Highlands...If you ask me any question about [Marina], I can explain it rationally. She's got webbed toes, Nijinsky had webbed toes."[13]

The authenticity of the *Local Hero* idea was given credence by events that followed the arrival of the production team in the village of Pennan. The locals really did smell money. They believed that a big Hollywood operation with bottomless pockets would change their lives — or at least make a difference to an out-of-the-way place with a shrinking population, few jobs and a sea wall that badly needed reinforcing against the tides. Pennan got behind their own Gordon Urquhart, the pub landlord Les Rose who brought in a lawyer and an accountant for negotiations, and was heralded by regional press as the 'real Local Hero'[14]. As the film's producer Iain Smith tried to explain to them, there was actually a tight budget and they had to stick to it. "We were the idealistic film makers encountering the locals who were much more interested in reality than we could ever have imagined."[15] In the end the production paid out around £10,400 to Pennan, some to a general village fund, some to local committees, and a fee to individual villagers for disturbances.

There was a postscript when Donald Trump built his 'world-class' golf resort on sand dunes just up the coast from where parts of *Local Hero* were filmed. A documentary film, *You've Been Trumped* (2011), recorded the villagers' protests and their refusal to bow down to the Trump Corporation's campaign. This led to Forsyth's one and only film review in *The Guardian*:

I make things up for a living. I don't get out much and I haven't allowed a newspaper in the house for thirty years, so I truly live in a world of fiction. I've got by with Louis B Mayer's definition of a documentary being a film without girls in it…Recently however, I've been obliged to confront reality head-on in the form of the film *You've Been Trumped*. It turns out that an old piece of fiction of mine, *Local Hero*, bears unavoidable comparison with real life events in Aberdeenshire…With the rest of the audience that day I came out into the daylight dazed and shocked, with a numb feeling of individual impotence. Our usually unchallenged feeling of smug security as citizens of a mature democracy had been rocked…It's Donald Trump's job in the film to stir things up and mess things around. How well does Trump accomplish this? I'd say pretty well. In fact he evinces some true talent and even relish for rooting around in the sticky brown stuff and delivering it to the whirling fan. But there are glaring deficiencies in the drawing of this character. He seems to seriously lack certain human dimensions. There are whole sides to him that are missing. A writer who'd dreamed him up wouldn't be standing in line for any Oscar, no sir. This character breaks all the rules of drama. For a start, he has no arc. Stick with me, this is gold dust, I learned it in Holly-wood.[16]

Local Hero made a smallish profit of less than $1 million and Bill won a BAFTA as Best Director. He went out drinking along with Martin Scorsese after the ceremony and, for a laugh, ended up switching his trophy with Paul Zimmerman, who'd just picked up the Best Screenplay BAFTA for *King of Comedy*. *Local Hero* was also said to be the "favourite film" of Al Gore, the politician famous for his environmentalist mission (which he didn't see as being inconsistent with a lifestyle that included multiple mansions and private jets). In 2010, a US radio presenter reminded Bill that Al Gore was a fan, perhaps expecting him to be pleased. Bill's response was a picture of polite distaste. Not a flicker of an expression, a simple "that's right" — which said it all.

*

It's easy to forget *Comfort & Joy* is a Christmas film. The title comes from 'God Rest Ye Merry Gentleman' and its glad tidings, the carol that best evokes scenes of avuncular lamb-chopped hosts and their rose-lit oak-panelled rooms, the tables loaded with victuals. The film plays with the myth of seasonal jollity and togetherness through its own sombre wandering through our modern version, the hot department stores and streets of shoppers, the strings of electric fairy lights, the quiet offices and empty homes; Christmas scenes that come with a creeping sense of how we don't really feel the magic the way we're meant to. Christmas is the ultimate sweet-toothed escape, an annual period of compensation for our angst and woes, just like the treats peddled by the Mr Bunny and Mr Softy vans every evening in Glasgow; like Maddy's insatiable sprees of shoplifting; all those munchable snacks that Dickie Bird voices the adverts for.

Forsyth had first started writing the script in the early Seventies. Over time it ended up being "almost a narrative of a couple of years in [his] life"[17], a film about the obsessions that can result from a loss of identity and sense of purpose.

> "Like Dickie, I went mad for about three or four months. If the film had been longer, I think there would have been a point where someone said to Dickie, 'It's good to see you back on your feet again.' But he didn't know he was off his feet. That's certainly what friends said to me after a few months: 'It's great to see you together again.'"[18]

Identities are a kind of security blanket that can slip and fall off, making us more dependent on other comforts we can find, however trivial. It's not only Dickie, the popular local DJ, who struggles with who and what he is. Many of the characters (in this and his other films) are only living by the labels that have been given to them: that problem of perception and reality again. Forsyth said it was like TS Eliot's 'The Naming of Cats' poem: "cats have three names: the name you call it, then its proper name, then its secret name which only it knows. So somebody's business, or the way he or she spends the day, can be confused with the real person."[19]

Forsyth has pointed to connections in his mind between the *Comfort & Joy* script and the Preston Sturges movie *Sullivan's Travels* (1941) where a privileged film director of shallow, formulaic comedies insists on slumming around the soup kitchens and homeless shelters to gather material for a venture into serious social realism. His disasters on the road and eventual imprisonment lead him to realise that what people really need is some little moments of joy in their lives. He needed to make funnier comedies[20].

The film's storyline was the consequence of a mis-understanding. During the making of *Local Hero*, Bill chatted with Peter Capaldi, who told him about the family business and their fleet of ice-cream vans. Peter talked about the 'ice-cream wars' and the outbreaks of violence involved. Ice-cream wars, fine. A Scottish phenomenon with some rasp-berry-sauce topped oddness to it. What Bill didn't then know — as someone who was reading far more books than news-papers — was the real nature of those wars, how drug deal-ers were using ice-cream vans as a front. There was no fam-ily rivalry over recipes but criminals ready to use intimida-tion, violence and even murder to protect their valuable drug territories. It wasn't a whimsical re-writing of history, as it might have looked, but bookish naivety.

Dickie's character was written with the blithe, doleful charm of Bill Paterson in mind. With two Bills on set, Pater-son was known as 'Big Willy' — or by Forsyth, waggishly, sometimes as 'Wee Willy'. Paterson hadn't passed a driving test or obtained a licence, so he was driving the soft-top

BMW around Glasgow illegally. "I wasn't a danger to others around me — which was just as well, because I had Chris Menges, one of the best and most treasured cameramen around, strapped to the bonnet of the car."[21]

The lack of a satisfyingly happy ending was a problem for the studio again. Couldn't Dickie just end up finding love and a new beginning with Clare Grogan's flirty character? Not really. But the family reunion over an ice-cream fritter business probably wasn't in keeping with the rest of the film either, it wasn't chilly enough. Why not have Dickie return to his bachelor flat and find it full of new cushions and vases and knick-knacks? A meal ready for him on a table dressed with napkins and candlesticks, bottles of expensive wine and crystal glasses. Maddie has come back to him, dressed to kill. "Is any of this stuff actually yours?" asks Dickie. "No," says Maddie, winding her arms around him and looking back at all the material comforts she has brought back into his life. "This is all yours now."

Comfort & Joy lost money for Universal Studios. "I don't think that anyone at Universal actually made a phone call and said, 'Let's pull the plug on this.' But I think emotionally they did, on what basis I don't know, maybe something as simple as a slow weekend in New York. Maybe there was a baseball game or something. Those are the things that I see affect judgments: a slow weekend, a lukewarm review."[22]

*

Housekeeping (1980) was the first novel by Marilynne Robinson, a doctoral English lit student from Idaho who'd been

writing her dissertation on *Henry VI part two*. The book had
been recommended to Forsyth by actor Toni Kalem, best
known for playing Angie Bonpensiero in *The Sopranos*, on the
night of the New York Film Critics' Circle Awards. Bill had
just picked up the best script trophy for *Local Hero* and was
walking back to the hotel with Peter Riegert on "a wintry
Manhattan night" when they bumped into Toni and Peter
made the introductions. They got to talking about the writing and books they liked and Toni told him what a surprise
Housekeeping had been, its unusually solemn qualities[23]. She
left her own copy of the book at the reception desk of the
hotel for Forsyth to read, and its scant and lonely poetry soon
came to lodge itself into his imagination. In time it made
him want to be more than a reader: he'd make a film that
would be a "video promo for the novel". He took a year and
a half over turning the 220 page novel into a workable
screenplay, marking up a copy of the book and physically
cutting out pages to paste onto paper (Bill had made an enthusiastic start on this process before realising he'd probably
need two copies). The screenplay turned out to be almost as
long as the book because he couldn't bear to take things out.

Why had *Housekeeping* taken such a hold on him?
"Robinson...wrote from a lopsided perspective, an oddball
angle that Forsyth found suited him just fine," suggested one
film reviewer for the *Washington Post*[24]. In itself, that seems too
broad a conclusion. Talking about a particular painting,
Marilynne Robinson once remarked that "beauty is a casual
glimpse of something very ordinary...It's a brick wall with a
ray of sunlight on it."[25] Her reflections here, and in the ap-

proach to her novel, are an echo of the spirit of Forsyth, and the beautiful ordinariness of *Gregory's Girl* especially.

On one level, the plot is a simple coming-of-age story, but one stained all the way through with darkness. Two young sisters, Ruth and Lucille, are left with their grandmother in the town of Fingerbone after their mother has committed suicide. They fall into the care of eccentric aunt Sylvie, a distracted and fanciful figure. She's a drifter who's become used to sleeping fully clothed (in her bed or on one of Fingerbone's park benches), who fills the house with her hoards of old newspapers and tin cans. As they grow older, the novel looks at the pressures on the two girls to conform to the niceties of Fifties small town America; appropriate ways to dress, look and behave. Eventually this means Ruth and Sylvie have to face up to being outsiders to that small town circle and the consequences, the sadness of otherness, how adulthood isn't always a straight road to acceptance or what's safe or steady.

It's a quiet book, loaded with a sense of imminent loneliness. "There's a little bit of *Gregory's Girl* in Ruth and a little bit of the [Scottish] gloaming in these Rockies," noted the *Washington Post*[26]. However solid people's lives may look, their bonds and achievements and sense of self, time keeps running on, and then there's only memory left. Everything in *Housekeeping* is as fluid as the water in the town's death-bringing lake and the floods that arrive each year.

Forsyth intended Robinson's creation to speak for itself. He didn't always know exactly why they filmed all the scenes they did, it just seemed better to trust the book. But there are his own fingerprints here and there. In particular, as would be expected, in some of the visual jokes: when the house is flooded the girls sweep floating rubbish away into a cupboard and shut the door, only for it to float back out again in a little bobbing train; there's a store advert that reads "If you really want to please her/ Give your wife a fridge and freezer"; and the way in which a lettuce, one of the very few things that has survived Fingerbone's famous train crash, is picked up and held proudly for a group photo. Forsyth also makes more visually of the piles of newspapers and tin cans as signals of the obvious failure of Sylvie's housekeeping. The book's sadness is all there, rendered through the winter blues, greys and browns of the northwest countryside. If anything though, Robinson's bleakest lines and images have been taken out — like Ruth's constant fear that Sylvie will kill herself, just carelessly, out of a vague sense of curiosity. In the book, death stays close to them, as easy to accomplish as shutting their eyes. Sleep's best when you're "really tired", says Sylvie, "You don't just sleep. You die."[27] The poetic heart of the book — during Sylvie and Ruth's trip to a deserted island — is an exposition on the magic that comes from 'not-having' rather than our usual state of 'having'. This is given a visual interpretation by Forsyth rather than any narration from the book (because it's too blatantly literary?):

> For need can blossom into all the compensa-
> tions it requires. To crave and to have are as
> like as a thing and its shadow. For when does
> a berry break upon the tongue as sweetly as
> when one longs to taste it, and when is the

> taste refracted into so many hues and savors
> of ripeness and earth, and when do our
> senses know any thing so utterly as when we
> lack it? And here again is a foreshadowing —
> the world will be made whole. For to wish for
> a hand on one's hair is all but to feel it. So
> whatever we may lose, very craving gives it
> back to us again. Though we dream and
> hardly know it, longing, like an angel, fosters
> us, smooths our hair, and brings us wild
> strawberries.[28]

Something like the anticipation you feel before your ice-cream float arrives.

Robinson completed her story with an account of what happened to Sylvie and Ruth next, still together and wandering, taking part-time jobs waiting on tables; imagining, meanwhile, what Lucille's more conventionally successful life might be like, picturing her properly dressed in a tweed suit and amber scarf. Forsyth makes the ending more satisfying for movie-goers with his single desolate picture of Sylvie and Ruth running away from Fingerbone, taking the perilous route of walking the railroad track across the lake and disappearing into the mist.

One telling difference that Robinson disapproved of — although she loved the film as a whole — was the treatment of Lucille. Forsyth, she felt, had been too black and white about Lucille's need for acceptance and popularity. It was only human that Lucille would want to have friends, gingham dresses and Coca-Cola, argued Robinson. Forsyth, though, really doesn't stray from the text (and doesn't include some of Robinson's sharper digs at Lucille in the book: like how she's the type who cheats at Monopoly by hiding $500 bills; or Ruth's verdict that her sister was "of the common persuasion"[29]), instead he's emphasising the bittersweetness of their situation and the transience of things, a coming to terms with plain reality and the peace that could be found there; how the poetry of things might otherwise be excluded by the tense scrutiny and narrow standards of someone like Miss Royce, the Home Economics teacher, who 'saves' Lucille.

After taking an option on the rights to the novel, it took two years to raise the £5 million budget for production. The breakthrough came with the news that Diane Keaton would play the role of Sylvie (in exchange for half the film's entire budget). With this star power involved, Cannon — best known for its ninja films and *Death Wish* sequels — came up with the cash. The cast was assembled, locations were found in Nelson and Castlegar in Canada, and sets were built, including a vast wooden railway trestle, 125 feet long and 20 feet high. Then Diane Keaton pulled out, six weeks before filming was due to begin. She'd decided to do the crowd-pleasing comedy *Baby Boom* (1987) instead, and so Cannon bailed. "I walked the streets of New York thinking my life was over," said Bill[30]. He'd not wooed her enough, he kept thinking, a star like that, she'd needed more hands-on schmooze to keep her on-board.

Housekeeping (1987) was saved by the unexpected appointment of David Puttnam as head of Columbia Pictures, the first non-American to run a US studio. Strategists were recommending a move away from formula movie-making to re-build audience numbers, and Puttnam's name meant films with substance, highbrow concepts with mass appeal, like *Chariots of Fire* (and *Local Hero* of course), *Midnight Express* (1978), *The Killing Fields* (1984) and *The Mission* (1986). He was known around the industry for having said that he never would have made a dumb film like *Rambo: First Blood II* (1985), and that *ET The Extra Terrestrial* (1982) was spoilt by the ending (the alien should have stayed dead). Puttnam arranged the funding for *Housekeeping*, a project that screamed quality, and allowed there to be what Forsyth called a "search for a proper actress" to play Sylvie[31]. It was only later that he remembered how the project had all started. Toni Kalem was an actress wasn't she? Maybe she'd lent him the book because she'd been hoping for the part of Sylvie? "I could be so thick about those things."[32]

It wasn't always an easy novel to work with. The flooded house scenes had to be filmed indoors in a swimming pool with warm water to spare the actors. The water turned brown because of the furniture — becoming like a "sofa tea" said Forsyth[33]. The Canadian lake refused to freeze so the production crew had to build plywood decking over pond water and use a snow machine and chunks of styrofoam to re-create a wintry scene. The biggest problem for *Housekeeping* in the end turned out to be the demise of Puttnam's reputation. Things were going wrong everywhere for him. As would have been expected, Puttnam had preferred interesting lower-budget propositions (like Spike Lee's *School Daze* (1988) and a film about a talking penis, *Me and Him* (1989)) over standard Hollywood propositions, but the approach hadn't been met with approval from cinema-goers. At the same time he'd taken on the even greater risk of backing Terry Gilliam's byzantine fantasy *The Adventures of Baron Munchausen* (1989), and the budget was running out of control. It eventually lost Columbia $38 million. Forsyth himself suspected Puttnam had hired too many Brits for his own good. People were starting to gossip about the studio as 'British Columbia'. After Puttnam left, the studio and its new head weren't interested in spending anything on Puttnam projects, so *Housekeeping* was given low-key promotion and allowed to drift out of sight. The film lost around $4 million.

*

The next venture was meant to be Dylan Thomas's screenplay of *Rebecca's Daughters* (1948), a fruity, ruffle-necked romance built around a historical case of tollgate riots. In the nineteenth century, tollgates had been sprouting up on the main routes around towns in south Wales, sealing off pockets of land where tenant farmers needed to work and move their livestock. It was the last straw for small-time farmers already suffering as a result of land enclosure, high rents and demands from the church for tithes. The tollgates became the focus for protests against the greed and tyranny of the wealthy classes and were broken down and burnt. Besides being a story of a local uprising against 'the Man', Forsyth would have been attracted by a comical aspect to the rioting. The secret leader of the riots, their instigator and the quarry of soldiers brought in to squash any revolt, was 'Rebecca' — a man with a blackened face dressed up in women's clothes, a shawl and skirts. His followers were his 'daughters', other men wearing bonnets and long frocks. The idea for the rioters had come from a line in the book of Genesis in the Bible referring to Rebekah and her children and the useful destruction of gates. It meant a useful disguise — and, at the same time law-abiding locals could feel hidden inside an older tradition of religious virtue.

Dylan Thomas's screenplay was unusual in that it wasn't a typical text made up of dialogue and scene notes but was meant to be read. Thomas used his poet's skill to convey every shot with bravura: "Now we see it, through the rain, approaching us down a narrow, pooled and rutted country road, bare trees each side of it, tossing in a temper. Blown broken branches scrabble and scrape the wood-work and windows as the chaise lurches on, the horses streaming and breathing out clouds in the dusky gusty cold."

This time there was no money in the offing[34]. Instead, Forsyth ended up accepting a job working around someone else's script, a classic genre movie. Harry Gittes was a producer from the old school, a down-at-heel chancer who "drove around in [his] rusty old Volkswagen Beetle and was always on the move". He got in touch with Forsyth about *Breaking In* (1989) and they clicked. To impress him with his connections, Harry took Bill to Jack Nicholson's mansion, not even bothering to ring the doorbell before walking in. They watched the American football game with their host "on the biggest TV screen [Bill had] ever seen."[35]

The original script had been written by John Sayles, a thirtysomething writer/director who had a decent record of writing for mainstream cinema: B-movie horror films like

Piranha (1978), *Alligator* (1980) and *The Howling* (1981), as well as early drafts for *ET, The Extra-Terrestrial*. Sayles went on to have success with indie films like *The Secret of Roan Inish* (1994) and neo-western *Lone Star* (1996). His *Breaking In* was a 'mismatched buddy' story about Ernie, a safecracker feeling his age who takes on Mike as his young apprentice. Sayles was happy to leave Forsyth to do whatever he wanted with what was an old, unused script — and, in turn, Forsyth saw the job as mainly involving some updating. But that wasn't really what he'd been brought in for. Gittes and the Samuel-Goldwyn studio still saw Forsyth as a very particular kind of film man. He was there to add humour and get more warmth out of the buddy dynamic and inject a bit of — sure, you know — Scots whimsy.

By this stage, Forsyth was willing to explore a different formula, maybe see if he could create a popular hit by putting his mindful twist on a crime caper film:

> "a kind of experiment to see how far I have
> to go to find an audience in this country and
> how far the audience is prepared to come
> and see what I do. Kind of tippy-toeing to-
> ward them, and hopefully they'll tippy-toe
> towards me. And then we'll just see how far
> apart we still are. I make very accessible
> movies and I'd just like the audience to be
> exposed to them…Yeah, basically…Because
> I think there should be room for a filmmaker
> like me in the commercial marketplace. I'm
> not an obscure kind of artist or anything."[36]

Forsyth soon had his own ideas of what *Breaking In* should be. Even with a Sayles story and US studio wrapping, he wanted to make a "subterranean film" about a criminal who was "living in the shadows, anonymous", punishing himself for his crimes[37]. To make the film work, Forsyth (with a Calvinist upbringing still in his head and heart) knew there had to be a sense of threat and eventual punishment, a note of tragedy. The studio wanted the criminal pairing to get off with a short prison sentence to keep the mood upbeat, while Forsyth insisted on a more realistic 15 years. In the end there was a compromise on nine years.

The director wanted the lynchpin role of Ernie to be played by John Mahoney (Martin Crane in *Frasier*), but instead got pushed towards the big name of Burt Reynolds — which changed everything. The pathos of Ernie, trapped in a mess of crime and morality and self-loathing, is evaporated, because Reynolds is stone-faced and handsome, a macho blank. He's a good-looking guy who knows all the answers and no amount of limping or hesitancy was ever going to make his worries look like they meant anything to him. With Mahoney playing a smaller, more watchful man, Ernie would have kept the vulnerability that was needed to make the film work. (And just as an aside about the casting of Mike. At first glance it looks as if it could be Billy Greenlees. The mop of hair, the way he moves, as if Bill still had Eichmann in his mind somewhere).

Forsyth does manage to flavour the film with his own humour to an extent, by making fun of some of the clichés of cop movies. Like the mock chase scene where a flock of police officers follows Mike walking around a theme park as he carries on pretending to pick up litter as if nothing is happening; and the fooling of audience expectations when Ernie and Mike drop down into a store at night and find themselves face to face with a Doberman, ears pricked, watching them alertly. What follows isn't a thrilling race to safety, there's no last moment escape or torn trousers. The dog mooches around and sits and watches while Ernie works on the safe. Then a second Doberman appears, and there's an even better joke as the audience waits for this one to turn nasty, because Ernie has assumed it's the same dog and pats him roughly out of the way; but no, it's just as mild-mannered and disinterested. A wonderful exhibition of irony.

The film also re-emphasises Forysth's preoccupation with loneliness and the frailty of human relationships. After all they've been through together as a team, there's no understanding between them, and the final lines are another of Forsyth's parting shots (like Mac in his empty flat, Ruth and Sylvie on the railway bridge), they both think of each other as losers: "Poor kid," says Ernie ruefully. "Poor old guy," says Mike.

"To me, *Breaking In* is an awkward little movie," wrote Forsyth in 2019. "It's not an American film and it's not a European film; it's ungraspable what it is…I really felt like a foreigner in America at that time, trying to make a classic genre movie that any American could have made with one eye shut."

Breaking In also lost about four million dollars.

*

Burbank, California. We're in the office of Warner's president Terry Semel, one of the most powerful men in Hollywood[38]. He's sat behind a desk with the size and sheen of a grand piano; three telephones and a gold fountain pen in front of him. Semel is a solid figure in a black suit with a hard brushed wave of dark hair. And he's furious.

"Can anyone tell me what this film is supposed to be about?"

There'd been another miserable test screening of Warner's new $40 million Robin Williams film. Forsyth takes his cue and sits up, but this only makes Semel more impatient.

"*Not* you," he barks.

Being Human should be remembered as Forsyth's major work, the coming together of ideas he'd been sketching out in his previous films — not as a flop that cost investors $35 million. In a way, it's the only true Forsyth film. He'd made *That Sinking Feeling* for the GYT; *Gregory's Girl* was a "calling card"; *Local Hero* was David Puttnam's idea; *Comfort & Joy* turned into a kind of riposte; *Housekeeping* and *Breaking In* were other people's stories. *Being Human* was the chance to turn all the literature and art of his interests and thinking into a stream of moving pictures. Pure, original Forsyth.

The idea for the film's premise came from the reworking of a proposal he'd hated. Would he make a film with Bill Murray? Of course. Would he make a film of Bill Murray as a time traveller, going to hell and undergoing a body-swap? No thanks. As a premise though, it had something. It was another Hollywood trope involving a contortion of fantasy, but one that could be subverted. It could be made real and say something real. Not an easy sell at any stage, but Forsyth worked hard at making the *Being Human* pitch clear to studio executives:

> In this script there are six main characters who inhabit different periods of time, from pre-history to the present day. But there is just one story. Because we blend into one developing narrative the lives that we show. There is no suggestion of time travel or reincarnation or any other tricksy or mystic device. We can do in real time and with real characters what other movies strive to do with immortal time travellers and ghosts. Our story is thoroughly based in reality and the magic we are dealing with is real, human magic...The key to allowing the audience to enjoy this human connection at the heart of the film is that one actor will play the six individuals. The feeling will be of the endless, glorious playing and replaying of the simple drama of being alive. We end the film with a present-day hero, but by that time we will be seeing this modern man in an entirely fresh light...By then perhaps, we will be able to see ourselves in this novel perspective, too[39].

The subtleties of the story, with all of its stray melancholy endings, make for a curious film. Mysterious, and inherently more poetic than cinematic; what has since been acknowledged among a small circle of film critics as being "an ambitious think-comedy — a Charlie Kaufman film before there was a Charlie Kaufman."[40]

Forsyth described the opening to the last, present day chapter of the story like this:

> A trip from Queens to New Jersey at five o'clock on a Friday afternoon is going to look like a dream sequence whatever you do with it, and that's fine. Hector's trip to his children has more meaning for us than a simple journey from A to B. We will be aware of our other Hectors, and the journeys home that they did or didn't manage to make. This car trip will pull the threads together. And after so many images of the natural world, a world little altered by man, the PANORAMIC SHOTS of New York in all its mad glory will place our Hector in a new dimension. If there is a breathtaking moment in this film, when everything comes together, when all the pieces fit, then it will be somewhere around here that it happens. Six thousand years ago we left Hector on a beach, aching for his family. If the traffic allows, tonight in New Jersey Hector will complete his journey.

In the beginning, Warner Brothers could see possibilities, and with the steadying presence of Robin Williams onboard (not John Malkovich, as Forsyth had wanted), they were prepared to come up with $20 million in funding and a global distribution deal. "At the time Warners said: 'It'll either be wonderful or it won't make a buck'...," said Bill. "Really they wanted to buy my idea but not my sensibility and I wanted their money but not their propagandist crap. These things were never said, of course. You can be so easily beguiled. I spent a year writing it and then I just put a stamp on it and sent it away to my agent in America."[41] Given the scale of the budget, Warners stayed in tight control: "all the money was buying me was an absolutely rigid schedule," he complained, arguing he wasn't being given the time he needed to work with the actors. One of the immediate demands, of course, was for a happy ending with Hector giving his son a big hug of reconciliation. Forsyth knew he had no choice. "In a crude way, it is a $20 million hug."[42] He at least made the change more sympathetic to the rest of the piece by getting the daughter to tell Hector that's what he had to do, no choice.

The studio's hopeful wonder crashed and burned after the first screenings with executives. What the hell was it? What had happened to the novelty of the plot idea and the big manic personality of Robin Williams? Anything that could have been good about it was wrecked. Swallowed up in an ocean of sad-seeming boredom. Forsyth enjoyed telling the story of how an elderly lady coming out of a preview screening had asked him if was involved with the film. Oh yes, he said. Well, she told him sharply, he should go dig a hole and bury it.

Meanwhile, the studio was going to do everything it could to make some money back on their investment. That

started with bringing in 'film doctor' DeDe Allen[43] to make
drastic cuts to the length of *Being Human*, from 160 minutes
down to 85, including the removal of an entire chapter
where Hector is a nineteenth-century surveyor mapping the
land. In the new round of tests, audiences still found it too
long at 85 minutes. Then they added a voice-over as a way
of trying to engage audiences early, making them feeling less
stranded, and provide an element of kookiness which turned
out to be horrible. Theresa Russell's contribution is arch and
cloying. Like a piece of art covered in day-go stickers attempting explanations.

After a year of delays, a 120 minute version was finally
jettisoned into the world by Warner's in May 1994. An ugly-
looking exercise in fly-tipping: bolted on opening credits and
no promotion. Straight to video in the UK. US critics saw it
as the failure of a once-beguiling sense of humour, someone
who was just trying too hard. It was what happened when "a
director with a gossamer comic touch tries to become commercial," wrote *Entertainment Weekly*, "the movie is so flat and
banal it's like a Mel Brooks parody in which someone forgot
to put in the jokes...Its five astonishingly limp parables might
have been spun by a depressed Aesop who forgot to take his
Prozac."[44] A "dreary mess" decided *Rolling Stone*, "we expect
more from Williams and Forsyth than a movie that hectors
us to stop and smell the roses."[45] *Variety* found the film to be
"more than two hours of patience-eroding tepid drama and
non-comedy...the picture shockingly reveals no philosophic-
al connective tissue, no elements that have been meaningfully placed and built so as to coalesce into rewarding meaning at the end."[46]

As we'd expect, Forsyth had produced an ambitious and thoughtful film that went against all the Hollywood rules of serious cinema; and in the case of such a stubborn and ambitious piece of work, there was nowhere to hide, no room for the concessions and distractions of love stories and jokes. *Being Human* was the *Gregory's Girl* proposition taken to an extreme, made fierce and radical, but also worked out, embellished, smoothed and finessed over a much larger canvas. The Forsyth installation with some warehouse space.

Hector is the grown-up Gregory, the anti-hero who keeps running away from problems and threats. What could have been visceral action scenes, the meat and drink of historical drama, happen somewhere else, or are left confined to the corner of the screen, like the battling knights in the medieval age chapter.

> PRIEST: So, the mad knights are at it again...what were they, Swiss or English?
> HECTOR: I don't know. They all look the same to me.

Instead we see the actual implications for people of the action, the litter of death, the humiliations and awkwardness. Like this, when a fatally wounded knight in armour is laid onto a table:

> SOLDIER: Must be sore in there. Is it your dada?
> [The Squire looks at him and nods his head. Hector looks with sympathy at the boy.]

> SOLDIER #2: If he's got a little head it might be alright. Has your dada got a big head?

The director's gaze is even more intent and protracted across the film's simple landscapes. The silences are longer. The inability of people to communicate in any reliable way is a constant, and made explicit in the section featuring the relationship between the medieval Hector and Beatrice. Having no common spoken language is not a problem when it comes to their physical attraction, bodies speak for themselves, but there is eventually no language that allows Hector to explain his longing for home, why he needs to leave her and the warm and homely place she has offered to him.

We're shown different ways in which people struggle to 'read' the world and make sense of its signs, the mistaken 'knowledge' they create. The Roman soothsayer cuts the liver from chickens as a way of divining the future. In an unused scene, this time from the pre-history chapter, the raiders' priest thinks the pile of stones they find on the cliff must be part of a religious ritual, and there is a debate over whether they should throw Hector off the cliff to "help the voyage". The Priest:

> walks around the pile of stones, checking it out from all sides as if it was some infernal machine that he didn't know the workings of. He squats down and squints through it to the watery sun emerging from the clouds far out to sea. He looks across to Hector, now sitting

on the grass. The Leader sits down beside
him. They sit together like friends. The age-
less intimacy of sacrificer and victim.

Nineteenth century 'progress' doesn't bring people closer to
truth.

They are building a pile of stones, a cairn.
They work quietly, methodically. The only
sounds are of their breathing and the
CLICK-CLACK of the stones. We feel the
echoes of our many previous Hectors and
their piles of stones, built for this or that purpose. Our doomed surveyors are acting out
the same ritual, this time in the name of science.

Instead of relying on a basis of questionable rationality, being human means not knowing, accepting instead the confusion, and unknowability, of our relations with things and
others — especially others — and how the confusion can be
magical in itself.

We feel the echo of another night when a
man watched someone sleep and dream. He
handles some of the things spilling from her
bag, lying beside him. Her dried flowers and
herbs, which he sniffs, her little bottles and
phials. Witches brew? Or simply an early version of a cluttered handbag? We don't know

what is passing through Hector's mind. Perhaps he is trying to work out how he came to
be lying with the strange, wonderful, un-
knowable creature by his side. And how
many people have done that through the
ages, in caves or by campfires, or in suburban
bedrooms? There are many ways in which we
will be able to connect with this perplexed,
flea-ridden man, far away from home, hud-
dling by a fire in the forest, trapped in his
time, as we all are.

Being Human follows the tracks of the different ways societies
have found ways to organise people and influence how they
understand the world around them. Trying to reduce and
control the idea of what's true. Replacing a simple-minded
being with a kind of living that is dependent on made-up
and limiting realities: from slave ownership and religious
wars to financial obligation and debt.

HECTOR [present day]: Well, I'm glad you
two are thinking about the old planet. I'm
proud of you. Look how beautiful everything
is. Sometimes I think it's people that make it
all wrong...we walk around with all our problems...

Hector keeps trying to return to his family but can't ever
quite find a way through the man-made tangle of things.
Among the Warner studio executives there was the belief

that Hector's story was one of progress along a road of spiritual growth — and Forsyth was not going to contradict them (not out loud anyway) if that belief made them happy.

For fans of Forsyth, the film ends with the wonderfully satisfying return of an old joke from *That Sinking Feeling*, as if we've come full circle. It's when Hector and his daughter, Betsy, and son, Thomas, are sitting on a beach at night around a camp fire, looking at the stars growing brighter as the royal-blue of the sky darkens. They don't really know their dad, he's not been around, and it's been a very difficult weekend together. But after the nerves, the frustration and disillusion with each other, they've reached some kind of acceptance. Maybe they can get along for a while. There's a moment of quiet between them that emphasises the mystery that's everywhere around them on the beach. In each grain of sand, every shadow from the firelight. A mystery that covers everything like a dew. What was all this stuff anyway?

> BETSY: Wait a minute... I know... the whole universe is inside a speck of dust that's lying in a ball of fluff in the cuff of a pair of pants hanging over the back of a chair...

> HECTOR: No...I'll tell you...the whole thing...stars and everything...is sitting on the skin of a bubble of milk in a bowl of corn-flakes...and somebody's just about to eat it.

Forsyth once said that making *Being Human* had been a big mistake. He could have just sat down and written a poem instead[47].

*

Andy and Conchita have got friends round for their first wedding anniversary. Andy's dressed in a big velvet-bow tie and ruffled shirt and he's cooking them his special ravioli for dinner. Eric's in the living room giving advice on the best lighting for the anniversary snaps, comparing the spec of his digital camera with Billy's. Steve has had to take over in the kitchen because he's been too worried about what's happening to the seasoning.

The party-goers finally settle and find their places around the table. Charlie is about to stand up and begin his 30 page speech when the doorbell rings. Greg first, white-faced. Then Susan. They've had a row. He's never going to be serious about anything, Susan whispers bitterly to Conchita (a former go-go dancer) over vodka and cokes in the kitchen. And guess who he's been seen meeting up with? Only the new Climackston FC manager, Dorothy Swift.

Then, a secret only known to Billy comes out. He's witnessed it all through a windae: a Chinese corporate giant is going to buy up the school and knock it down for luxury housing. There are tricks and schemes to foil the plans. A chase involving Andy in his cornflakes truck. An excitable Phil Menzies guards the Chinese while they're tied up in the changing rooms, torturing them with his endless football tactics and theories. And finally, they're back in the country park, the whole cast, because the school has been saved for another day. Twilight falls, strings of summer lights in the trees are sparkling, and there's a stage and a party in the park. Susan's ready and dolled up in front of a microphone, and — hold on — is it Gregory's birthday?

That's what *Gregory's Girl 2* was meant to be. The entire logic of modern film-making said that's what it should have been. Audiences and critics would have purred over the nostalgia and the peppering of cute references, no matter how stupid and inane the plot was. Bill Forsyth made a perverse non-sequel instead, contrary to the expectations anyone would have had for a sequel; one that was on a different planet to the new wave of Scottish movies and their seemingly cool, edgy attitudes, like *Trainspotting* (1996), *The Acid House* (1998), *Orphans* (1998) and *Ratcatcher* (1999) — the films that may not have been made at all if not for Forsyth's achievements.

It wasn't his idea in the beginning. Clive Parsons, the producer of the original, was all set to make a TV series based on the original *Gregory's Girl* story and had asked Bill to help him write a pilot.

> "I got a little bit possessive about it and said: 'Why don't we make a film rather than the TV thing?' So that's how it started, it wasn't something I was yearning to do…I could hear people saying: 'Well, what's wrong with him if he's got to go back to 25-year old ideas?' So I was very determined to run a mile from the original, run as far from the original film as I could."[48]

He wanted to make something about what really happened to the older Gregory, the kind of man he would become. Calling it *Gregory's Two Girls* (1999), he soon realised, was a big mistake — because it was a title that immediately signalled sequel antics. There are a few nostalgic visits to scenes from the original, but not much for the casual Forsyth fans: a park bench located where Gregory and Susan had once danced together; another bench in the park north of the town where Dorothy went for her runs. There's sight of the blue bridge between the flats in Abronhill, as well as the Trio fish and chip shop. And there are some other, more discreet echoes. Greg is aged 34 (Bill's age when the first film was made); Greg's new 'girl', Carly McKinnon, was born in 1981[49].

The return to Climackston is a gloomy one, almost dystopian in its vision of a modern Scotland that's going backwards, its character and ambition withering, powerless in the face of global business and its impressive, ever-smiling persuasions. American Football is now the school's obsession and girls want to be part of it, not as players, but cheerleaders with glittery pom-poms and sexy routines. Local power is concentrated in the hands of Fraser Rowan, local-boy-made-good, and the owner of a giant tech company which is very much part of the global industrial complex: good HR and CSR on the surface, but an inhuman trade in its black heart. The company publicly makes a great deal of its role in

recycling old computers for schoolchildren in Africa while at the same time hiding away its development of electronic devices for torture booths. Appealing to the government authorities is no use. They are only interested in expediencies. How they can protect regional enterprise and some useful cronies, not geographically remote issues like human rights. As Maddie's American boyfriend observes of Scotland, its people are fortunate to have such a picturesque and tranquil landscape, but it's easy (and dangerous) to fall asleep, because the world as a global system is still alive, full of injustice and tragedy and causes to fight for. Contrary to the prevailing Nineties mood, history was far from at an end. Through grown-up Gregory Forsyth questioned the nature of political commitment, the difference between having principles and actually doing something about them: "The New Labour showboat was on the waves, and all these ideas — the idea of local participative politics, issue politics, all of that — you either tied yourself to a tree or made sure you bought the right coffee, and you felt you were doing something."[50]

The fans of the original film, which included many of the critics, knew they were going to be disappointed. But the extent of the disappointment was a surprise to them.

> "So *Gregory's Girl* is 17 years old, and well may you hope that, in honour of the anniversary, Miss Clare Grogan — a veteran of the first film - might appear, bringing her ra-ra skirt out of retirement and giving us all a rousing on-camera chorus of Happy Birthday, just for old times' sake [wrote Peter Bradshaw in *The Guardian*]. But, sadly, no. Gordon Sinclair is the only star from the original brought back... the movie turns out to be a bit of a mess: an uneven romp with all the plausibility of a Children's Film Foundation feature or an old Scooby-Doo episode. And though young Gregory Underwood has grown up, it is clear that Bill Forsyth hasn't: the feel and the atmosphere of *Gregory's Two Girls* show it to be

weirdly marooned in that late 70s/early 80s
period of Mr Forsyth's pomp… Once Forsyth
and his fey, cuddly pictures were thought to
be the quintessence of our film industry;
rightly or wrongly, the fashion is now for zappier, sexier stuff, with Jude Law rather than
John Gordon Sinclair."[51]

It's the kind of review that inspires the same melancholy feelings as *Gregory's Two Girls* itself. Everybody seems to just want
Fraser's zappier, sexier world, even *The Guardian*. Consumer
mag *Empire* was similarly brassy about its lack of interest in
anything other than cheap pleasures:

"The blueprint for a Gregory sequel is not
hard to imagine, but unfathomably, what we
actually get is painfully lumpen comedy…
and it's just shite…So offbeam and distracted
is the writing, that between interminable
ramblings about political insurrection, Forsyth resorts to 'beaver' gags and ruinous slap-
stick…To add insult to deep injury, there is
only one damn scene with any football in it.
And no Claire Grogan. Criminal."[52]

The reviews suggested none of them had ever seen
Comfort & Joy, or *Housekeeping*, let alone *Being Human*, and had
no sense of what kind of film-maker Bill Forsyth actually
was. To them he'd just popped up in the busy movie sched-
ules with another quaint comedy. With the smallest handle

on the context they might have realised how honest and interesting a sequel *Gregory's Two Girls* was, the integrity and intelligence involved. If proof was needed that *Gregory's Girl* was more than just a commercial formula, then Forsyth's sequel spells it out — in a destructive kind of way — at every step. Was the romantic innocence of Gregory's character ever meant to survive the opening wet dream sequence, the one where he has sex with one of his pupils in the gym hall, the headteacher and police banging on the door? When the references to Nabokov only shove *Lolita* back into audience faces? If it felt inappropriate to some viewers then, in New Labour's climate of worthy self-awareness — now, in an age where any reasonable discussion of a subject like male attraction to girls under 18 is impossible, it's made the film seem unwatchable, because it's said to be such a serious lapse in judgment on Forsyth's part. Nothing to do with a writer reflecting on the different sides of human experience, but an indefensible act of heresy. A sin.

> Gregory might seem to live a morally upstanding life — he is a teacher attempting to inculcate his charges with ideas of social and economic justice, [wrote Ben Lambert for MUBI in 2021] but his romantic pursuit of a girl in one of his classes corrupts everything within and around him[53]. It is only towards the end of the film, when he firmly rejects said pursuit, that he can begin to reclaim his status as a valid moral actor; and even then it is implied that he will have to pay a heavy

restitution before doing so…the central
bleakness of its conceit has seeped out into
the film's overall aesthetic, that the sense of
thinness and productive exhaustion is the
point. The sequel to one of the most joyful
films ever made becomes, in Forsyth's contrary hands, an anti-enjoyment.[54]

*

After his many different essays in film-making, Bill Forsyth
felt as if he'd run out of places to go. "I was actually fairly
happy with [*Gregory's Two Girls*] and I had lots of ideas. But
the film business kind of changed under my feet," he said in
2016. "I do not know where my movies would be shown except in Britain — people would not go to a mall to see them.
I hate to say it, but the feature movie is fading away, and I do
not feel attracted to making movies for television."

Since 2003 he's been living with his partner Moira
Wylie, an actor from the Scottish film and theatre world[55].
They retired together to a rural village across the firth from
Edinburgh, a medieval landscape in sight of the Lomond
Hills that has been used as a character landscape for the TV
boxset world of *Outlander*. It's a quiet life on the hillside, looking forward to the *Times Literary Supplement* falling through the
letterbox each week; having the time to spend ambling round
book shops; occasionally making it to film festivals and catching up with old friends; working most days on the writing of
this or that — there are ten or more scripts on the go,
screenplays at different stages, if anyone comes knocking

with funding. But recent creative projects have gone nowhere, one way or another. In 2009 there were hopes of a new Forsyth-written and directed film, known as *Exile* or *A New Boy*, but the financing didn't happen. Nor did a script for HBO about astronauts marooned on a Mir spacecraft for six months. In 2013, Bill and producer Iain Smith began to collaborate on a TV series for BBC Scotland about the global digital marketplace and the alienation and poverty it could lead to among traditional communities: "Local folk with three jobs rubbing up against globe-straddling billionaires in their Highland retreats in a fictional internet capital of the Highlands. Our hero is an out of work and out of time journalist with no digital skills, trying to write his way out of disastrous circumstances, trying to make sense of a world he can't comprehend, trying to do it all in written shorthand." The BBC wanted harmless content suited to a cosy Sunday evening slot, another *Call the Midwife*. Not this. Not something that questioned the make-up of 21st century wealth and power: the vast, parasitical growth of digital tech and insidious enterprise. The BBC tried to tutor Forsyth into writing the script they wanted, and then lost interest. "The saddest thing is I put my heart into it as I love writing things that Scottish people get more from than anyone else," said Forsyth. "It would have made a hugely satisfying swansong for me, and I'm sure it would have chimed with many of the local issues and emotions of the moment."[56] Forsyth was then asked to leave his co-writing role on a musical adaptation of *Local Hero* for the Edinburgh Lyceum theatre in 2019 — his need to keep to the integrity of his original vision had become a problem and he subsequently asked for his name to be taken off the production's credits.

Forsyth never watches his own films. Why would he? "The only reason you'd choose to watch a film you'd made would be to find fault with it."[57]

Bill Forsyth in Kelvingrove Park for the *That Sinking Feeling* 40th anniversary reunion, 2019. Courtesy of Celine McIlmunn.

*

The Glasgow streets were crowded now, hot with sunshine and busy with tourists coming in and out of fast food places on a Friday evening. I still had hours to wait until the train, so I went and sat in a paved square near Glasgow Central. There was a busker in a tracksuit with big waves of Seventies hair and a chest of gold-looking chains. He was belting out some old classics into a microphone, his mates standing round him, waiting until he packed up and they could go to a bar someplace. I sat and wrote up more of my Cumbernauld notes with a pad and a biro, checked my emails and WhatsApp.

A man came striding into the square, saw me sitting there and hesitated. He changed direction and came towards me. Short and solid, muscular, carrying a backpack. It happened in every city; someone would ask for money and I never had cash on me, not since Covid, and not often before then. It was embarrassing just to hold my hands up, pat my pockets and do my best to look apologetic.

"What you writing?"

"Sorry?"

"What you writing there?"

The way he moved, walking with purpose and intent, suggested some kind of tension inside of him. He wanted to get somewhere, or away from somewhere. Did he really want to know what I was writing about? *Gregory's Girl* flashed into my head. The mysterious character of Forsyth. His artist's way of seeing, the literature that had influenced him. The warmth and genius of innocence he'd found in the GYT. And most of all, the importance of being human. 'Being' as a better way than 'living'; how it opened up ways to slip under or around the insistent noise of modern life and its conventions. I pushed it all out of my head again, fast. I didn't want to start a conversation about a project that might sound lame. Obscure at best. Irrelevant to a world where people have brains burnt with anxiety, because their relationships have turned to crap, where there's nowhere to live, not enough to eat.

"Notes," I said, "just getting my notes together —"

"Ah right," he said. He'd got the message.

"Just asking, cause I've started to keep a diary," he said, "and I wondered, y'know. I'm ex-army and when I was back I had PTSD. All that. So I keeps this diary of when I've done something kind, and when I've been an arsehole, and that kinda helps me. Ok pal —"

And he was off, with the same kind of urgent stride, leaving me feeling stupid. I should have told him everything. He would have got it. Or been happy to listen if he hadn't.

---

[1] John Dingwall, 'Movie director Bill Forsyth looks back on giving Peter Capaldi his big break and the remastering of *Gregory's Girl*', *Daily Record*, 25 April 2014.

[2] Bill Forsyth: "Film has given me time, my life, a space to learn and be creative", *Film Talk*, August 3 2015.

[3] Kevin Courrier, Interview with film director Bill Forsyth, *Critics at Large*, 1985.

[4] Gerald Peary, 'Bill Forsyth', www.geraldpeary.com, September 1985.

[5] Forsyth's first choice for Felix Happer, Brian Keith (1921-1996) had been typecast as a burly, square-jawed villain in TV series and Disney westerns.

[6] Allan Hunter, 'Being Human', *Sight and Sound*, August 1994.

[7] Jonathan Murray, 'Cornflakes versus Conflict: An Interview with Bill Forsyth', *Journal of British Cinema and Television*, Vol. 12, 2015.

[8] Ibid.

[9] Dominique Toyeux, 'Tidings of Comfort and Joy, an interview with Bill Forsyth', *Cinema Cessenta*, March/April 1986.

[10] Jonathan Hacker, *Take Ten: Contemporary British Film Directors*, Clarendon Press, 1991.

[11] Mark Kermode feature with Bill Forsyth, BBC *The Culture Show*, 18 November 2008.

[12] *The Making of* Local Hero, documentary film, 1983.

[13] Rita Kempley, 'Everyday of Bill Forsyth', *The Washington Post*, 15 October 1989.

[14] Evening Express, 19 March 1983.

[15] Robert Fish ed., *Cinematic Countrysides*, Manchester University Press, 2017, p111-112.

[16] Bill Forsyth, '*Local Hero* and Donald Trump: "a malign mix of bullying, muscle flexing and craven politicians"', *The Guardian*, 17 October 2012.

[17] Abbey Bender, Bill Forsyth Talks About Pioneering Scottish Cinema, MUBI, 3 October 2019.

[18] Gerald Peary, ibid.

[19] Ibid.

[20] Just like the advice given to Woody Allen by the super-intelligent alien visitors in *Stardust Memories* (1980): "You wanna do mankind a service? Tell funnier jokes."

[21] *When Bill Paterson met Bill Forsyth*, BBC Scotland, 2011.

[22] Gerald Peary, ibid.

[23] Interview with Jim Healy, Dryden Theatre, New York, April 11 2010.

[24] Rita Kempley, 'The Shimmering Spirit of *Housekeeping*', *The Washington Post*, 8 January 1988.

[25] Sarah Fay, 'Marilynne Robinson, The Art of Fiction No.198', *The Paris Review*, Fall 2008.

[26] Rita Kempley, ibid.

[27] Marilynne Robinson, *Housekeeping*, Faber & Faber, 1980, p119.

[28] Ibid, p152/3.

[29] Ibid., p93.

[30] Interview with Jim Healy, ibid.

[31] Ibid.

[32] Ibid.

[33] Forsyth was so immersed in the text he probably didn't realise he'd pinched this phrase. Robinson refers to the water in the house as a "tea of hemp and horsehair".

[34] It must have been frustrating to see a *Rebecca's Daughters* film released in 1992, starring Peter O'Toole. The director was Karl Francis (best known for working on *Weekend World*); the screenplay had been developed by Guy Jenkin (the co-writer with Andy Hamilton of the *Drop the Dead Donkey* and *Outnumbered* sitcoms).

[35] Bill Forsyth, 'On Making *Breaking In* with Burt Reynolds', *Talkhouse*, 4 October 2019.

[36] Rita Kempley, 'Everyday of Bill Forsyth', ibid.

[37] 'An Afternoon with Bill Forsyth', FilmForum, 5 October 2019.

[38] Terry Semel was appointed president and chief operating officer in 1982 and has been credited, alongside business partner Robert Daly, with Warner Brother's financial turnaround. In 2001 Semel took over as CEO at Yahoo, reviving the company's fortunes. In 2023 he was living in a nursing home receiving care for Alzheimer's.

[39] All quotes from the film come from the *Being Human* third draft, January 1992.

[40] Stephen Metcalf, 'Where is Bill Forsyth?', *Slate*, 15 June 2009.

[41] Allan Hunter, ibid.

[42] Ibid.

[43] Allen is regarded as one of the legends of film editing, having worked on *Bonnie and Clyde* (1967), *Dog Day Afternoon* (1975) and *Reds* (1981) etc. She was Warner's Vice-President in Charge of Creative Development at the time of *Being Human*.

[44] Owen Gleiberman, *Being Human* review, *Entertainment Weekly*, 20 May 1994.

[45] Peter Travers, *Being Human* review, *Rolling Stone*, 9 May 1994.

[46] Todd McCarthy, *Being Human* review, *Variety*, 5 May 1994.

[47] *Gregory's Girl* DVD, audio commentary — Bill Forsyth and Mark Kermode, 2019.

---

[48] Jonathan Murray, ibid.

[49] Carly McKinnon, angel-eyed Frances, moved to Canada and worked as a journalist for *The Varsity*, the University of Toronto's student newspaper. She only returned to acting in 2022, when she appeared alongside Clare Grogan and Dawn Steele (who'd also been in *Gregory's Two Girls*) as teachers in *My Old School*, the re-telling of the true story of Brandon Lee, the 30 year-old who went back to his old school for another chance at life, fooling Bearsden Academy in Glasgow into thinking he was 17.

[50] Jonathan Murray, ibid.

[51] Peter Bradshaw, *Gregory's Two Girls* review, *The Guardian*, 15 October 1999.

[52] Ian Nathan, *Gregory's Two Girls* review, *Empire*, 1 January 2000.

[53] This is unfair. Greg had a dream. He's excited and flattered that Frances might be interested in him — but at no point is there any 'pursuit' of Frances.

[54] Ben Lambert, 'Notebook Primer: Bill Forsyth', MUBI, 29 July 2021.

[55] Moira Wylie had been married to the actor Donald Campbell, who was born in Glasgow but spent most of his professional career in Canada. Besides acting in and directing theatre productions, Moira herself has continued to take parts in interesting film projects: the movie of Kerouac's *On the Road* (2012), Samuel Beckett's mother in *Meetings with a Young Poet* (2013) and *On the Basis of Sex* (2018).

[56] Judith Duffy, 'Makers of *Gregory's Girl* and *Mad Max* declare war on the BBC', *The Herald*, 3 April 2016.

[57] *Gregory's Girl* DVD, audio commentary — Bill Forsyth and Mark Kermode, 2019.

12. Endings

"You know, there's definitely something in the air tonight, Charlie."

n David Thomson's bible for cinephiles, *The New Biographical Dictionary of Film*, our *Gregory's Girl* story is described as leading to a dead end: "It may simply be that Forsyth is a melancholy man who has gone as far as he can, like Bartleby the Scrivener."[1] Bartleby, the absurdist Herman Melville character[2], began his work in a legal office with great success, but then politely refused to do anything more, unwilling to be part of a system he didn't believe in. "I prefer not to," responded Bartleby to any requests. He spent his days staring out of the office window into the red brick wall opposite, a curiously inert philosopher whose passivity had engulfed him.

Times passes anyway. Our interests change, passions turn cold and end up being hard to understand. Writing in 2016, Bill Forsyth himself expressed a feeling of obsolescence, of how he felt like the Professor in Ingmar Bergman's *Wild Strawberries* (1957). "I'm now living as a temporary immigrant and relative stranger on a planet that belongs to a different race: the young."[3] A film about youth had made him, and now generations of youth were shutting him out. Ever the fatalist, it wasn't like it was a problem. "It's an activity that fascinates me," he said of film-making, "but I don't feel like I'm doing anything important."[4]

*

Back in Luton, looking at the Oriental girl in the picture, it wasn't escape I'd been searching for, not fantasy, I was really only interested in the magic that turned out to be real.

As we get older we feel as if we know everything anyway, closing doors and windows behind us as we go. It means, just as one example, that we don't have a way of talking about the ordinary magic of things, what we find in our relations to places and moments in time, how they take us by surprise — not often even a language for thinking about them with ourselves. Certainly nothing close to what the Greeks and Romans had in paganism, their everyday mythology that meant every dull field, every stream and rock and sky was streaked with bright veins of meaning. We have the clear and obvious rules of science instead: the world as a meaningless (but measurable) blitz of atoms.

So we keep on having to try and make our own private kinds of language to help make sense of the truth of what we see and feel. And that's what Forsyth ended up doing in *Gregory's Girl*, one of his films about being. "I love things that admit the magical in our lives. Magic comes from somewhere — it's not spurious," said Forsyth. "Maybe it comes from primitive people in our past trying to cope with things

358

they didn't understand. But I like to locate it in very ordinary situations."⁵ *Gregory's Girl* is a crack in the side of the mountain, those adamant surfaces of our hard modern reality, offering up some glimpses of an ordinary, overlooked magic.

So it only looks like a dead end — a bunch of half-forgotten films — when the resonance of a piece like *Gregory's Girl* is still out there working in the landscape of our culture, in everyday conversations, in our references and daydreams; still vivid in our minds.

Ganin, Nabokov's hero in *Mary*, wonders over the same kind of mystery.

> 'And where is it all now?' mused Ganin.
> 'Where is the happiness, the sunshine, where
> are those thick skittles of wood which crashed
> and bounced so nicely, where is my bicycle
> with the low handlebars and the big gear? It
> seems there's a law which says that nothing
> ever vanishes, that matter is indestructible;
> therefore the chips from my skittles and the
> spokes of my bicycle still exist somewhere to
> this day.'⁶

On old VHS tapes and DVDs. The chips and fragments of *Gregory's Girl* also still exist in our imagination — not plain memories of a story or images, but a place filled with a familiar bittersweet loneliness, whether as a memory of past times or something that's still with us now. It lives with us, this place, a reminder of a particular way of looking at things, of how to keep on seeing the magic in the ordinary.

Not just a single view through a window, but a place with its own light and air. There's not much of a story to remember, no meaning or purpose to take to heart. And that's where the happiness of it comes from, because there's no happiness in rules and laws and prescriptions anyway (the formula of Hollywood stories), only in the stream of things — how they look and feel, the 'thereness' of things — and the way we make the most of that inescapable uncertainty and insecurity. And it doesn't matter what Forsyth's specific intentions for *Gregory's Girl* might have been. Our response to the film is a flicker of what's left of our remaining resistance to the onslaught of formulaic entertainment, its heroes, its assumptions, its propaganda. Whether we're conscious of it or not, we still prefer some poetry.

*

It's just a little film and I'm taking it too seriously, I know, by looking for mysteries where (maybe) there are none. Future generations won't bother. Why would they? Not with little mysteries, or even with watching such a minor piece at all. Research suggests that children's 'default mode' is building up earlier — because there are so many more digital stimulants and less time for boredom or daydreaming — and the window for imagination, romantic or otherwise, is shrinking.

[1] David Thomson, *The New Biographical Dictionary of Film*, 6th edition, Knopf, 2014.

[2] Herman Melville, *Bartleby, the Scrivener: A Story of Wall Street* (1853)

[3] Bill Forsyth, 'Charlie Gormley: Long Shot to Hollywood', *Long Shot* DVD.

[4] Kevin Courrier, Interview with film director Bill Forsyth, *Critics at Large*, 1985.

[5] Graham Fuller, 'The Bill Forsyth saga: a new film from the director of *Local Hero*', *The Listener*, 19 November 1987.

[6] Vladimir Nabokov, *Mary*, Penguin, p40/41.

Printed in Great Britain
by Amazon

24646683R00209